STUDIES IN IMPERIALISM

general editor John M. MacKenzie

When the 'Studies in Imperialism' series was founded more than twenty years ago, emphasis was laid upon the conviction that 'imperialism as a cultural phenomenon had as significant an effect on the dominant as on the subordinate societies'. With more than fifty books published, this remains the prime concern of the series. Cross-disciplinary work has indeed appeared covering the full spectrum of cultural phenomena, as well as examining aspects of gender and sex, frontiers and law, science and the environment, language and literature, migration and patriotic societies, and much else. Moreover, the series has always wished to present comparative work on European and American imperialism, and particularly welcomes the submission of books in these areas. The fascination with imperialism, in all its aspects, shows no sign of abating, and this series will continue to lead the way in encouraging the widest possible range of studies in the field. 'Studies in Imperialism' is fully organic in its development, always seeking to be at the cutting edge, responding to the latest interests of scholars and the needs of this ever-expanding area of scholarship.

Sex, politics and empire

MANCHESTER
1824

Manchester University Press

AVAILABLE IN THE SERIES

Sex, politics and empire

A POSTCOLONIAL GEOGRAPHY

Richard Philips

MANCHESTER UNIVERSITY PRESS
Manchester and New York

distributed exclusively in the USA by Palgrave

1004669955

Published by **MANCHESTER UNIVERSITY PRESS**
OXFORD ROAD, MANCHESTER M13 9NR, UK
and ROOM 400, 175 FIFTH AVENUE, NEW YORK, NY 10010, USA
www.manchesteruniversitypress.co.uk

Distributed exclusively in the USA by
PALGRAVE, 175 FIFTH AVENUE, NEW YORK, NY 10010, USA

Distributed exclusively in Canada by
UBC PRESS, UNIVERSITY OF BRITISH COLUMBIA,
2029 WEST MALL, VANCOUVER, BC, CANADA V6T 1Z2

British Library Cataloguing-in-Publication Data
A catalogue record for this book is available from the British Library

Library of Congress Cataloging-in-Publication Data applied for

ISBN   0 7190 7006 6 *hardback*
EAN   978 0 7190 7006 8

First published 2006

14 13 12 11 10 09 08 07 06   10 9 8 7 6 5 4 3 2 1

Typeset in 10/12pt Trump Mediaeval
by Graphicraft Limited, Hong Kong
Printed in Great Britain
by CPI, Bath

CONTENTS

FIGURES AND TABLE

Figures

Table

GENERAL EDITOR'S INTRODUCTION

The operation of the British model of imperialism was never consistent, seldom coherent, and far from comprehensive. Indeed, the existence of what were in effect several British empires rendered the emergence of such a model impossible. Yet ideas, administrative methods, and legal provisions did of course pass through its systems. This book reveals the manner in which these propositions can be followed through the exportation of aspects of sexual politics from the so-called metropole in the later nineteenth century. Purity campaigns, controversies about the age of consent, the regulation of prostitution and the passage and repeal of contagious diseases laws, as well as a new legislative awareness of homosexuality, were all part of the sexual currency of the late Victorian age. Proponents of these developments were invariably aware of the potential imperial dimensions of their concerns. Indeed, as in the case of the age of consent issue and the regulation of prostitution in military contexts, India was a prime locus of such anxieties. The imperial territory could be as much a central focus as domestic society.

The strength of this work is that it deals in the complex spatial geographies of imperial sexual politics. By examining theorisation about the alleged sexual iniquities and purities of the urban and the rural, fears about supposed military debauchery and the related tendency towards inter-racial sex, as well as the quasi-anthropological debates about the sexual propensities of other 'races', the author demonstrates the manner in which the (often bourgeois and religious) alarm about the sexual habits of the age brought together metropolitan and colonial locations into a single, if complex, mental system. Yet both surveys and applications were patchy. Diverse patterns emerge from the analysis of the sexual politics of a West African colony (Sierra Leone), Australian territories (South Australia and New South Wales) and the largely separate 'empire' of India. As with so many other aspects of imperialism, these matters were largely interactive and reciprocal. Dominant rulers and settlers, as well as the indigenous peoples and subordinate classes at whom provisions were invariably directed, indulged in processes of acceptance, rejection, and modification. Concepts of imperial sexuality, while circulating and diffusing through a variety of media, travelling protagonists, and administrative instruments, were never truly replicated across the colonial spectrum.

Thus, polemicists, journalists, religious and colonial authorities in a variety of colonial settings seldom slavishly followed the notions that emerged from London. Moreover, we should always remember the significance of the gulf between intention and effect, for example between legal enactment and its operation 'on the ground'. This is paralleled by the dangers in taking what can sometimes be seen as propagandist theorising at face value. Richard Burton's notion of the 'Sotadic Zone', so deeply implicated in his visions of the distinctions among different forms of civilisation and the putative lack of it among those peoples he despised as backward, reflects this. So does the African bourgeois insistence (for example) on the absence of homosexuality among black societies on the continent, a contention very easy to disprove. In his conclusion, Richard Phillips, in a salutary passage, carries his examination and critique of the geographies of colonial sexuality into the post-colonial period. So many of the complexities are still with us. On the issue of homosexuality, for example, a tolerant South Africa can be juxtaposed against an intolerant Zimbabwe or Nigeria. In the Anglican Communion, the Archbishop of Cape Town and his predecessor Desmond Tutu can insist on a parallel between racial discrimination and persecution on grounds of orientation, while political and religious authorities respectively in Zimbabwe and Nigeria can prosecute just such discrimination with gusto. And if these diverse geographies occur in continental terms, they can also emerge in the national: the appointment of a gay bishop in New England contrasting with fundamentalist rejection in the South and elsewhere in the USA.

In recent years, an exceptionally rich historiography of issues of sexual politics in the imperial setting has emerged. This book adds a number of additional and highly significant perspectives from the point of view of human geographies within the spatial dimensions of the British Empire. And those spaces were always beset as much with resistance and contestation as with the exercise of power and the law. In these many ways, the 'mapping' of the contours of the polemical and moral, religious and administrative, legal and social aspects of diverse sexual politics is here achieved with great clarity.

John M. MacKenzie

ACKNOWLEDGEMENTS

This project was researched and written with support from the British Academy, the Government of Canada, the Royal Geographical Society and the Universities of Salford and Liverpool.

I would like to thank colleagues and friends who read and commented on drafts of this work: Dennis Altman, Alison Blunt, Elleke Boehmer, Antoinette Burton, Brian Dickey, Mark Duffett, Dave Featherstone, David Hilliard, Philip Howell, Rhys Jones, Bill Lawton, Alan Lester, Philippa Levine, Miles Ogborn, Gordon Pirie, David Pivar, Jane Samson and Stephen Slemon.

I am grateful for comments and questions from members of a number of institutions, at which I was invited to present preliminary findings. These include departments of Geography, English, Law, History and Women's Studies at the Universities of Cambridge, Liverpool, Manchester Metropolitan, Minnesota, Open, Queens (Canada), Royal Holloway University of London, SOAS, Sussex, Toronto, Wales (Aberystwyth) and York (Canada).

On the production side, thanks go to Gustav Dobrzinsky for Cartography, and Ron Price, copy-editor for Manchester University Press. And I gratefully acknowledge permission to publish revised versions of material that has appeared in print elsewhere. An earlier version of the material in Chapter 3 appeared as 'Imperialism and the regulation of sexuality: colonial legislation on contagious diseases and ages of consent', *Journal of Historical Geography*, 28: 3 (2002), 339–362. An earlier version of material in Chapter 4 appeared as 'Hereogeneous imperialism and the regulation of sexuality in British West Africa', *Journal of the History of Sexuality*, 14: 3 (2005). An earlier version of material in Chapter 7 appeared as 'Writing travel and mapping sexuality: Richard Burton's Sotadic Zone', in James Duncan and Derek Gregory (eds), *Writes of Passage: Reading Travel Writing* (London, Routledge, 2000), pp. 70–91.

This book was researched and written in Sydney, Adelaide, London and Milan. For their hospitality and friendship during my time in Australia, I thank Ruth Frappell, Natalie Jamieson and Stephen Whiting. For the same in London, special thanks to Craig Lind, Mark Malindine, John Bowman, my sister Helen, and Alison Blunt. For everything else during this time, particularly the happy months in Northern Italy, I thank Matteo Lodevole.

Richard Phillips
Liverpool

INTRODUCTION

Mapping the tyranny

> I beg you to take a map of the world, and mark in the two hemispheres every place where you see this abominable system has been established by England. It will give you an idea of the extent of the tyranny.[1]

Inviting people to think about a familiar problem in an unfamiliar way, Josephine Butler (figure 0.1) hoped to open their political horizons and critically renew their project. The familiar problem, a preoccupation not only of feminists and moralists but also military and medical professionals, was the legal regulation of prostitution, which had been repealed in England a year earlier but remained in force in much of the British Empire. Butler argued that the way people and government treated prostitutes and other sexual outsiders – a category in which we might include sexually active younger people and those with lovers of the same sex or a different race – spoke volumes about their domestic and imperial society, about the way it was and the way they wanted it to be. She campaigned for the rights of prostitutes in England and India, against the double standard of their oppression: the willingness of Englishmen to exploit others while taking liberties for themselves. Certainly, many liberties were taken in the name of empire. 'The expansion of Europe', as the libertarian historian Ronald Hyam approvingly put it, 'was not only a matter of Christianity and commerce, it was also a matter of copulation and concubinage.'[2] He illustrated how their active sex lives helped Europeans through months and years in penal colonies and resource frontiers, military camps and farming settlements. For Hyam these were 'essentially harmless pleasures',[3] but for Butler they spoke of power: that of a morally bankrupt imperial order.

One did not need to share Butler's moral stance to see the connections between sexuality and imperial power. It was widely recognised – tacitly or explicitly, by family members, medical workers, schoolteachers,

[1]

0.1 Signed postcard (c.1868) of bust of Josephine
Butler

owners and employees of plantations or mines, by governments – that
sex was important not only for the pleasure (for some) but also the
business of empire. Colonisation schemes were organised around sexual
arrangements. The heterosexual nuclear family was chosen as the
building-block for the agricultural colonisation of large parts of the
world in the nineteenth century: the family farm.[4] The unmarried man
was the vehicle for other imperial projects. Though likely to be sexually frustrated and emotionally lonely, he was also conveniently mobile
and affordable, an effective soldier or plantation worker.[5] Prostitutes
were deployed within the same projects, serving armies and frontier
settlements. As Philippa Levine argues, 'prostitution was a critical
artefact of colonial authority, a trade deemed vital to governance but
urgently in need of control'.[6] Colonial authorities made sex a central
plank of what Lenore Manderson calls the 'moral logic of colonialism'.[7]
Legal critics Kristin Mann and Richard Roberts generalise:

Colonialism sought to impose a new moral as well as political order, founded on loyalty to metropolitan and colonial states and on discipline, order, and regularity in work, leisure and bodily habits. By regulating such things as health, sanitation, leisure, and public conduct, law played a vital role in moral education and discipline.[8]

Richard Rathbone argues, more generally still, that English law was 'one of the most obvious manifestations of the colonial presence', a means by which 'Government imposed its will'.[9] But, while colonial companies and governments carefully formulated and enforced rules about who should, could or could not marry, and about who could or could not have sex with whom, where and when, they did not do so with a free hand. Activists such as Butler – known as purity campaigners – took an interest in the regulation of such intimate and morally charged areas of their own lives and the lives of others.

The unfamiliar if not entirely original political idea that she proposed – framing abstract social and political problems in cartographic or more generally geographical terms – arguably had the potential to freshen the rhetoric of a twenty-year-old movement against state-regulated

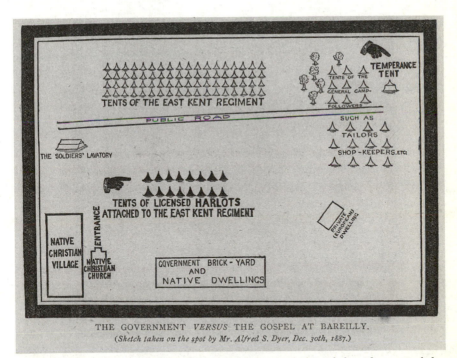

THE GOVERNMENT *VERSUS* THE GOSPEL AT BAREILLY.
(*Sketch taken on the spot by Mr. Alfred S. Dyer, Dec. 30th, 1887.*)

0.2 The caption to this 1887 sketch by Alfred Dyer complained that 'the tents of the Government harlots confront the troops from morning to night' and are 'in full view of the entrance to the native Christian Church'

[3]

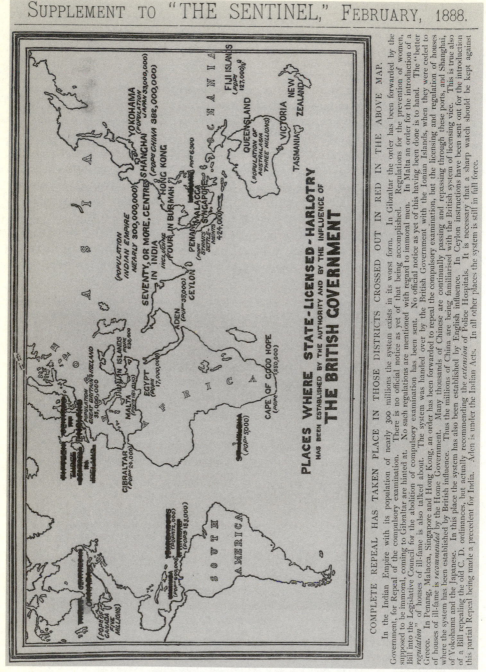

0.3 'State-licensed harlotry' in the British Empire. Map by Alfred Dyer, 1888

prostitution. It promised to open up and develop forms of political action that could not be imagined in other ways. Some of Butler's fellow-campaigners saw the point, and used similar tactics. Alfred Dyer appealed even more directly to the geographical imaginations of his public, publishing maps of military and state-regulated prostitution in the British Empire. In one, depicting a military cantonment in India, he claimed to show 'how lust is forced upon the British soldier, and how the native population is corrupted, by the British government in India' (figure 0.2). In another, locating regulation on the global map of empire, he echoed Butler's cartographic polemic, impressing readers with the extent of the 'state licensed harlotry' (figure 0.3). Butler's rhetoric and Dyer's imagery suggest that geographical imagination was therefore potentially significant for those involved in this imperial sexuality politics – the movements against regulation and associated campaigns for and against aspects of sexual and moral law in the British Empire. These politics were dominated in the Victorian period by three areas of legislation:

- Contagious Diseases (CD) Acts and Ordinances regulated prostitution in designated areas. Their provisions varied over time and between places, but generally these laws required female prostitutes to submit to medical inspections and confined those diagnosed with syphilis or gonorrhoea to detention wards of 'lock hospitals'.[10]
- Various forms of criminal and family law governed the age at which girls and young women could lawfully consent to sex without penalty to either themselves or their male sexual partners (sex with other girls or women was not legally recognised).[11]
- Sex between men was not so much regulated as prohibited in the British Empire, though the form of this prohibition varied. In England the Criminal Law Amendment Act (1885) set a two-year jail term for sex between men. In most other parts of the Empire, approximations of earlier British laws remained, allowing judges to impose harsher penalties for a narrower range of male same-sex acts.[12]

The political events surrounding these laws were concentrated historically into the final decades of the nineteenth century. These were busy and dramatic years in the history of British imperialism, years in which the British were aggressively expanding their geographical and political reach. The coincidence between what historian James Morris once called the 'climax of empire'[13] and a particularly intense period in sexuality politics, which transformed many aspects of the regulation of sexuality, raises questions about how, precisely, sexuality and imperial power were connected – how, to unpack and apply to the imperial field Michel Foucault's more general point, sexuality constituted 'an especially dense transfer point for relations of power'.[14]

Geographical imagination, which created new possibilities for intervention in imperial sexuality politics, might do the same for those seeking to understand empire and sexuality in historical perspective. Historians of sexuality and empire have begun to see, if not develop, the political and intellectual advantages of thinking geographically, and the disadvantages of not doing so, or not doing so enough. Cultural historian Frank Mort makes this explicit in a critical review of his own work on the history of sexuality and its embroilments with power – in a book entitled *Dangerous Sexualities* – which 'took social geographies . . . entirely for granted':

> In that sense it operated with the established conventions of most historiography, viewing space and place as a relatively passive backdrop against which 'real' cultural processes were enacted. The urban geographies of Manchester and London, for example, which featured so prominently in the environmental campaigns for nineteenth-century sanitary and philanthropic reform, were simply assumed 'to be there', as were the more localised spaces of the church and schoolroom, which were the *habitus* of so much moral education . . . In a rather different sense, the mental environments and psychic spaces which were the focus of moral reform also remained unexplored, despite the growing impact of Freud's topography of the mind by the early twentieth century. This neglect of social and symbolic geography remains a characteristic feature of research on sexuality. While recent cultural histories have amply demonstrated the significance of language in generating sexual meanings, they have continued to underestimate the spatial dimensions of these codes.[15]

Mort's point – and my point of departure – is the suggestion that space is ultimately more than a backdrop against which these historical processes unfold, and more than an outcome of such processes.[16] As both an imaginative realm and a real world, it is something more fluid and more productive.

Mort locates this spatial turn within a 'post-Foucauldian' vision for the understanding of sexuality, and it is important to explain this point since the contemporary focus on histories, but not geographies, of sexuality and on sexuality's embroilments with power can be traced largely to Foucault, the French philosopher and historian. Foucault showed that it is possible to think of sexuality not as a natural biological essence but as a historically changing social construct which emerges from and in turn channels and produces social power relations. In histories of sexuality, he demonstrated that the ways in which people understand and live their sexual lives has changed over time, and this has been a function of power, most immediately of individuals and institutions such as doctors and the medical establishment, and more fundamentally of the social order that authorises them. Speaking of sexuality in terms of historical epochs, and identifying periods and moments during and at which sexualities were transformed, Foucault fulfilled the literal promise of his *History of Sexuality*, but left the geography of sexuality largely implicit. On the global level, he distinguished between broad sexual regions, particularly with respect to a division between societies in which erotic arts produce what he called the truth about sex – China, Japan, India, Rome and Arabo-Moslem societies – and those in which this kind of truth is elicited by legal, medical, educational and other forms of confession – 'our civilisation' or 'the West'.[17] As Peter A. Jackson has pointed out, Foucault had not completely ignored the geographies of sexuality,[18] but his geographical typology was incomplete, ordered around a problematically imperial division between Occident and Orient and sweeping in its characterisation of those broad global regions. Pointing to the emergence of new sexual categories, Foucault elided the geographies in which they were produced and variously adopted and contested. Diane Watt and I have argued that his '*history* of sexuality has a (hidden) geography' – that structured around relations between the mainly metropolitan institutions that discursively constituted and regulated sexualities and their provincial and colonial hinterlands.[19] Thus, for instance, the homosexual, a category that Foucault traced to Europe circa 1870, might be located more specifically in European sites of legal, religious and medical practice. Conversely, it should be recognised that the category was not suddenly adopted throughout Europe, nor has it been; rather it has coexisted with other ways of understanding and living sexual lives. Concentrating on developments in various 'hegemonic centres',[20] Foucault was less interested in the places in which other constructions of sexuality persisted within the West, and indeed with differences within non-Western sexual cultures. Asked by French geographers about the lack of geographical specificity in some of his work on society and power, he answered:

If I . . . allow the frontier to wander about, sometimes over the whole of the West, that's because the documentation I was using extends in part outside France, and also because in order to grasp a specifically French phenomenon I was often obliged to look at something that happened elsewhere in a more explicit form that antedated or served as a model for what took place in France. This enabled me – allowing for local and regional variations – to situate these French phenomena in the context of Anglo-Saxon, Spanish, Italian and other societies. I don't specify the space of reference more narrowly since it would be as warranted to say that I was speaking of France alone as to say I was talking about the whole of Europe. There is indeed a task to be done in making the space in question precise, saying where a certain process stops, what are the limits beyond which something happens – though this would have to be a collective undertaking.[21]

And yet, a geographical perspective should do more than Foucault seems to suggest here – the relatively trivial matter of making boundaries more precise.

Possibilities for a deeper understanding of the geographies of sexuality and empire are signalled, if not developed, in historical and postcolonial works on the subject. The interpretive methods, concepts and language in Ann Laura Stoler's major work on imperial sexuality politics, for instance, are profoundly spatial. *Carnal Knowledge and Imperial Power* is peppered with spatial metaphors and spatial references: sites, borders and locations, streets and homes, maps and cartographies. Stoler speaks of 'place and race',[22] 'moral environments',[23] 'sites of social engineering'[24] and the 'social geography of empire',[25] to cite just some examples. Similarly, other critics draw upon and mix spatial metaphors. Judith Walkowitz, for instance, writes that 'the topography of the social underground has been extensively delineated';[26] Rudi Bleys, that European imperial outreach encompassed and produced 'a geography of perversion and desire';[27] while Philippa Levine argues that 'colonial definitions of sexuality served to map a geography of racial borders'.[28] The final chapter in Levine's major work on prostitution in the British Empire, *Prostitution, Race and Politics*, concentrates on the geographies of sexuality politics: 'Space and place: the marketplace of colonial sex' draws out the elements of such an historical geography, picking up threads that have run through the book – on themes such as 'landscape and colonisation', 'sex in the streets', 'the brothel' and 'sex in the city'. Through these geographical vignettes, Levine maintains that the authorities attended to spatial detail because, 'if the prostitute was to be interrogated, she had also to be placed . . . within the colonial landscape'.[29] And yet, these threads appear simply to have floated to the surface of this book, relegated to the place where an appendix might be. Levine's argument that in the politics of culture 'where' is as complex and powerful a category as 'who' raises more questions than it answers. So, more generally, do the geographical threads and spatial terms in her work and in that of other critics and activists, from Stoler to Butler. Yet, despite or perhaps because they are tentative and slippery, these hanging threads provide points of departure, from which to begin a more systematic exploration of empire, sexuality and space.

Empire, sexuality . . . and space

To develop the claim that geographical imagination will open up new forms of understanding and intervention in sexuality politics, and to ask where this might take postcolonial criticism, it is first necessary to say more about *geographical imagination*. This is a complex and contested term. Most simply, it encompasses a 'sensitivity towards the significance of place and space, landscape and nature in the constitution and conduct of life on earth'.[30] It has been applied to a particular form of critical thinking, most notably by Derek Gregory's exposition of *Geographical Imaginations* in social and cultural theory, but it has equally been used with reference to particular forms of fine art and popular culture, from landscape paintings to adventure stories.[31] Geographical imagination has been located within hegemonic forms of social power such as imperialism and nationalism, but also within counter-hegemonic forms, where resistance is located and conceived within 'spaces of resistance'.[32] Geographical imagination is therefore an open term, broad enough to refer to very different sorts of thinking by different sorts of people. This openness can be an advantage, so it important not to foreclose the term with premature definitions. Nevertheless, some distinctions and clarifications will help to explain what it might mean to think *geographically* about empire and sexuality.

First, distinctions can be drawn between material and metaphorical spaces, and more specifically sexual spaces.[33] Jane Ussher identifies a 'perennial material–discursive divide', distinguishing geographies composed of 'signs and signifiers' from those of 'corporeality, action and flesh'.[34] Broadly distinguished from their material counterparts, metaphorical sexual geographies have been identified in cultural and mental representations. Raymond Williams noted that the city, for example, has been imagined as an immoral geography, the country as its purer and healthier counterpart.[35] Rana Kabbani has shown how Europeans – including painters, writers, travellers, anthropologists and geographers – identified the Orient with various forms of sexual perversity, freedom and tradition.[36] Distinctions between material and metaphorical spaces also structure the regulation of sexuality, and more generally the contested processes of regulation. Geographies of law, including sexual law, are themselves tangibly real, but do not constitute a discretely material sphere. Davina Cooper identifies spaces of representation within legal discourse and shows how these structure law and legal practice. In *Governing Out of Order* (1998), she draws out a number of distinct ways in which law and geography intersect, generalising that law is fundamentally *spatial* in its contexts (in which legal questions and conflicts are played out), its *discursive formations* (by which legal demands and issues may be grounded, strengthened through territorialisation) and its *material practices* (including specific forms of situated enforcement). Similarly, Nicholas Blomley draws out 'the inherent – and inherently ideological – representations of space that are fundamental to legal understandings and practices'.[37] These revolve around what he calls a 'power/space nexus'[38] within the legal construction of space and the spatial construction of law.[39] Though they may be distinguished, material and metaphorical sexualities and sexual geographies are not always distinct. Alison Blunt and Cheryl McEwan generalise that postcolonial geography is oriented towards the analysis of 'spatial images such as location, mobility, borderlands and exile' at the expense of 'more material geographies',[40] though they acknowledge that the distinction between discursive and material is often blurred, since 'discourse itself is intensely material'.[41] Moreover, the material and metaphorical are recursively related, producing and produced by each other. Michael Brown has shown how the metaphorical sexual geography of the closet both structures lives – identities and specific experiences – and is reproduced by them.[42] Similar forms of interplay between metaphorical and material geographies may be traced in the field of imperial sexuality politics. Most concretely, for example, areas with reputations for sexual promiscuity may have been targeted for increased regulation. Less obviously, more abstract geographical ideas may also have informed regulatory systems, for example, when geographical ideas about boundaries inform the contestation of more abstract boundaries, such as between sanctioned and unsanctioned sexual conduct. These distinctions and dynamics echo others, drawn above, between the spaces of activism and criticism.

A second distinction can be made between absolute and relational sexual geographies, and between particularist and comparative approaches to them. I will suggest that the sites of sexuality politics were mutually connected, generating and patterning geographies of sexuality politics. It will be necessary to investigate the relationships between places, personal and institutional, biographical and social, informal and formal, which constituted and produced this 'geography of connection'.[43] This means acknowledging and exploring the connections between places but also, less obviously, within them. Thus, for Mort, the specific urban historical geographies of sexuality in London were also relational geographies, which reflected the city's wider connections and power relations: 'the capital's importance as the centre of empire, and latterly of post-colonial migration, has thrown up a series of extraordinarily complex cultures of sexual otherness'.[44]

Similarly, for Antoinette Burton, it was impossible to think of London or England as a pre-defined or self-contained home base. Burton aims to 'interrogate the assumption that the nation has always been an a priori, coherent whole and that fragmented identities and cultures of movement are characteristic of contemporary postcolonial modernity exclusively'.[45] Levine proposes a more general way of thinking about this and other imperial geographies of connection, speaking of the British Empire as 'a set of relations . . . frameworks structuring political, economic, and cultural exchanges'.[46] To better understand this sense of a relational geographical totality, within which political actions may be productively located, it helps to turn to Frederic Jameson's use of the term 'cognitive mapping'. Borrowing and reanimating a term from applied environmental psychology – originally used to describe mental representations that people form to navigate and understand living environments – Jameson traces the need for cognitive mapping to a disorienting world, thrown together and torn apart by imperialism.

> The truth of that limited daily experience of London lies . . . in India or Jamaica or Hong Kong; it is bound up with the whole colonial system of the British Empire that determines the very quality of the individual's subjective life. Yet those structural coordinates are no longer accessible to immediate lived experience and are often not even conceptualizable for most people.[47]

The purpose of cognitive mapping, as Jameson sees it, is to 'inscribe a new sense of the absent global colonial system on the very syntax of poetic language itself, a new play of absence and presence'.[48] Butler and Dyer cognitively mapped when they represented the global and the local but globally positioned geographies of regulation, and also when they showed individuals how they belonged to social totalities that reached from British women to their 'sisters' in the red-light districts of Bombay or Freetown. Cognitive mapping means searching for a visual or spatial language capable of representing, understanding and ultimately changing the world. It means representing the global system, but also the localities that comprise it, and the connections between them. In Burton's more straightforward terms, it means bringing disparate sites – domestic and imperial – 'into the same field of debate'.[49]

To locate sexuality politics is not just to position them within this multidimensional – material/metaphorical, real/representational, absolute/relational – and still somewhat slippery plane, but to explain their positions, the patterns they comprise. It can be to ask where political developments first appeared, and how – also when and to what extent – they spread. Historical geographies of imperial sexuality politics can be difficult to describe, not only because laws changed frequently, as did the propensities of the various authorities to enforce them, but because these regulations applied to a variety of territorial units. In this, as in other areas of law, geographical legal structures were complex. Blomley identifies what he terms a 'patchwork of diverse and often opposed legal spaces', not only between but within 'supposedly seamless systems of national law' and other (often apparently unified) legislative unit areas.[50] The geography in which laws were made and enforced, complex enough within and between sovereign states, was still more complex within empires, particularly where those empires were composed, as the British Empire was, of a great variety of political forms, with different legislative and legal systems. It may be possible to identify legal territorial units, in which forms of sexual regulation were formulated and/or enforced, though it will be necessary to distinguish each in terms of its specific political and legal system and relationships. Thus, for example, it is possible to identify India and South Australia as legal territorial units, with respect to the letter but not the enforcement of the law on consent. India had one law, South Australia another, but their interpretation and enforcement was much more coherent in the latter. In the South Asian possession, its recognition was mediated by numerous and complex *internal* territorial, political and legal systems. Of course, with populations of approximately 250 million and one-third of a million, these were radically different entities. Pieces in the legal patchwork were not only uneven in size but confusingly overlapping and varied in depth. In this, they reflect the more general complexity of geographies of law, composed of differently proportioned, intersecting and interacting geographical entities.[51] Variability in the geography of law within the British Empire was a function not only of the different systems adopted by the British authorities through historical circumstance or strategy but of the variable depth of colonial rule. It was not only specific laws, but also the imperial system that underpinned them, that met with resistance or was at least negotiated. To the extent that the British asserted a right or a desire to govern, they did so unevenly. But the legal geographies of empire were never simply the frameworks for governance; they were produced through and were productive of imperialism.

This brings the discussion from broad questions about how to think geographically about sexuality and empire to more specific questions about how, as Mort put it, 'a historical geography of sexuality' might 'be conceived',[52] as well as how a postcolonial geography might be envisaged. Before following these projects through by mapping and

interpreting the historical geographies of sexuality politics – the material geographies of regulation and resistance and the metaphorical
geographies of the political imagination and rhetoric – it is necessary
to say more about what this might achieve and where it might take
postcolonial criticism.

Beyond 'the British experience': postcolonial criticism and methods

Though postcolonial projects are, of course, diverse, many share the
aims of explaining and contesting imperial power and ways of seeing.
Postcolonial geography brings a specific perspective to this, though,
as Blunt and McEwan acknowledge, this sub-field has far to go.
'Postcolonialism and geography are intimately linked', they note, and
yet 'there have been few sustained discussions about what might
constitute a postcolonial geography'.[53] They propose that this academic inquiry and political project should focus on 'understanding
the spatial dynamics of power, identity and knowledge'.[54] It should
explore how imperial power was and is both constituted and resisted
geographically: how it was produced by, and was productive of,
geographies. Taking up these questions, this book examines the
spatial dynamics of power with respect to the contested regulation of
sexuality.

Another general postcolonial project is to challenge Eurocentric
versions of history and geography in which, as Marks puts it, 'we' did
this to or for 'them',[55] and visions of the present and future in which
the same must be true. Postcolonial geographies stand to contest the
assumed passivity of the non-European and colonised worlds, to demonstrate that people and places 'on the margins' could also be active,
making their own histories, if not of course in conditions of their own
choosing. It can be difficult to strike a balance between recognising
the force of the centre, on the one hand, and the productivity of the
margins, on the other. To critique Eurocentrism, it is important to
acknowledge – without overstating – the latter. This book, aiming
towards a measured reorientation of the ways in which empire and
sexuality are understood, analyses the spatial constitution of imperial
power, but also teases out the multiple points at which this was
produced and contested.

Preliminary investigations of sexuality and imperialism have tended
to re-inscribe imperial/colonial binaries which attribute the production of sexualities to the imperial centre. Hyam, for example, presented empire as a widened field of sexual opportunity, which liberated
but did not fundamentally change British sexualities. His survey of

[13]

empire and sexuality, as the subtitle of his oft-cited work makes clear, privileged 'the British experience', by which he meant the experiences of British *men* in the colonies. Hyam's account was not only one-sided – something that might be forgivable in the interests of focus; it rested on an ahistorical and Eurocentric understanding of sexuality. For Hyam, empire simply liberated the British, whose sexualities came before their colonial adventures, were freed rather than formed in the fields of empire. Critical of such an approach, Philip Howell generalises: 'Experiences in the metropolis – sexual policies, attitudes, assumptions, identities and subjectivities – are too often represented as removed or translated fully formed to the colonies, which occupy therefore only a marginal and subordinate place.'[56] Foucault's history of sexuality, for all its insights about reciprocal relationships between sexuality and power, suffered from some of this Eurocentrism, locating histories of sexuality within Europe. In a sustained postcolonial critique of Foucault's *History of Sexuality*, Stoler has done much to relocate histories of sexuality among relationships between European and non-European worlds *within* imperial power relations.[57] She argues that metropolitan sexualities were produced through the interplay between metropole and colonies. She disrupts discrete metropolitan sexualities by situating European sexual discourses and sexualities in their wider and racialised imperial contexts, and by empirically examining the production and regulation of sexualities in particular colonial formations. With reference to racially structured colonialism in the Dutch East Indies and French Indochina, she shows how racial boundaries were produced, policed and naturalised through the tight and often anxious regulation of sexuality.[58] Other postcolonial critics, notably Anne McClintock, disrupt metropolitan sexualities (and related constructions of race, class and gender) through their analyses of ambivalence and hybridity, which unsettle the otherwise apparently seamless imperial order.[59] By exposing the tenuous production of sexual (and other) means of imperial binaries, such as centre–margin, white–black and coloniser–colonised, Stoler and McClintock demonstrate the significance of critical histories of imperial sexuality for wider postcolonial projects concerned with deconstructing imperial binaries and worldviews. Their work leads a vibrant field of postcolonial criticism, which takes sexuality as a key indicator of imperial power, and asks how sexualities were produced and performed not only by Europeans but also by others.

Looking beyond the British experience, this book de-centres the metropolitan within histories of sexuality. It widens the field of view to include sexuality politics within a range of non-metropolitan sites and relationships between them. This is partly a matter of recovering and mapping forms of colonial agency. There are some useful pointers in the critical literature on sexuality politics which might help to position this project. It has been argued that *agency* with respect to the regulation of sexuality was socially and spatially dispersed. Alan Hunt argues that agency was dispersed geographically, and 'that moral regulation movements form an interconnected web of discourses, symbols and practices exhibiting persistent continuities that stretch across time and place'.[60] But, while he traces the social and spatial dispersal of Victorian moral regulation projects in Britain and the US, showing how they were directed as much from below as from above, as much from the margins as from the centre, he does not look beyond those imperial centres. He is not alone in that respect, for most of the important studies of the regulation and constitution of sexuality in the Victorian and Edwardian periods examine now well-charted metropolitan ground. Walkowitz's studies of the regulation of prostitution and the sexual life of Victorian London represent the tip of this iceberg. Similarly, those outside the US and Britain who have addressed questions of moral regulation have tended to examine events in England rather than their own countries.[61] Introducing a historical essay about prostitution in New South Wales, Judith Allen commented that though 'prostitution historiography has expanded during the last decade' (the 1980s), most of the work was British, American or European, both in origin and in geographical scope.[62] As one Australian researcher remarked: 'There has been very little attention given by historians in Australian to the ideas and activities of social purity organisations . . . and their attempts to influence the regulation of social conduct'.[63] More recently, this imbalance has been corrected, in part, by Manderson, Howell and particularly Levine. The picture they paint is valuable but incomplete, concentrating on the regulation of prostitution at the expense of other areas of sexual life, and on times and places in which an important but narrow form of regulatory politics applied. One of the aims of this book must be to shift the balance from CD laws back towards a bigger picture, not ignoring the regulation of prostitution but placing it in the wider political and geographical landscape. Another, more general, aim is to explore how regulation and resistance stretched across time and space, both *within* imperial centres and *between* imperial centres and colonial margins. This means enquiring about the wide range of people who became involved in sexuality politics and the relationships between them, including the activist networks that spanned and integrated much of the Empire, also reaching beyond into continental Europe and the US. It means exploring the places in which and between which interventions were situated.

In practical terms, the first thing to do is to map broad historical geographies of regulation and resistance, to show how specific laws and movements 'stretched across time and place'.[64] The 'big picture' of imperial sexuality politics, which this assembles, will provide preliminary answers to questions about where political innovations come from and where they go, and how they change *en route*. Of particular interest in this mapping are the non-metropolitan sites in which political ideas are actively generated or mediated: these places and processes are examined more closely through detailed case histories. In order to examine a wide yet manageable range of sites of sexuality politics, four contrasting sites have been selected from within the British Empire (figure 0.4). As the following introductions outline, these sites illustrate a variety of regulatory experiences: some raised the age of consent early and confidently, others later and reluctantly; some innovated with strong forms of CD legislation, others trailed with weaker forms or none at all. The sites also present contrasting pictures of political process: purity campaigners were much more

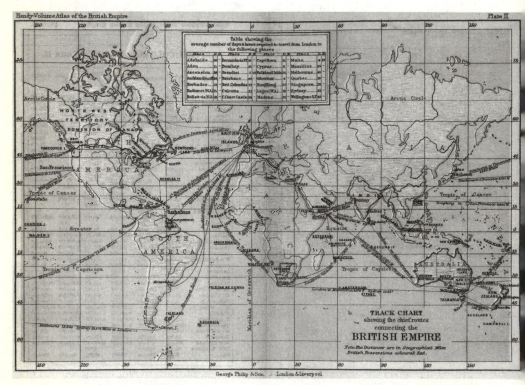

0.4 1886 map showing Britain's colonial possessions and the maritime routes between them

interested in and more prominent in some than in others; legislative activity was equally localised. The contrasting experiences reflect variable conditions for political engagement. The three colonial case studies in this book correspond to Stoler's political typology of sites of sexuality politics.[65] They range from a limited form of responsible government by the dominantly white settler society of South Australia to a complicated system of locally administered colonial but somewhat locally responsive rule by the British minority in India, to direct and relatively absolute colonial rule by the tiny British minority in Sierra Leone and their bosses in London. The four sites also varied in other ways, of course, including their respective geographies, societies and economies. These differences and profiles, which demand a brief introduction before being considered in more detail in successive chapters, situate and may later help to explain differences with respect to contrasting experiences of and trajectories within imperial sexuality politics.

The first of the case studies in this book, the West African colony of Sierra Leone, consisted of a promontory of swampy land, rising to forest and mountains, spanning just 25 by 15 miles (see figure 4.4). Founded by private investors in 1787, it became a Crown Colony in 1808, before being extended in 1896, when the Protectorate of Sierra Leone was annexed, but governed on distinct administrative terms. The British and other Europeans, arriving by ship, commonly described sparkling vistas of a small settlement – Freetown (originally named Granville Town) – framed by ocean, mountains and forest. Up close their descriptions varied but were rarely so complimentary, being generally dominated by descriptions of chaos, disease and death. They labelled this colony, and sometimes the region as a whole, 'the white man's grave'.[66] Many Africans saw the colony differently, and some explicitly contested these negative accounts.[67] The common thread in these descriptions, however, was that of a colony, perched in a few settlements on mosquito-infested swampy land between ocean, forest and mountain, inhabited by a mixture of peoples – composed of Creoles (liberated Africans), local Africans, Arab traders and European colonists – whose social and racial order was often less rigid that that of most of the rest of the British Empire. This small colony, with its mixed and transient population, and its skeletal, undemocratic government, formed the setting for a certain strand of British imperial sexuality politics, which was marked by a departure from otherwise common forms of regulation and resistance. Sierra Leone stood out from the imperial geography of regulated prostitution – the 'map of tyranny' identified by Butler and investigated by Levine and others. Its transient oceanic population – in particular its contrast between

Christian, class-conscious, largely anglophile Creoles, on the one hand, and diverse Africans, on the other – proved fertile ground for a vibrant, eccentric, moral politics which creatively borrowed and departed from political counterparts in other places.

Bombay (see figures 5.1 and 5.2), largely a creation of European colonialism, had grown from a backwater in the ancient Indian and Arabian Ocean trading system to a major centre in the increasingly global economy, first in the hands of the Portuguese (from 1534) and then (from 1661) the English (not yet politically united with the Scottish).[68] The latter systematically recruited migrants to the city, originally a small and swampy island, offering religious and economic concessions that attracted Hindus, Muslims, Jews, Christians and Parsis, who made Bombay into a 'cosmopolitan trade mart'.[69] Describing Bombay at the end of the nineteenth century, an English writer asked his readers to imagine

> a great city, of over 800,000 souls, lying on the shores of a beautiful sea, sparkling in the sunshine, glorious in the monsoon, backed by grand mountains, with many a castellated peak nestling in palm groves, with hundreds of sea-going vessels anchored in its harbour, with two busy lines of railway piercing it, broad thoroughfares and grand buildings, with a most active and intelligent mercantile community, both European and native; with its lawns crowded day and night with pleasure and leisure seekers, and its brightness added to by the most brilliantly dressed ladies in the world, the Parsees.[70]

Of course, there were many other ways of seeing Bombay, not all so detached or privileged, though some elements of the story would remain. It was, from any perspective, a large commercial port and centre of government. In contrast to Sierra Leone, Bombay was governed by a powerful administration, particularly in the late 1860s when a newly appointed municipal commissioner enjoyed virtual *carte blanche*. A number of political activists emerged in and/or based themselves in the city, using its media and other communications to advance local and broader political projects. These included British and Indian purity – and allied – activists, who campaigned on issues such as the age of consent and the regulation of prostitutes, the presence of whom was frequently noted and sometimes regretted by moralists, health officials and military officers.

Bombay has since been renamed Mumbai, and this raises a question about place names which is both practical and political. Acknowledging that general policies on place names involve simplification, eliding differences in how places were seen and known, and the politics of different peoples' identifications with them, I have nevertheless decided to use the most meaningful contemporary terms. It is appropriate to speak of *Bombay* because most people did at the time. In other cases, including the perennially difficult question of whether to speak of 'England' or 'Britain', I have decided to use different terms according to context. As Levine observes, 'English' and 'British', 'England' and 'Britain' were used inconsistently and confusedly, often 'collapsed into one another'.[71] Nevertheless, after the union between Scotland and England early in the eighteenth century, 'British' was generally applied to imperialism, and was also used to describe the wider sphere of British influence and diaspora. On the other hand, most laws regulating sexuality were not strictly British, many such as the Criminal Law Amendment Act (1885) applying to England and Wales but not Scotland; nor does 'British' describe the scope of some other laws, including the CD Acts, which applied also to parts of Ireland; since they were neither English nor British. I refer to these laws as 'domestic'.[72] Equally, as the first chapter explains, most metropolitan purity movements were English rather than British, and 'English' was generally invoked in purity rhetoric and used to describe 'national' activist organisations. Though it is not possible to arrive at an entirely uncomplicated policy on the use of these terms, it is therefore most meaningful to refer to 'Britain' when referring to the Empire but not to metropolitan sexuality politics; then, the terms 'English' or 'domestic' are more often appropriate.

The centre of English sexuality politics, Victorian London was also the largest city the world had then known, with a large and socially and ethnically diverse population that reached 4 million in 1871 and only continued to grow.[73] The hub of international shipping and national rail, it was also the industrial and commercial centre of the British Empire, the largest empire the world had known. It was equally important politically, as the centre of British parliamentary democracy and the seat of the generally less responsive statutory departments and agencies that directly and indirectly governed the colonies and India. Lobbyists and activists, recognising this concentration of power, were also particularly active in London, visible in the city's newspapers and on its streets, where they demonstrated and acted on a variety of issues, some of which were concerned with sexuality and more specifically the sexual life of the capital. Judith Walkowitz[74] and Lynda Nead[75] have shown how the city, with its great mass of people, its anonymity and its juxtaposition of rich and poor, powerful and vulnerable, provided an unprecedented range of sexual opportunities, which were a source of pleasure to some but anxiety to others. This reflected London's role as a great meeting-place – a hub of global transport and communications, a space of connection and concentrated political power. As Miles Ogborn[76] has shown, metropolitan growth and life, in the context of broader processes of social and governmental modernisation, provoked and made possible a new agenda for sexuality politics, with new and enhanced forms of regulation and resistance. This wide-ranging politics was concerned with the city itself, but also with the wider society in which it was located, and especially with places identified as immoral and/or unhealthy, as naval ports and army garrisons often were. British domestic sexuality politics was therefore concerned with general legislation, with such matters as the age of consent and with area-specific legislation, notably the CD Acts.

South Australia and New South Wales (see figures 3.1–3.5), remote from England geographically, were among the closest politically. From the middle of the nineteenth century, their political systems and legislative processes replicated those of the imperial Parliament. Like most other dominantly white settlement colonies in the British Empire, government was devolved partly from London to the elected colonial governments, based in Adelaide and Sydney. Governments were also swayed by other forces, including the local media, churches and politicised citizen and campaign groups. Adelaide was one of the first footholds of British settlement in South Australia, which was formally colonised in 1836. Douglas Pike characterised the colony as a 'paradise of dissent',[77] shaped by independently minded colonists, who asserted ideals of civil liberty, social opportunity and religious freedom, and who secured responsible government for themselves within twenty years, in 1857, when their population was still less than one-third of a million. Though served by nearby Port Adelaide, the people of Adelaide were oriented primarily towards their agricultural hinterland and the ideals that shaped its colonisation. Whereas pictures and descriptions of Sydney emphasise the harbour and its merchant and military traffic of ships, passengers and seamen,[78] those of Adelaide tend to portray the city's wide, orderly streets and to emphasise its many churches and its legislative buildings (see figure 3.2). Perhaps as a consequence, the people and politicians of Sydney showed less interest in sexuality politics than their counterparts in Adelaide, who made initiatives and took their own political direction, marked – with respect to issues such as the CD Acts and age of consent – by engagement and independence of mind. Both colonies converged and diverged with England and other parts of the Empire in intriguing and significant ways.

These African, Indian, English and Australian case studies present contrasting and connected perspective on the geographies – the sites themselves and the connections between them – of imperial sexuality politics. They respond to Burton's call to bring the domestic and imperial sites of sexuality politics 'into the same field of debate',[79] and Edward Said's to chart the 'overlapping territories' and 'intertwined histories' of empire[80] – calls that, as Derek Gregory has recently noted, have generally fallen on deaf ears.[81] The comparative methodology of this book is not isolated, of course: Levine's work on prostitution, Elleke Boehmer's and Alan Lester's on anti-colonial resistance, Jane Jacobs's on cities, and Deirdre Coleman's on women's travel, all illustrate the power of juxtaposing disparate colonial sites, drawing convergences and divergences, relationships and distances into relief.[82] Dagmar Engels and Shula Marks are candid about the reasons some prefer to decline Said's challenge, deciding not to systematically compare India and Africa on the grounds that, '[f]aced with today's increasing specialisation of professional and historical knowledge, and the consequent accumulation of historical monographs, such a systematic comparison would call for an almost impossible range of reading'.[83] There is certainly some risk in casting one's net widely: most obviously, the possibility of knowing sites less well than individual area specialists might; and the inevitability of presenting less empirical detail on each site. But comparative research can illuminate processes that may not be visible within individual places, and also position those places within a wider framework, charting dispersed and connected political histories and geographies.

Asserting and exploring the power of geographical imagination for activism and criticism, the chapters that follow bring a new dimension to histories of empire and sexuality, and contribute to broader postcolonial projects, particularly those concerned with an analysis of imperial power, a critique of Eurocentric ways of seeing and the development of a postcolonial geography. The organisation of this book reflects its geographical orientation. The sequence of chapters is not linear, in the sense of developing a single thesis about the geographies of sexuality and empire. Nor is it chronological, describing a series of developments through time. It is more a collage, an assemblage of spatial processes and perspectives, which have coexisted historically and can do so conceptually. Every compositional choice comes at a price, of course, for when one structure is chosen, others are declined. Levine seeks a way round this by dividing her analysis of prostitution in the British Empire in two, chronological history followed by more fragmentary ideas and notes. This is clever, but Levine has really written two books, the second of which illustrates and confirms the power of thinking and writing outside the chronological box: spatially rather than temporally, for instance. I would argue that what is, in effect, Levine's second book need not have been appended or subordinated to the first; it would stand alone. I present this book, therefore, as a free-standing exploration of spatial politics and of the spatiality of imperialism, which explores Butler's claim that geographical perspectives may open up new fields of understanding and political action.

Notes

1 J. E. Butler, *Revival and Extension of the Abolitionist Cause* (Winchester: John T. Doswell, 1887), p. 13. Butler's publications and letters are reprinted, with those of other purity campaigners, in J. Jordan and I. Sharp (eds), *Josephine Butler and the Prostitution Campaigns: Diseases of the Body Politic*, 5 volumes (London: Routledge, 2003).
2 R. Hyam, *Empire and Sexuality: The British Experience* (Manchester: Manchester University Press, 1990), p. 2.
3 Hyam, *Empire and Sexuality*, p. 152.
4 R. C. Harris, 'The simplification of Europe overseas', *Annals of the Association of American Geographers*, 67 (1977), 469–483.
5 A. L. Stoler, *Carnal Knowledge and Imperial Power: Race and the Intimate in Colonial Rule* (Berkeley: University of California Press, 2002).
6 P. Levine, *Prostitution, Race and Politics: Policing Venereal Disease in the British Empire* (New York: Routledge, 2003), p. 227.
7 L. Manderson, 'Colonial desires: sexuality, race and gender in British Malaya', *Journal of the History of Sexuality*, 7:3 (1997), 372–388, at 373.
8 K. Mann and R. Roberts, *Law in Colonial Africa* (London: Currey, 1991), p. 3.
9 R. Rathbone, 'Law, lawyers and politics in Ghana in the 1940s', in D. Engels and S. Marks (eds), *Contesting Colonial Hegemony: State and Society in Africa and India* (London: British Academic Press, 1994), pp. 227–247, at 231.
10 The first of the English CD Acts (1864) provided for regulation in designated areas; this temporary legislation expired in 1866, when it was renewed with the CD Act (1866) and succeeded by the CD Act (1869), which extended coverage to a series of additional areas. This Act was suspended in 1883 and repealed in 1886. In India the Cantonments Act (1864) provided for regulation in military zones; the Indian CD Act (1868) extended regulation to civilian areas, before being repealed in 1888. See: J. R. Walkowitz, *Prostitution and Victorian Society: Women, Class and the State* (Cambridge: Cambridge University Press, 1980).
11 E. J. Bristow, *Vice and Vigilance: Purity Movements in Britain Since 1700* (Dublin: Gill & Macmillan, 1977).
12 F. B. Smith, 'Labouchere's amendment to the Criminal Law Amendment Bill', *Historical Studies*, 17 (1976), 165–175; R. Aldrich, *Colonialism and Homosexuality* (London: Routledge, 2003).
13 J. Morris, *Pax Britannica: Climax of an Empire* (London: Faber, 1968).
14 M. Foucault, *History of Sexuality: An Introduction* (London: Penguin, 1978), vol. 1, p. 103.
15 F. Mort, *Dangerous Sexualities: Medico-Moral Politics in England since 1830*, 2nd edn (London: Routledge, 2000), pp. xxii–xxiii.
16 This extends an argument, advanced most coherently by Doreen Massey, that social relations such as class, gender and race are spatially constituted: see: D. Massey, *Space, Place and Gender* (Cambridge: Polity, 1994).
17 Foucault, *History of Sexuality*, p. 58.
18 Peter A. Jackson, 'Mapping poststructuralism's borders: the case for poststructuralist area studies', *Sojourn*, 18:1 (2003), 42–88.
19 R. Phillips and D. Watt, 'Introduction', in R. Phillips, D. Watt and D. Shuttleton (eds), *De-Centring Sexualities: Politics and Representations Beyond the Metropolis* (London: Routledge, 2000), pp. 1–18, at 1.
20 Foucault, *History of Sexuality*, vol. 1, p. 127.

21 M. Foucault, 'Questions on geography', in C. Gordon (ed.), *Power/Knowledge, Selected Interviews and Other Writings 1972–1977* (Brighton: Harvester Press, 1980), pp. 63–77, at 67–68.
22 Stoler, *Carnal Knowledge and Imperial Power*, p. 112.
23 Stoler, *Carnal Knowledge and Imperial Power*, p. 129.
24 Stoler, *Carnal Knowledge and Imperial Power*, p. 131.
25 Stoler, *Carnal Knowledge and Imperial Power*, p. 138.
26 Walkowitz, *Prostitution and Victorian Society*, p. 44.
27 R. C. Bleys, *The Geography of Perversion: Male-to-Male Sexual Behaviour Outside the West and the Ethnographic Imagination 1750–1918* (London: Cassell, 1996), p. 9.
28 P. Levine, 'Orientalist sociology and the creation of colonial sexualities', *Feminist Review*, 65:1 (2000), 5–21, at 11.
29 Levine, *Prostitution, Race and Politics*, p. 297.
30 D. Gregory, 'Geographical imagination', in R. J. Johnston, D. Gregory, G. Pratt and M. Watts, *Dictionary of Human Geography* (Oxford: Blackwell, 2000), pp. 298–301.
31 D. Gregory, *Geographical Imaginations* (Oxford: Blackwell, 1994); R. Phillips, *Mapping Men And Empire: A Geography of Adventure* (London: Routledge, 1997); G. Huggan, *Territorial Disputes: Maps and Mapping Strategies in Contemporary Canadian and Australian Fiction* (Toronto: University Of Toronto Press, 1994).
32 S. Daniels, *Fields of Vision: Landscape Imagery and National Identity in England and the United States* (Cambridge: Polity, 1993); J. P. Sharp, P. Routledge, C. Philo and R. Paddison (eds), *Entanglements of Power: Geographies of Domination/Resistance* (London: Routledge, 2000); S. Pile and M. Keith (eds), *Geographies of Resistance* (London: Routledge, 1997).
33 M. Brown, 'Closet geography', *Environment & Planning D, Society and Space*, 14 (1996), 762–769.
34 J. M. Ussher (ed.), *Body Talk: The Material and Discursive Regulation of Sexuality, Madness and Reproduction* (London: Routledge, 1997), p. 1.
35 R. Williams, *Country and the City* (London: Hogarth Press, 1985).
36 R. Kabbani, *Imperial Fictions: Europe's Myths Of Orient* (London: Pandora, 1986); see also: R. Aldrich, *Seduction of the Mediterranean: Writing, Art and Homosexual Fantasy* (London: Routledge, 1993); A. McClintock, *Imperial Leather: Race, Gender and Sexuality in the Colonial Contest* (London: Routledge, 1994).
37 N. Blomley, D. Delaney and R. T. Ford (eds), *Legal Geographies Reader: Law, Power and Space* (Oxford: Blackwell, 2001), p. xix.
38 N. K. Blomley, *Law, Space and the Geographies of Power* (New York: Guilford Press, 1994), p. 58.
39 Blomley, *Law, Space and the Geographies of Power*, p. 58; D. Cooper, *Governing Out of Order: Space, Law and the Politics of Belonging* (London: Rivers Oram Press, 1998); Blomley, Delaney and Ford, *Legal Geographies Reader*.
40 A. Blunt and C. McEwan (eds), *Postcolonial Geographies* (London: Continuum, 2002), pp. 1–2.
41 Blunt and C. McEwan, *Postcolonial Geographies*, p. 5.
42 M. Brown, *Closet Space: Geographies of Metaphor from the Body to the Globe* (London: Routledge, 2000).
43 M. Ogborn, *Spaces of Modernity: London's Geographies, 1680–1780* (Guilford Press, London & New York), p. 19.
44 Mort, *Dangerous Sexualities*, p. xxv.
45 A. Burton, *At the Heart of Empire: Indians and the Colonial Encounter in Late-Victorian Britain* (Berkeley: University of California Press, 1998), p. 71.
46 I. C. Fletcher, L. E. N. Mayhall and P. Levine, *Women's Suffrage in the British Empire: Citizenship, Nation and Race* (London: Routledge, 2000), p. xiii.
47 F. Jameson, 'Cognitive mapping', in C. Nelson and L. Grossberg (eds), *Marxism and the Interpretation of Culture* (Chicago: University of Illinois Press, 1988), p. 349.

48 Jameson, 'Cognitive mapping', p. 349.
49 Burton, *At the Heart of Empire*, pp. 160–161.
50 Blomley, *Law, Space and the Geographies of Power*, p. 58.
51 Blomley, Delaney and Ford, *Legal Geographies Reader*.
52 Mort, *Dangerous Sexualities*, p. xxiii. Partial answers to this question include works by Judith Walkowitz, Miles Ogborn, Lynda Nead and Philip Howell, which are cited throughout this book.
53 Blunt and McEwan, *Postcolonial Geographies*, p. 1.
54 Blunt and McEwan, *Postcolonial Geographies*, p. 5.
55 S. Marks, 'History, nation and empire: sniping from the periphery', *History Workshop Journal*, 29 (1990), 111–119, at 112.
56 P. Howell, 'Prostitution and racialised sexuality: the regulation of prostitution in Britain and the British Empire before the Contagious Diseases Acts', *Environment & Planning D, Society and Space*, 18:3 (2000), 321–340, at 321.
57 A. L. Stoler, *Race and the Education of Desire: Foucault's History of Sexuality and the Colonial Order of Things* (Durham, NC: Duke University Press, 1996).
58 Stoler, *Carnal Knowledge and Imperial Power*.
59 McClintock, *Imperial Leather*, p. 5.
60 A. Hunt, *Governing Morals: A Social History of Moral Regulation* (Cambridge: Cambridge University Press, 1999), p. 9.
61 Australia's foremost historian to have addressed the subject in depth, F. B. Smith, has done so with reference to England and the US.
62 J. Allen, 'The making of a prostitute in early twentieth-century New South Wales', in K. Daniels (ed.), *So Much Hard Work: Women and Prostitution in Australian History* (Sydney: Fontana, 1984), pp. 192–232, at 195.
63 J. Jose, 'White Cross League and sex education in SA state schools 1916–1929', *Journal of the Historical Society of South Australia*, 25 (1996), 45–57, at 46.
64 Hunt, *Governing Morals*, p. 9.
65 Colonies based on small administrative centres of Europeans (as on Africa's Gold Coast) differed from plantation colonies with sizeable enclave European communities (as in Malaya and Sumatra), and still more from settler colonies (as in Algeria) with large, heterogeneous and permanent European populations: Stoler, *Carnal Knowledge and Imperial Power*, p. 54.
66 C. Chamier, *Life of a Sailor, by a Captain in the Navy* (London: Richard Bentley, 1832), p. 264.
67 For example W. Rainy, *The Censor Censured; or, The Calumnies Of Captain Burton on the Africans of Sierra Leone* (London: George Chalfont, 1865).
68 P. Balsara, *Highlights of Parsi History* (Bombay: Young Collegians' Zoroastrian Association, 1981 [1963]).
69 M. D. David, *Bombay, the City of Dreams: A History of the First City in India* (Bombay: Himalaya Publishing House, 1995), p. 2.
70 J. M. Mitchell, *In Western India: Recollections of My Early Missionary Life* (Edinburgh: David Douglas, 1899), vol. 1, pp. 68–69.
71 Levine, *Prostitution, Race and Politics*, p. 7.
72 Walkowitz, *Prostitution and Victorian Society*.
73 T. Boyle, *Black Swine in the Sewers of Hampstead* (New York: Viking Press, 1989), p. 212.
74 J. R. Walkowitz, *City of Dreadful Delight: Narratives of Sexual Danger in Late-Victorian London* (London: Virago, 1994).
75 L. Nead, *Victorian Babylon: People, Streets and Images in Nineteenth Century London* (New Haven, CT: Yale University Press, 2000).
76 M. Ogborn, 'Law and discipline in nineteenth-century English state formation: the Contagious Diseases Acts 1864, 1866 and 1869', *Journal of Historical Sociology*, 6:1 (1993), 28–54.
77 D. Pike, *Paradise of Dissent: South Australia 1829–1857* (Melbourne: Cambridge University Press, 1967 [1957]), p. 1.

78 R. Gibson, 'Ocean settlement', in R. Gibson (ed.), *Exchanges: Cross-Cultural Encounters in Australia and the Pacific* (Sydney: Museum of Sydney, 1996), pp. 91–111.
79 Burton, *At the Heart of Empire*, pp. 160–161.
80 E. Said, *Culture and Imperialism* (New York: Vintage, 1993), p. 1.
81 D. Gregory, 'Post-colonialism', in R. J. Johnston, D. Gregory, G. Pratt and M. Watts, *Dictionary of Human Geography* (Oxford: Blackwell, 2000), pp. 611–615, at 614.
82 E. Boehmer, *Empire, the National and the Postcolonial, 1890–1920* (Oxford: Oxford University Press, 2002); D. Coleman, *Maiden Voyages and Infant Colonies: Two Women's Travel Narratives of the 1790s* (London: Leicester University Press, 1999); J. Jacobs, *Edge of Empire: Postcolonialism and the City* (London: Routledge, 1996); A. Lester, *Imperial Networks: Creating Identities in Nineteenth-Century South Africa and Britain* (London: Routledge, 2001).
83 D. Engels and S. Marks (eds), *Contesting Colonial Hegemony: State and Society in Africa and India* (London: British Academic Press, 1994), p. 5.

CHAPTER ONE

Spreading political knowledge: English newspapers, correspondents, travellers

> Like people and schools of criticism, ideas and theories travel – from person to person, from situation to situation, from one period to another.[1]

English purity campaigners saw their own country as a net exporter of the ideas, laws and movements that drove sexuality politics around the world. Josephine Butler claimed that 'England has been sending forth to all these parts of the world two streams, one pure and the other foul'.[2] She echoed the words of Ottobah Cugoano and Olaudah Equiano, who had asked many years earlier how 'a fountain' could 'send forth at the same place sweet water and bitter?'[3] Claiming and alluding to African political forebears, Butler tacitly acknowledged that the abolition of slavery had not simply been an English victory, and that slaves and other Africans had played a part. Nevertheless, she invoked the moral responsibility that many of the original abolitionists had shouldered and claimed for England. Other English purity activists made similar claims about the responsibilities and influence that went with power. For Ellice Hopkins, the new abolitionism was a metropolitan project that had been exported to the rest of the world, ensuring that 'other nations followed the noble repentance of England'.[4] William T. Stead (1849–1912), an English journalist equally convinced that the eyes of the Empire were fixed on England, and more specifically on himself, asserted that his interventions in metropolitan sexuality politics would result in a 'shuddering horror . . . that will thrill throughout the world'.[5] Claims such as these, laying moral responsibility at the feet of the English, but in the process reasserting English influence, betrayed a mixture of strategy and arrogance.

A form of diffusion?

Parallels and coincidences in global sexuality politics, past and present, have sometimes been attributed to the *diffusion* of ideas and identities. Michael Mason used this term to describe the spread of new forms of sexual morality through Victorian society,[6] Dennis Altman, the spread of gay and lesbian identities through the modern world,[7] Larry Knopp and Michael Brown, the spread of queer culture and politics within the contemporary USA.[8] But what does the term mean? A standard dictionary definition of 'diffuse' is 'to disperse or be dispersed from a centre; to spread widely, disseminate'.[9] Some patterns – increases in the age of consent in England ahead of many other parts of the Empire, for example – seem to suggest that innovations were originating in England and then spreading to other parts of the Empire.

Geographers have elaborated more generally on this compellingly simple idea:

> A stone is tossed into a pond. The consequent splash forms a large wave immediately around the entry point. Within a second, waves are starting to move out in a circular pattern across the surface of the water. Some seconds later, very small ripples are disturbing the weeds on the far side of the pond.[10]

Peter Haggett explains that the stone may take the form of a virus in a susceptible population or information in a communication system, and that the pond may be composed of individuals or social groups. The idea of diffusion can be modified and complicated to allow for waves moving at different speeds, originating off-centre,[11] mediated by human 'hopes and fears', and by 'power, personality and relationships'.[12] Consistently, however, diffusion involves 'the ability to spread outwards or to disperse from one or more limited centres to a wider geographical area'.[13] In each case, an *innovation* spread from one place to another over time, advancing in 'waves of adoption',[14] through a combination of simple proximity (a 'neighbourhood effect') and hierarchical connection.[15]

The idea of diffusion, structured as it is around centres and margins, places that respectively innovate and adopt, act and are acted upon, resonates with understandings and ideologies of colonialism. Some of the most powerful interpretations of colonialism, such as Carl Sauer's analysis of the dispersal of cultural traits from origins, or 'cultural hearths',[16] and Frederick Jackson Turner's analysis of westward expansion as a 'tide of innovations moving remorselessly outwards from the Eastern Seaboard',[17] revolve around ideas about diffusion. More generally, James Blaut identifies 'diffusionism' with 'the colonizer's model of the world':

This belief is *diffusionism,* or more precisely *Eurocentric diffusionism.* It is a theory about the way cultural processes tend to move over the surface of the world as a whole. They tend to flow out of the European sector and toward the non-European sector. This is the natural, normal, logical, and ethical flow of culture, of innovation, of human causality. Europe, eternally, is Inside. Non-Europe is Outside. Europe is the source of most diffusions; non-Europe is the recipient.[18]

For Blaut, 'diffusionism' is broader than the more specific and abstract idea of spatial diffusion and more politically committed, more closely embedded in a Eurocentric worldview. But while he deconstructs its assertion that 'Inside innovates, Outside imitates',[19] Blaut does not consider the possibility that sometimes this is precisely what happens, if only because the centre, constructed and self-appointed as it is, uses its power to invent and export. Though ultimately I follow Blaut in challenging the ideological underpinnings of diffusionism, I propose to explore the extent to which this notion does explain spatial and temporal patterns in the emergence of systems of regulation and forms of resistance. Did innovations in regulation and resistance emerge at central points and spread outwards? The mechanisms and processes by which English sexuality politics was exported might, for instance, involve channels of communication such as the postal service and inter-colonial and international media, and be channelled through personal and social contacts and networks. Without discounting the possibility that movements spread in multiple directions – such processes are considered in later chapters – this chapter examines the processes by which purity movements may have spread from England to other parts of the British Empire.

English purity campaigners were conscious of the importance, and in some cases the reciprocity, of their relationships with activists in other countries. As Butler put it 'Our work is world-wide . . . No nation now "liveth to itself or dieth to itself", any more than the individual.'[20] They not only cooperated with their counterparts on the Continent, but openly borrowed from them. For instance, regulation had been introduced in France much earlier on – in 1802 by Napoleon – and the French had an equally long history of resistance from which the English were able to learn. Butler, who worked with colleagues in France, Belgium, Switzerland and elsewhere, advised her countrywomen and men to learn languages and acquaint themselves with 'the efforts and conflicts of reformers of other lands'.[21] The leader of the National Vigilance Association (NVA), a leading English purity campaign group, 'found that to keep the work on watertight national lines would at best achieve only partial success, and at worst might end in disillusion and collapse'.[22] He argued that international cooperation was important, not only because European countries had similar experiences, but because those experiences were linked, notably by the international traffic in prostitutes in which young women were allegedly procured in one country and shipped off to another. Touring Europe in 1898–99, he helped to plant national committees and establish links between them.[23] Despite the leadership that this illustrated, English activists generally understood that within European purity movements they were participants – sometimes borrowing ideas, sometimes offering them – rather than leaders.

Outside of Europe they were less modest, positioning themselves at the centre of the British Empire and English-speaking world, where they felt a sense of responsibility and/or political opportunity. Their campaigns responded to, criticised and mirrored contemporary imperialism, asserting that activists around the world watched events in England, particularly London. Mrs Ormiston Chant, who campaigned for the closure of London's Empire Theatre, reputedly a meeting-place for prostitutes and gay men, claimed to have 'roused' Londoners 'to keen interest' and also 'the whole of England, and many people in other countries, such as France, Germany, India, South Africa, and the United States'.[24] She asserted that London interested the world both because of its unprecedented debauchery and because of its ideas, its innovative political culture; metropolitan purity activists claimed both an international profile and a direct international influence. The NVA claimed, for example, of its campaign against allegedly obscene publications in general and the French author Zola in particular:

> No victory could have been more complete or far-reaching. Throughout the length and breadth of the United Kingdom publishers declined to sell. The Australian colonies seized and confiscated them, and a late Member of Parliament said, after his return from a journey to India, that nothing had struck him more forcibly than the marvellous effect which the English prosecution had had upon the Indian booksellers.[25]

To activists and organisations such as Chant and the NVA, London was what Steven Marcus[26] once termed a 'shock city', a cutting-edge social and political formation that other cities – cast as less developed and lower down the political hierarchy – were inspired or destined to copy.

That hierarchy was understood by many English activists as a structure through which English laws were extended to colonies or devised for them. Alfred Dyer catalogued CD Acts and ordinances in British colonies, dependences and territories, condemning what he saw as a British imposition on the lives of millions of colonial subjects, including '200,000,000 of our fellow subjects' in India alone.[27]

Campaigners distinguished regions of absolute (if differently ordered) imperial rule such as India and Sierra Leone from those with degrees of autonomy such as the Dominion of Canada and the Australian colonies, but argued that British influence held sway to a different extent in either country. Butler claimed that in independent colonies 'the system has been established by their Parliaments, at the instigation, however, of, or on the urgent advice given by, officials and experts in England'.[28] She spoke of *our Government's imposition* of the drink and opium traffic, and of legalised vice, to the destruction of the bodies and souls of conquered races wherever we have planted our flag'.[29] For Butler, regulation revealed the more general immorality of colonialism. As she put it, 'There is no creature in the world so ready as the Englishman to destroy, to enslave, to domineer.'[30] To others, such as Charles Bell Taylor, MP, colonialism was not fundamentally corrupt: it could be put right.[31] It would be simplistic to label some purity campaigners anti-imperial and others imperial reformists, but whether they sought to dismantle or reform imperialism, purity campaigners and critics asserted and acted on the general power of English people over their colonised counterparts. Invoking the imperial power of which she was often critical, Hopkins argued that English purity movements would inevitably 'influence in the world at large'.[32] She reflected a tendency among English purity campaigners to identify, on some level, with the power of those they sought to influence and often to oppose. Butler, for example, decided that she must speak for those less powerful than herself. Anticipating Gayatri Chakravorty Spivak's analysis of subaltern subjectivity,[33] which renders the subaltern (disempowered colonial subject) unable to represent herself, 'to speak', she declared colonial prostitutes unable to represent themselves. She condemned on their behalf 'the violation of their persons, and the special horrors incidental to the regulation system?'[34]

English purity campaigners recognised distinctions within both Indian and English society, which further complicated the hierarchical geographies of sexuality politics. They commonly placed England above Wales and Scotland, in both their rhetoric (recall, for example, Butler's claim that *England* was sending forth political streams) and their organisations. Though some of the *national* organisations that they formed and supported were 'British', English purity activists distinguished the constituent nations of Great Britain and generally assumed the leading role. As late as 1886, the *Sentinel* reported the emergence of 'the first purity campaign in Wales'.[35] Similarly, a year later *The Christian* stated that 'the agitation in favour of the repeal of State-regulated vice abroad has not hitherto taken root in Scotland',[36] though it informed readers that English deputations to Scottish meetings were trying to change that. The leading role, claimed for England, was sometimes linked to the organisational structure of purity societies, including those identified with larger and/or institutional bodies, such as churches. Thus, for example, the CEPS (Church of England Purity Society) formed in England – the domain of the Church of England – then spawned and corresponded with White Cross organisations (the White Cross Movement in 1883, Army in 1884, League in 1895) in Scotland, Ireland and the colonies – finding 'allies in the Dioceses of Bombay, Colombo, Gibraltar, British Guiana, Lucknow, Singapore, Pretoria, Sydney and Victoria'.[37]

This hierarchical geography was further sub-divided between large and smaller cities and between town and country. Thus, for example, Dyer regarded Bombay as a gateway to India, a strategic point from which to influence the large rural population. The Quaker publisher that supported his publishing house in Bombay stated: 'Though only one-twentieth of the people live in towns of over 20,000 population, yet it is from the large cities and centres of education that influence mainly spreads.'[38] As the Bishop of Bombay put it, 'Christianize Bombay, and all Western India will be Christian.'[39] In India, as in other countries, campaigners focused strategically on large and important cities, from which they hoped the movements would trickle down to smaller cities, towns and villages.[40]

Campaigners identified channels of influence, within and between the levels of this hierarchical space, which established formal connections and/or possibilities for linkage. The CEPS, formed in London (at Lambeth Palace) in 1883, resolved to 'take advantage of the existing framework of the Church, and to establish a branch in every Diocese in England and the Colonies'.[41] Other kinds of connections, such as shared languages, were also instrumental in opening channels. Despite Butler's advice to activists to learn and work in foreign languages, they campaigned largely in English, which strengthened their involvement in British-ruled settlement colonies and in the US, and heavily limited their involvement in parts of the British Empire where only a minority spoke English. Channels were also structured by real or perceived political compatibility. Thus, for example, English purity campaigners considered it relatively straightforward to export models of political action to the US or to self-governing British colonies, but more complicated and potentially impossible to export the same to less compatible political systems such as those of British India. Overall, they saw English-language self-governing colonies and independent nations as the most suitable sites for the extension of English campaign models. Accepting this version of events, American purity campaigners such as Benjamin De Costa, a New York Episcopalian minister who visited England and met Hopkins, Butler and Stead before establishing an American White Cross Army, perceived themselves as 'just behind' their English and European mentors.[42]

Metropolitan purity campaigners saw England as a centre from which innovations in regulation and resistance diffused hierarchically and contiguously, reaching geographically, socially or politically 'close' countries such as the Australian colonies and the US before more 'distant' others. But to what extent did this Eurocentric, or more specifically Anglocentric, understanding reflect the reality? In what follows I explore how ideas and movements, to borrow a term from Edward Said, 'travelled': in what directions, to which destinations and with what effect. I trace the processes by which and the extent to which specific campaigns may have spread from England to other parts of the British Empire. Focusing on purity movements, I consider and illustrate three mechanisms for this diffusion – news, correspondence and travel – doing so with primary reference to purity movements within and between England, Australia (Sydney in particular) and India (Bombay).

Inter-colonial news: 'the Modern Babylon' reported around the Empire

The image of ripples spreading outwards from the centre of a pond seems particularly apt to describe the spread of information about English campaigns; indeed, it is an image that historians of social purity movements have often employed. For example, Mariana Valverde argues that 'ripples of the Stead scandal' reached Canada and invigorated emerging purity movements there.[43] The 'Stead scandal' consisted of a series of articles collectively headed the 'Maiden Tribute of Modern Babylon', printed in London's *Pall Mall Gazette* in July and August 1885. Penned by journalist and editor William T. Stead (1849–1912), they told the story of a 13-year-old girl, procured and sold into prostitution, and expanded on the wider context of this incident through reports about the findings of a 'Secret Commission'. Designed to 'thrill throughout the world',[44] Stead's allegations do appear to have sent waves of information and ideas to many countries, prompting journalistic and political interventions around the Empire and beyond.[45] By reconstructing the flows and movements of Stead's scandal, it should be possible to understand some of the connections that formed and bound together the wider terrain of sexuality politics.

Stead's articles were distributed, reproduced, syndicated, reported and copied in newspapers around the world, and – according to his biographer – in 'every corner of the British Empire'.[46] Readers who did

not see original copies of the *Pall Mall Gazette* found faithful repro-
ductions of its leading story on their own front pages. Virtually iden-
tical reports appeared in many North American newspapers: coverage
in the *Toronto Daily Mail* was very similar to that in the *New York
Times*, the *New York Herald* and the *Chicago Daily Tribune*. In each
case, the story was printed in similar form on the front page.[47] The
Toronto Daily Mail allowed the sensation to dominate the opening
columns of the front page through July, pushing Canadian news –
including the nationally much more significant Riel Rebellion, which
threatened the westward expansion of the young nation and reflected
racial unrest within it – to inside pages and/or less prominent columns.[48] These newspapers attributed their syndicated stories to the
same source – the Mackay–Bennett commercial cable, based at the
Herald Bureau, London. First reports of the *Pall Mall Gazette* stories
took a little longer to reach some other parts of the world, though
when they did they were much the same. Thus, the *Sydney Mail*, in
a report from London dated July 9, reported: 'Under the guise of
effecting reform in the matter of the social evil, the *Pall Mall Gazette*
has been publishing articles which are creating an immense sensation. The paper has been expelled from the clubs and bookstalls.'[49]
There was no comment at this stage on the potential relevance of
these stories to Australia. Despite the uniformity in content, attribut-
able to the news agencies and syndicates, reports of the Stead scandal
did vary in the contexts of their publication. Different stories and
advertisements appeared alongside them, and they were bought and
read by people with different cultural literacies. Though drafted in
London and distributed from there, and not always actively modified
at the points of their reception, stories could not travel wholly intact.

The contextual mediation of Stead's story was more evident where
it was more actively reported and commented on. In some cases, the
stories were appropriated and retold with local settings in the hope
of invigorating local campaigns. The 'Maiden Tribute' was restaged
and/or retold, adapted to local settings and political agendas, from the
lumber camps of Wisconsin to the settlement fields of Tasmania.[50]
Local journalists introduced local colour in the form of vocabulary, perspective and analysis. The *Australian Christian World* gave extended
coverage to the stories in January and February 1886, including a
digest of English media reactions to them and to Stead's continued campaign, and finally considered their relevance to Australia.[51] Drawing
out the relevance of Stead's example, it stated:

> The work of reform must not be confined to England, but in the words
> of the champion leader of this movement, wherever and so long as ever

these crimes exist must we be resolved to do anything and everything to stem their torrent. And they do exist in Australia; for a prominent journalist told me that such facts as contained in the "Tribute," &c. might be found in Sydney every night if people cared to look for them.[52]

The paper concluded that Australians might not equal their European mentors – 'We cannot all be Luthers or Steads; we cannot all be martyrs or heroes' – but they could at least try: 'we can each do our feeble share'.[53] Reporting a speech in which Stead took credit for legislative change in England, the *Australian Christian World* identified the ripples both of his story and of its political impact:

> In Tasmania the age of protection was, before last year, ten. Then it was proposed to bring it to the British standard of thirteen. The *Pall Mall* arrived in the midst of an agitation for raising the age to sixteen. The Government were obdurate, and would only consent to raise it to fourteen. A Mr. Dangerfield, of Hobart Town, then wrote to the newspapers to this effect: 'If the House does not raise the age above fourteen, I will publish a Maiden Tribute of Modern Tasmania that will cause great scandal.' Frightened senators threatened to bring Mr. Dangerfield to the Bar of the House, but they thought better of it, and raised the age of consent to fifteen.[54]

It is possible to find many more examples of purity activists around the world commenting on the relevance of the 'Maiden Tribute' to their local and national situations, and using it to launch new initiatives. In Chicago, Clifford Roe began his major contribution to national purity movements with reference to Stead and the *Pall Mall Gazette*.[55] Like other American purity activists in the nineteenth and early twentieth centuries,[56] he 'rode the popularity of the Stead exposé'.[57] In Australia, the Bishop of Sydney did something similar, launching an Australian branch of the White Cross League with reference to 'the ghastly disclosures recently made in England of an organized and systematized trade in the corruption of young girls', which led him to 'fear that, perhaps in different and less organised forms, similar evils exist here'.[58] And in Montreal, members of the Society for the Protection of Girls and Young Women also used Stead's campaign as a springboard for their own.[59] Each of these examples illustrates how stories of London's vice, published originally in London, filtered into distant corners of the Empire (and beyond), assuming local forms and significance, and effecting the spread of a campaign.

It will ultimately be necessary to more critically assess the apparent diffusion of English news and campaigns, to consider the possibility that the contextual acts of writers, publishers and campaigners were not simply derivative, and to question the originality and causal influence of metropolitan acts. First, however, it is important to consider other mechanisms by which English purity movements may be said to have spread from England, particularly throughout the Empire.

Correspondence: Ellice Hopkins and Dr Richard Arthur

Butler advised activists to exploit their contacts with correspondents and friends in the colonies, writing letters that would inform and influence them.[60] Archives of her own correspondence, at the Women's Library in London and the Special Collections of Liverpool University, demonstrate that Butler practised what she preached. Letter-writing formed part of her sustained efforts to establish joint action against regulation across the Continent and to extend English campaigns throughout the British Empire.[61] Analysis of the (well-known and very large) Butler correspondence archive is beyond the scope of this section, which aims to draw out some of the ways in which letters widened the horizons of English campaigns. A focused illustration of this is provided by correspondence between the English and Australian activists Ellice Hopkins and Dr Richard Arthur, and by links between some of the campaign organisations with which they were associated, in particular the English and Australian wings of the CEPS.

Hopkins, who has been described as 'representative of the new-style purity feminist',[62] was an ambitious campaigner with wide horizons who wrote pamphlets for overseas White Cross Leagues – she claimed that they were 'read at meetings held in Australia and America'[63] – and kept up correspondence with activists around the world. Hopkins sought some of the credit for this, writing: 'I sometimes humbly think that the moral drains of *one* hemisphere are enough to be forced through the channel of a single heart. But it has pleased Providence to give me *both*, and Australia and New Zealand have just added themselves on . . . (not very improving for my head).'[64] She boasted: 'My work grows and grows. I have the Antipodes added on, and have almost as much work in Australasia as in the three kingdoms.'[65] Ultimately, it will be necessary to critically examine and qualify Hopkins's imperious self-importance, but not before entertaining the suggestion that her letters did play a part in the diffusion of purity movements. Hopkins showed particular interest in Australia, where her principal correspondents included Richard Arthur, with whom she remained in 'constant' touch 'up to the time of her last illness'.[66] Arthur (1865–1932) had trained as a medical doctor in England before emigrating to Sydney in 1891, where he was involved in social purity and social hygiene campaigns, and served as an elected member of the Legislative Assembly (MLA) of New South Wales.[67]

The relationship between Hopkins and Arthur was asymmetrical, the former using their correspondence to promote her own publications and projects in Australia. For example, she sought Arthur's advice on how best to adapt *The Power of Womanhood; or, Mothers and Sons* (1899) for the Australian market, asking whether the English edition should be adapted 'with regard your school system for boys?'[68] Hopkins also asked Arthur to provide statistics and facts about Australian conditions regarding 'the degradation of women which I am told exists' that 'would make my appeal to the Australian women so much more definite'.[69] He complied, helping the English author to dominate the Australian market for purity literature, even as she rejected his own submissions to the White Cross League series, on the grounds that no new manuscripts were required.[70] The Australian edition – the sixth – of *The Power of Womanhood* was published in 1902, three years after the English and American editions.[71] Hopkins presented the book as the natural extension of a campaign from England, within the British Empire, and dedicated it to 'the Mothers of Australasia in deep and grateful affection'.[72]

> The great British Empire, the greatest civilising, order-spreading, Christianizing world-power ever known, can only be saved by a solemn league and covenant to her women to bring back simplicity of life, plain living, high thinking, reverence for marriage laws, chivalrous respect for all womanhood, and a high standard of purity for men and women alike.[73]

Hopkins referred to the information provided by Arthur, stating for instance that she was 'of course aware that the colonial school system is probably in some respects different from ours',[74] and acknowledging that 'the last few pages I know apply to the mother country far more than to colonial life'.[75] Hopkins was also indebted to Arthur for promotional support, once her publications appeared in print. For example, he recommended booklets by the Englishwoman within his own pamphlets, such as 'The Training of Children in Purity', in which he quoted Hopkins and advised every mother to obtain a copy of her booklet.[76] Australasian White Cross League pamphlets and pledge cards, which Arthur printed and circulated, bore both English and Australian contact details. Hopkins's self-promotion and enlistment of support appears to have worked. She claimed to have been told that 'Australia gobbled up an edition of my book in a few weeks' and that it 'is doing immense good'.[77] If Australia did indeed gobble up *The Power of Womanhood*, this was partly due to the support and endorsement the book received from local activists such as Arthur.

Despite the advice she sought, and received, on adapting her work, Hopkins made only minor amendments to her text and indeed to the campaign models and organisations that she helped to devise for Australian consumption. Arthur worked for many years in one such organisation, the Australian White Cross League, which he served as honorary treasurer. This work complemented his activities as an MLA, which included a lengthy campaign to raise the age of consent in New South Wales (see chapter 3). In both these areas, Arthur acknowledged debts to English campaigners including Hopkins and Stead. He claimed to be awaiting an Australian Josephine Butler to 'rouse men and women to the tragedies passing every day before their eyes', and called for a journalist like Stead who might 'show to our hypocritical, willingly-blinded eyes the horrors that lie concealed in our city'.[78] In the absence of such figures, he took it on himself to replicate, as far as possible, English campaigns in the Antipodes. In this, he appears to have had some success. Between them, Hopkins and Arthur do appear to have contributed to the successful launch of the White Cross Movement in Australia. In 1885 the CEPS claimed that the White Cross League, which had been founded by the Bishop of Durham, was 'developing' in Australia, as well as in 'America' and India.[79] Hopkins's biographer claimed that the Australasian organisation was 'inaugurated by her and by her books', and that it represented 'the most active, as it is the most recent, development of her work'.[80] The Australian White Cross League, which was founded in Sydney in 1902,[81] endorsed this view, stating in successive annual reports that 'the work of the White Cross League was initiated . . . by Miss Ellice Hopkins'.[82]

It is easier to chronicle the actions than measure the achievements of this organisation. The Australasian White Cross League was prolific in distributing leaflets and arranging and delivering lectures to young men and boys. In 1904, the League's general secretary and lecturer, R. H. W. Bligh, reportedly travelled for nine months throughout South-Eastern Australia, delivering hundreds of lectures and upwards of 50,000 booklets.[83] The League invited readers to sign a purity pledge, which would quietly confirm their commitment to high moral standards among both men and women. It is not known how many people signed the pledge, or what difference their signatures might have made. The organisation maintained that it *had* made a difference, citing anecdotal evidence – for instance, it printed a letter 'from a suburb of Adelaide' which stated: 'I found a little booklet in the road yesterday, entitled *True Manliness*.' The writer expressed appreciation and offered moral and financial support to the printers of this booklet.[84] There is no evidence that the letter was genuine, and no way of assessing the difference that Hopkins's booklet may have made to its sender, or the difference its changed sender may have made to society. The image of a derivative purity pamphlet found lying on the ground in suburban Adelaide does, however, provide a persuasive if possibly fictional image of the diffusion of texts and campaigns from England to the colonies. This completes the picture, sketched in this section, of how correspondence channelled ideas, texts and movements from England to other parts of the world, through asymmetrical relationships.

It will be necessary to write more sceptically of the role that Hopkins's letters may have played, and to critically reassess the apparent passivity and deference of her Australian correspondent and the organisations in which he worked. The CEPS was never a centralised organisation, and its devolved structure cautions against interpreting the Australian CEPS or the White Cross League as mere replicants.[85] It will also be necessary to critically re-examine the imperiousness – the self-important Anglocentric worldviews – of campaigners such as Hopkins. The chapters following develop these points, criticising the imperialism of English purity movements while also identifying the limits of their political reach, and shifting the focus from English to colonial political actors.

Travel and travel-writing: Alfred Dyer

Perhaps the most tangible way in which purity campaigns were extended was through travel. In the first instance, activists travelled to build networks, gather information and publicise their cause. Many of them travelled frequently, doing so for days, weeks or even years at a time. One of their aims was to meet fellow-campaigners whom they already knew through newspapers and letters, in supportive and informative encounters. For instance, the Reverend Joseph Kirby, a prominent South Australian purity campaigner, began his political career as a peripatetic activist, travelling and working in Queensland, New South Wales and South Australia, and consolidated his later work with visits to London and Bombay, where he met Butler, Stead and then Dyer.[86] One reason purity activists travelled and published travel accounts was to extend and support existing campaign networks. For example, both William Coote's European tour in 1898–99 and Henry J. Wilson's tour of the US in 1876 were designed to promote specific campaigns and help establish campaign groups and networks. Coote wanted to establish a network in opposition to the so-called 'white slave trade' (the traffic in young women for prostitution),[87] Wilson to found and support abolitionist societies (which sought the abolition of CD laws).[88] Another reason for travel was to gather information, primarily to widen and strengthen English campaigns on behalf of other places, largely by influencing English public and parliamentary opinion. Sometimes the tours were media events in their own right, which used the profile of travellers or the newsworthiness of their visits to draw media attention to their cause. For example, Elizabeth Andrew and Dr Kate Bushnell's tour of India in 1891–92 was designed to gather information and raise the profile within purity movements of the places they visited. Butler had asked Andrew and Bushnell to make the trip, to gather and disseminate facts about the toleration and regulation of military prostitution in British India. Similarly, the English Quakers and purity activists Alfred and Helen Dyer toured India in 1888. Anticipating the potential contribution of activists 'on location', whose 'vantage in India' might both inform and extend the English campaigns,[89] the *Christian* supported and publicised the Dyers's Indian tour, printing letters and articles they sent back.

Before he ventured into travel and travel-writing proper, Alfred Stace Dyer (1849–1926) used quasi-travel narratives to strengthen the overseas work of English purity campaigns. In *Slavery Under the British Flag* (1886), he took readers on a virtual tour through the sites in which regulation was established, within a kind of immoral geography of British imperial governance. Images and metaphors of travel establish connections between disparate locations, Dyer sounding almost like a tour guide as he leads readers on, inviting them to follow from place to place, to 'pass on to the British Empire in India', for instance.[90] Contextualising regulation, he provided a kind of human – historical, cultural, demographic, political – and physical geography lesson. He informed readers, for example, that Burma was a large, recently colonised, country bordering China and India,[91] and that India was the most important part of the British Empire, with a population of 200 million, compared to Great Britain and Ireland's 35 million.[92] Interest in India – shared with many other purity campaigners – was also evident in Dyer's work as editor and publisher of the *Sentinel*, in which capacity he published a variety of exposés on regulation, which described its effects on particular people and places, notably Calcutta, Madras and Bombay, illuminating these reports with a variety of maps and illustrations.[93] The periodical regularly visited Bombay, and gave prominent coverage to the activities of purity activists and organisations there, notably Wallace Gladwin (editor of the campaign journal *The Indian Purity Trumpet*[94] and founder of a White Cross League in the city[95]) and the Bombay Social Purity Alliance.[96] The *Sentinel* explained that Bombay was both the second most populous city in the British Empire and, alongside Madras, 'the centre of operations for the Contagious Diseases System throughout India'[97] (see figure 1.1).

1.1 Front page of *The Christian* showing a map entitled 'Government versus God in India'. The caption reads: 'Map showing seventy-five of the Centres in which the British Government has established the system described in Mr. S. A. Dyer's letters in THE CHRISTIAN'

Reporting the visit to India in 1888, Alfred Dyer, in whose name the articles appeared,[98] strategically deployed the medium and conventions of travel-writing to strengthen his case:

> By careful investigation and inquiry amid the scenes of the official enormities in question, I have collected evidence that is incontrovertible. In some cases I have seen the things which I shall describe. In others, my information has been gained from Christian missionaries and ministers . . . and others.[99]

Dyer began by asserting that 'good people at home'[100] had found it difficult to believe that the British Government in India could behave as alleged in relation to prostitution. He continued by presenting an eyewitness account in support of the allegations. Asking readers to trust what he had 'seen' with his own eyes, Dyer confirmed that 'licensed harlots in India were moved from place to place with British regiments on the march, under the sanction and direction of the authorities'.[101] The rhetoric of presence and immediacy, conveyed through claims not only to have seen but to be seeing – written in the present tense – 'brought home' the Indian subjects, bringing them to life for English readers. On the other hand, Dyer evoked the detachment of a traveller, seeing military prostitution with a critical distance that apparently eluded his more established countrymen. Bringing a clear and critical eye to things that the English in India had grown accustomed to – things they could either not see or not see fault with – he described a visit to the barracks and camp of the 4th Rifle Brigade at Lucknow. There, he met the 'chukladarin, or overseer' of prostitutes, whom he 'entreated to leave her sinful occupation', but was refused, told of 'the lucrative commission which she received [and] flourishing before our eyes as she spoke the jewellery and ornaments with which she was covered'.[102] Credible and vivid details, gathered through direct observations, encounters and conversations, give Dyer's account a sense of reality, translating sweeping and abstract allegations into specific human scenarios, in real time and place. The minutiae of the workings of official policies on prostitution – details of tents used by prostitutes at Lucknow, for instance[103] – convey something of its normalisation and, to Dyer, its horrifying acceptance.

It is often difficult to measure the impact of individuals within movements that spanned decades and involved many thousands of people. However, campaigners in England attached considerable importance to the contributions of colleagues, including the Dyers, who fought purity battles on the Indian front.[104] Dyer featured prominently in Maurice Gregory's version of events, which claimed that he had 'unearthed a hideous series of facts',[105] which forced the Government to act.[106] A more objective measure of Dyer's influence, an Anglo-Indian newspaper that supported regulation, also credited 'Dyer & Co.' with influence – by which it meant influence on English public opinion and members of Parliament.[107] Following Dyer's reports in the *Christian*, questions were asked in the House of Commons by Mr Williamson and Professor Stuart, and Sir J. Gorst, the under secretary of state for India, stated in reply: 'If anything like the practices alleged by Mr Dyer prevails in India, measures will be taken to secure that any such practices shall be stopped forthwith.'[108] When, in June 1888, the House of Commons voted for total abolition of government regulation of prostitution in India, the *Christian* attributed some of the credit to Dyer, stating that he 'and his Parliamentary backers at home . . . deserve the heartiest thanks of the British nation for securing this result'.[109] It reported that every speaker but one condemned 'the practices exposed in Mr Dyer's letters' and attributed the positive result to public opinion, which had been 'solely created' by them.[110]

Travelling and campaigning: the Dyers in Bombay

Activists also travelled with the intention of spreading and transplanting campaigns. On their Indian tour, the Dyers found one of Bombay's leading Christian and social purity publications without an editor and decided to take up the challenge, and that kept them in Bombay from 1888 to 1898, when they finally left for health reasons. Exchanging his editorship of the *Sentinel* for that of the *Bombay Guardian* – a well-established, 'undenominational, evangelical, weekly newspaper' established in 1851 by the Indian branch of the Society for the Abolition of Vice[111] – Dyer took many of his political ideas and strategies with him, transplanting a purity agenda. Doing so, he responded to Butler's call for 'men and women going forth to India and our Colonies to do the work which we have done at home'.[112] Like Butler, who regarded the 'repeal of the system in our Colonies as a logical sequence of its repeal at home',[113] Dyer asserted the more general belief that 'so far as root principles are concerned, legislative action in Crown possessions should follow the course of British Imperial law', subject to minor variations 'to suit local conditions'.[114] He tried to bring this about, first by informing the English public (as I have shown), then by trying to spread the campaign to and within India.

Dyer appears to have been a vehicle for the diffusion of purity campaigns from England to, and then within, India, taking to Bombay

the professional and political skills he had acquired in London. Some
English purity campaigners subscribed to ideas about hierarchical
diffusion, expecting influence to spread from principal cities, trickling
down to smaller centres and rural areas. Writing to the *Christian* in
1887, Gladwin explained how this would work, stating that the people
of India 'travel about much' by train, and that 'the travelling masses
will tell all the news'.[115] In a leaflet for advertisers, the printers of
the *Bombay Guardian* asserted the potential of a Bombay newspaper, pointing out that with a population of 900,000 Bombay was
the 'second largest city in the Indian Peninsula' and 'gateway to the
300,000,000 of India'. It claimed that Bombay would provide a point
of access to India's English-language readership of 16,000,000.[116] Dyer,
attempting to spread ideas to India, used channels such as these. As
the author of *The European Slave Trade in English Girls* (1880), he
had started the chain of events that ended in significant legislative
change in England.[117] As the publisher and editor of influential pamphlets and periodicals – the *Sentinel* alone sold up to 250,000 copies a
month – Dyer made an important contribution to the English purity
movements, while he also honed skills in the media, writing and
publishing, and cultivated political contacts.[118] Books he had written
and/or published – such as *Facts for Men on Moral Purity and Health*
(1884) – circulated in large numbers, not only in England but overseas, where they were endorsed and distributed by organisations
such as the Australasian White Cross League.[119] Contacts that he had
made – notably with another Quaker purity activist, George Gillett
(1837–93)[120] – also widened the geographical horizons of Dyer's work.
Like a number of other English purity campaigners, he 'turned his
zest towards India',[121] and more specifically towards Bombay, not
only because the city was seen as a gateway to the subcontinent, but
because of more local factors. First, upwards of 10,000 prostitutes
worked in Bombay at the time,[122] effectively with the sanction of
military and/or civil authorities. Second, it was an important node
in the opium trade, exporting large quantities of the drug to China,
again with official sanction. Announcing Dyer's Indian appointment,
the *Sentinel* accur-ately predicted that he would use the *Bombay
Guardian* to 'vigorously attack the traffics in impurity, intemperance,
and opium'.[123] Given its general function as a Christian weekly intended for a reader-ship of all ages and both sexes, this newspaper
was to remain muted on sensitive moral issues, forcing Dyer to seek
another outlet for more explicit criticism. To that end he initially
co-edited with Gladwin and Gregory the monthly *Banner of Asia*,[124]
which was published in Bombay (through the *Bombay Guardian*) and
London (through the *Sentinel*) and continued as a separate title until

1896, by which time the war against regulation was largely over (figures 1.2 and 1.3).[125]

To the extent that they exported purity movements from England to India, individuals such as Dyer and Gladwin worked within organisations and socially defined channels. On his original visit to India and in his appointment to the *Bombay Guardian*, Dyer was supported by the Friends' Association. This Quaker organisation had saved the *Bombay Guardian* when its long-serving editor died,[126] appointing a committee of trustees to manage a fund which it established to support the newspaper's machinery and printing costs, effectively subsidising its production and dissemination. Appointing Dyer to edit the newspaper, the Association asked him to 'spread in the Eastern Hemisphere the knowledge of the Gospel of our Lord and Saviour Jesus Christ', and also to oppose 'the Traffics in Vice and Opium and in Intoxicating Liquors' in the same sphere.[127] Dyer already knew some of the trustees, including Gillett, his co-conspirator in *The European Slave Trade in English Girls* campaign, then honorary secretary of the Friends' Association for Abolishing the State Regulation of Vice (since 1873).[128]

Effectively working for an English employer, Dyer also worked in an 'English way', importing many of the tactics that he and other English campaigners had used previously. He imported, marketed and distributed purity literature, including some of his own titles, which were also circulating throughout many parts of the British Empire.[129] Dyer also imported the journalistic tactics that had been tried and tested by purity campaigners in England, asserting that similar problems demanded similar responses. Reporting a court case in 1890, for instance, the *Bombay Guardian* claimed that a number of London clubs 'perpetrated . . . the deepest conceivable forms of wickedness',[130] and that a similar establishment had emerged in Bombay, 'the members of which have made themselves wealthy by a trade in human flesh'.[131] Dyer implicitly compared himself with Stead, linking his imprisonment in Bombay's Bycullah Gaol in 1894 (for publishing a statement by certain missionaries, alleging malpractice by officials[132]) with Stead's high-profile stay in Holloway in 1885 (he was sent to prison for breaking the law when researching the 'Maiden Tribute').[133] In another extension and adaptation of English models of purity activism, Dyer reminded readers of the traffic that had once existed between England and Europe. He argued that essentially the same thing was happening 'between certain European countries and English possessions in the East',[134] and that the authorities should respond as they had in England, by raising the age of consent, asserting that 'it is certainly not too much to ask that the Viceroy of India in Council

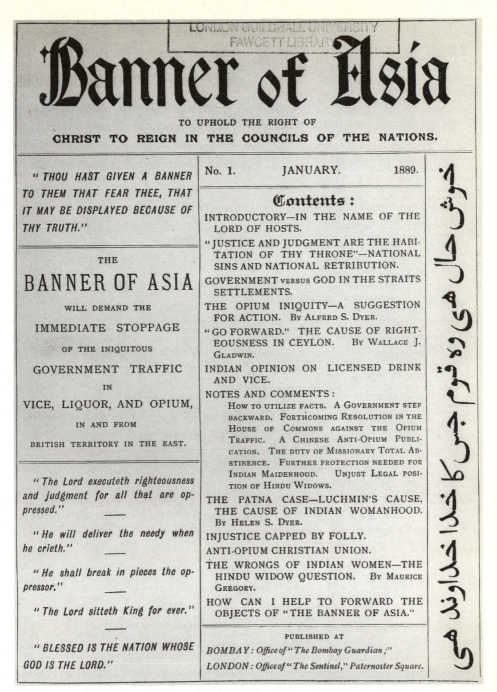

1.2 The monthly *Banner of Asia*, published at the offices of the Bombay Guardian, was used to lobby government and promote campaigns on moral issues such as opium and prostitution

1.3 Inside cover of *Banner of Asia*, first issue, showing advertisements for purity publications and organisations

should enact a law, for the whole of the British Indian Empire, upon the lines of the Criminal Law Amendment Act of 1885'.[135]

In addition to specific narratives and strategies, Dyer imported something more fundamental: a way of seeing Indian moral geography. As a large city, a railway terminus and a port, a region with a hot climate and non-white inhabitants, Bombay had many characteristics that English observers conventionally associated with immorality and sexuality. Through this lens, Dyer could plausibly characterise the city as 'the worst spot in the British Empire',[136] and he could even claim that 'Piccadilly at its worst at mid-night is MORALITY ITSELF compared to the European vice quarters at Bombay. The scenes to be seen there in broad daylight are too awful for description.'[137] Furthermore, he could conclude such conventional descriptions with equally conventional interventions, ranging from outreach activities to work on board European vessels in the harbour.[138] Helen Dyer employed similar rhetoric in her accounts of Bombay, which focused on European immorality and rescue work:

> Crushed and humiliated in spirit by the increase of drinking dens in the European quarter of Bombay, wherein many soldiers and sailors were drawn to ruin, Wallace Gladwin began to pray that God would incline some heart to open Gospel work for this needy class. He spent one whole night on his face before God.[139]

Situating Bombay within an immediately recognisable immoral geography, both Alfred and Helen Dyer asserted that the city's immorality should be a concern of purity campaigners everywhere: a concern, as Alfred put it, of 'the entire Christian population of this city, and the Empire of which it is the metropolis'.[140]

To that end, both Alfred and Helen Dyer were involved in direct activism along the lines of English purity movements. They co-founded a vigilance committee in Bombay and supported or supportively reported projects that had been initiated by others. In addition to their work on regulation and opium, they supported campaigns for pure literature,[141] temperance[142] and moral restraint.[143] The Dyers tried to integrate the Indian movements that they helped found into wider, more established networks. Just as he brought news of India to English campaigners, Dyer devoted some of his Indian publications to news of, for example, the 'liquor crisis in England',[144] the 'Great moral crusade in Japan',[145] the 'Pledge of the Peking prohibition of opium society'[146] and the enactment of colonial versions of the Criminal Law Amendment Act, for example in South Australia.[147] Informing readers in India about the latest developments in England, and vice versa, they played an important part in forming a campaign network than spanned different regions of the British Empire.

Their achievements in Bombay are difficult to assess. Dyer was a melodramatic figure whose claims should often be taken with a pinch of salt, and whose main achievements as a campaigner were probably behind him by the time he arrived in India – it was he who paved the way for Stead's successful campaigns in 1885. Nevertheless, the Dyers do appear to have heaped extra pressure on the Government to abolish regulation and the opium trade. Writing in 1888, Butler judged that Dyer was 'doing a great and good work, he is unearthing the crimes of our govt. and its unworthy officers. For denunciation, and as a scourge, he is a well chosen instrument.'[148] Directly through their immediate readership, and indirectly through the media that published and reprinted their reports, the *Bombay Guardian* and the *Banner of Asia* brought sensitive and provocative information to influential people. An independent observer claimed that the *Bombay Guardian*'s subscribers' list included

> businessmen, missionaries, military and civil officers, members of Legislative Councils, non-commissioned officers and private soldiers, railway men, Indians, both Christian and non-Christian, besides all who see it at libraries, and in England and America many who are entitled to be considered leaders in various fields of philanthropy and Christian effort.[149]

The impacts of these public opinion campaigns were in some cases traceable. Dyer, whose colleague called him 'the life and soul'[150] of the Anti-Opium Urgency Committee, which lobbied Parliament on the subject, both mobilised opinion in England and India, and arranged for fresh questions to be asked in the House of Commons.[151] Dyer's attempts to influence Indian public opinion were also noticed. If the *Bombay Guardian*, the *Banner of Asia* and the *Sentinel* are to be believed, a wide range of Indian 'native' newspapers noticed, responded to and supported Dyer's interventions and 'revelations':[152] the *Interpreter*, identified as a native paper based in Calcutta, was quoted as wishing 'Godspeed to Mr. Dyer's efforts'.[153] At most, the Dyers *grew* rather than planted English purity movements and publications in Bombay, working within structures that had been cultivated by others such as Gladwin (who disseminated purity literature and edited the *Purity Trumpet*),[154] the Bishop of Bombay (who took the chair when a White Cross Society was founded in 1886),[155] and missionaries such as the Rev. George Bowen (who edited the *Bombay Guardian* for over thirty years before Dyer).[156] Nevertheless, the Dyers's contribution was considerable, and this comprised of bringing ideas and perspectives into Bombay from England. Gladwin illustrated the difference this made, writing sycophantically that, even though he had lived in Bombay for years, it 'was only when [he] went to England and read some of Mr Dyer's books' that he understood 'the real character' – the real immorality – of British rule in India.[157]

Conclusion

This chapter set out to examine the means by which and the extent to which English sexuality politics were exported to other parts of the Empire. It found very tangible evidence of English impositions, though the evidence did not point simply towards a sphere of English influence.

On the one hand, purity activists tended to capitalise on – even to assert and reproduce – English influence, making the most of their privileged access to transport and communications technology and infrastructure. On the other, they attacked elements of British imperialism that they considered immoral – targeting the state regulation of prostitution – and worried about the responsibilities and ethics of holding so much power. Hopkins paused to reflect on how her activism was founded on class position and power, which brought privileged access to the media, and to publishing and campaign organisations and industries.[158] Butler privately criticised Dyer's attitudes towards the women he supposedly championed:

> His experiences are those of disgust and reprobation only, for the poor women, as well as for the men. My heart is racked with pity for them. I feel for them, if possible, more than for British women under the Acts. Mr. Dyer calls them 'brazen harlots' and all such bad names. But who made them so? They are all the more to be excused and pitied because they are only women, under the tyranny of men, but they are the women of a conquered and subjected race, coerced by our *imperial* hand.[159]

Worrying about the actions of '*our* imperial hand', Butler did not wholly personalise the criticism of Dyer, but instead acknowledged her own implication within the iniquitous imperial order. Recognising that she could not simply extricate herself from this, her pragmatic solution was to ask purity campaigners to think critically about their power, to monitor its use and ultimately to contest its foundation.[160] But, whether or not they were indeed self-reflexive, figures such as Butler and Dyer did their best to widen and transplant English purity campaigns. Hopkins's influence over Arthur and Stead's over newspaper editors and readers in many parts of the world evidenced their power to speak and be heard.

And yet, English influence was limited. Shortly after his arrival in Bombay, one of Dyer's colleagues had regretted that 'few in India besides the Missionaries have taken part in the highly important Repeal campaign',[161] and roughly the same could have been said after his departure. When Indian people did oppose regulation, they did so on their own terms – for example, dancers seeking exemption from the system and others simply evading it (see chapter 3) – rather than those of English purity activism. Dyer and his colleagues *did* make an impression in some respects, though the scale of their success must be qualified. They may have helped seal the fate of the opium trade, but not so much by drawing Indian people into their campaign as by informing English activists and lobbying the imperial Parliament in England. In any case, the opium trade was in decline at the time, so anti-opium campaigners such as Dyer were merely swimming with the tide of history.[162] Dyer and his colleagues were less significant players in struggles over the age of consent in India, an area in which Indians were much more important than English campaigners in securing legislative change, as the next chapter explains. Taking a back seat, the Dyers endorsed Indian struggles on the age of consent and related, controversial questions about the status of widows and the rights of women. Helen did so through a sympathetic biography of the social reformer Pandita Ramabai, with a Preface that asked English readers to support her work,[163] Dyer through the *Bombay Guardian*'s positive coverage of Behramji Malabari's age of consent campaign.[164] The age of consent had already been high on the political agenda when Dyer arrived in India, and his engagement in this debate was to be limited.[165] Other social purity initiatives, which the Dyers attempted to bring from England to Bombay, failed or were forced to change direction to adapt to local conditions and concerns. For example, Helen Dyer took over the management of a rescue centre, founded in 1877, but found it impossible to continue the Home of Hope according to the English principles on which it was founded, since she could find neither volunteer helpers nor employment for the women she rescued.[166]

By turning from Hopkins to Arthur and from Dyer to Malabari, or more generally from English to colonial agents of sexuality politics, it may be possible to get past the assumption that 'Inside innovates, Outside imitates',[167] and the Eurocentric ideology with which that assumption is associated. Chapter 2 shifts the perspective from English activists who exported political ideas to colonial counterparts who, at the very least, actively imported and appropriated them. Challenging any *derivative thesis* about colonial purity movements, it identifies productivity and activity within Indian readings of English purity texts, including political ideas and models.

Notes

1 E. Said, 'Travelling theory', in *The World, the Text and the Critic* (London: Faber & Faber, 1984), pp. 226–247, at 226.
2 Butler, *Revival and Extension of the Abolitionist Cause*, p. 4.
3 O. Cugoano, *Thoughts and Sentiments on the Evil and Wicked Traffic of Slavery and Commerce of the Human Species* (London: T. Becket, 1787), quoted by Coleman, *Maiden Voyages and Infant Colonies*, p. 1; Coleman also states (p. 38) that Equiano 'was almost certainly Cugoano's co-author'.
4 J. E. Hopkins, *Conquering and to Conquer* (London: Hatchards, 1886), vol. 1, p. 29.
5 *Pall Mall Gazette* (6 July 1885), p. 1.
6 M. Mason, *The Making of Victorian Sexuality* (Oxford: Oxford University Press, 1995); see, e.g., p. 19.
7 D. Altman, *Global Sex* (Chicago, IL: University of Chicago Press, 2001), p. 86.
8 L. Knopp and M. Brown, 'Queer diffusions', *Environment & Planning D: Society and Space*, 21:5 (2003), 409–424.
9 A. D. Cliff, P. Haggett, J. K. Ord and G. R. Versey, *Spatial Diffusion: An Historical Geography of Epidemics in an Island Community* (Cambridge: Cambridge University Press, 1981), p. 6.
10 Cliff *et al.*, *Spatial Diffusion*, p. 1.
11 Cliff *et al.*, *Spatial Diffusion*, 10.
12 K. Clark, *Innovation Diffusion: Contemporary Geographical Approaches* (Norwich: Geo Books, 1984), p. 27.
13 Cliff *et al.*, *Spatial Diffusion*, p. 1.
14 Clark, *Innovation Diffusion*, p. 7.
15 Clark, *Innovation Diffusion*, p. 7.
16 Cliff *et al.*, *Spatial Diffusion*, p. 10; C. O. Sauer, *Agricultural Origins and Dispersals: The Domestication of Animals and Foodstuffs* (Cambridge, MA: MIT Press, 1952).
17 Cliff *et al.*, *Spatial Diffusion*, p. 10; F. J. Turner, *Frontier in American History* (New York: Holt, 1920).
18 J. M. Blaut, *The Colonizer's Model of the World: Geographical Diffusionism and Eurocentric History* (New York: Guilford, 1993), p. 1.
19 Blaut, *Colonizer's Model of the World*, p. 1.
20 J. E. Butler, *Social Purity: An Address Given to Students at Cambridge* (London: Morgan & Scott, 1879), p. 34.
21 Butler, *Social Purity*, p. 34.
22 National Vigilance Association (NVA), *A Brief Record of 50 Years' Work of the National Vigilance Association* (London: NVA, 1935), p. 5.
23 NVA, *A Brief Record of 50 Years' Work*, p. 5.
24 T. Davis, *Actresses as Working Women: Their Social Identity in Victorian Culture* (London: Routledge, 1991); L. O. Chant, *Why We Attacked the Empire* (London: Marshall, 1895), p. 3.
25 NVA, *Work Accomplished* (London: NVA, 1906), p. 3.
26 S. Marcus, 'Reading the illegible', in H. J. Dyos and M. Wolff (eds), *Victorian City: Images and Realities* (London: Routledge & Kegan Paul, 1973), vol. 1, pp. 257–276.
27 A. S. Dyer, *Slavery Under the British Flag: Iniquities of British Rule in India and in Our Crown Colonies and Dependencies* (London: Dyer, 1886), p. 28.
28 Butler, *Revival and Extension of the Abolitionist Cause*, p. 14.
29 J. E. Butler, *Our Christianity Tested by the Irish Question* (London: T. Fisher Unwin, 1887), p. 29, emphasis added.
30 Butler, *Social Purity*, p. 36; Butler, *Our Christianity Tested by the Irish Question*, p. 29.
31 C. B. Taylor, *Speech on the Second Reading of a Bill for the Repeal of the Contagious Diseases Acts, 1866–69* (London: Effingham Wilson, 1883), p. 19.

32 Hopkins, *Conquering and to Conquer*, p. 29.
33 G. C. Spivak, 'Can the subaltern speak?' in C. Nelson and L. Grossberg (eds), *Marxism and the Interpretation of Culture* (Urbana: University of Illinois Press, 1988), pp. 271–313.
34 J. E. Butler, *Present Aspect of the Abolitionist Cause in Relation to British India* (London: World's Women's Christian Temperance Union, 1893), p. 10.
35 'The first purity campaign in Wales', *Sentinel* (September 1886), p. 105.
36 'A Scottish crusade against licensed sin in India', *The Christian* (25 November 1887), p. 11.
37 Church of England Record Centre, London (hereafter CERC), Church of England Purity Society, White Cross League Annual Report, 1898, p. 9.
38 Friends House Library, London (hereafter FHL), 10504/4, Bombay Mission Press.
39 Article by Bishop Thoburn, which was originally published in the *Indian Witness*, reprinted in the *Bombay Guardian* (15 March 1890), p. 10.
40 D. Pivar, *Purity Crusade: Sexual Morality and Social Control, 1868–1900* (Westport, CT: Greenwood Press, 1973).
41 CERC, Undated pamphlet by W. H. Heaton, 'Work of the Church of England Purity Society', pp. 7–8.
42 Pivar, *Purity Crusade*, p. 64.
43 M. Valverde, *Age of Light, Soap and Water: Moral Reform in English Canada, 1885–1925* (Toronto: McClelland & Stuart, 1991), p. 92.
44 *Pall Mall Gazette* (6 July 1885) p. 1.
45 S. J. Potter, 'Communication and integration: the British and Dominions press and the British world, 1876–1914', *Journal of Imperial and Commonwealth History*, 31 (2003), 191.
46 F. Whyte, *Life of W. T. Stead* (London: Jonathan Cape, 1925), p. 166.
47 'Topics of interest abroad', *New York Times* (7 July 1885), p. 1; 'London's sensation', *New York Herald* (8 July 1885), p. 3.
48 'A terrible traffic', *Toronto Daily Mail* (7 July 1885), p. 1.
49 *Sydney Mail* (18 July 1885), p. 149.
50 *Sentinel* (March 1889), p. 32.
51 *Australian Christian World* (1–29 January 1886).
52 'Stead part VI', *Australian Christian World* (5 February 1886), p. 708.
53 'Stead part VI', p. 708.
54 'Mr. Stead's release', *Australian Christian World* (12 March 1886), p. 787.
55 C. G. Roe, *Horrors of the White Slave Trade: The Mighty Crusade to Protect the Purity of Our Homes* (London: Roe & Steadwell, 1911), p. 13.
56 D. Pivar, *Purity and Hygiene: Women, Prostitution, and the American Plan, 1900–1930* (Westport, CT: Greenwood Press, 2002).
57 Pivar, *Purity Crusade*, p. 144.
58 Alfred Barry (late Bishop of Sydney and Primate), *An Address: The White Cross League* (Sydney: W. Brooks, undated) unpaginated.
59 J. P. S. McLaren, 'Chasing the social evil: moral fervour and the evolution of Canada's prostitution laws, 1867–1917', *Canadian Journal of Law and Society*, 1 (1986), 125–165, at 135.
60 Butler, *Revival and Extension of the Abolitionist Cause*.
61 Hopkins, *Conquering and to Conquer*, p. 79.
62 Mort, *Dangerous Sexualities*, p. 98.
63 R. Barrett, *Ellice Hopkins: A Memoir* (London: Wells Gardner, 1907), p. 233.
64 Letter dated 13 January 1902, quoted by Barrett, *Ellice Hopkins*, pp. 184–185.
65 Letter dated 22 December 1902, quoted by Barrett, *Ellice Hopkins*, p. 235.
66 Barrett, *Ellice Hopkins*, p. 184.
67 B. Nairn and G. Serle (eds), *Australian Dictionary of Biography*, vol. 7: *1891–1939* (Melbourne: Melbourne University Press, 1979), p. 103.
68 'The American edition I had largely to alter to take in their extensive day school system; would it be necessary to do the same with the Australian edition?' State

Library of New South Wales, Mitchell Library, Sydney (hereafter SLNSWM), MSS 473, Dixson Box 1, letter from Hopkins to Arthur, 7 December 1900.

69 SLNSWM, MSS 473, Dixson Box 1, letter from Hopkins to Arthur, 19 July 1899.

70 SLNSWM, MSS 473, Dixson Box 1, letter from Hopkins to Arthur, 19 July 1899.

71 J. E. Hopkins, *The Power of Womanhood; or, Mothers and Sons*, Australian edn (Sydney: George Robertson, 1902).

72 Hopkins, *Power of Womanhood*, p. ix.

73 Hopkins, *Power of Womanhood*, p. 165.

74 Hopkins, *Power of Womanhood*, p. 193.

75 Hopkins, *Power of Womanhood*, p. 193.

76 SLNSWM, 196A, 'Training of children in purity', pamphlet by Richard Arthur.

77 Barrett, *Ellice Hopkins*, p. 185.

78 R. Arthur, 'The protection of young girls', *Daily Telegraph* (Sydney) (21 November 1893).

79 CERC, Church of England Purity Society, White Cross League Annual Report, 1885, p. 13.

80 Barrett, *Ellice Hopkins*, p. 184.

81 J. Jose, 'The White Cross League and sex education in SA state schools 1916–1929', *Journal of the Historical Society of South Australia*, 25 (1996), 46.

82 SLNSWM, Australasian White Cross League Annual Report, 1918–19.

83 'Australasian White Cross League: an appeal for help', *Australian Christian World* (22 January 1904), p. 6.

84 SLNSWM, 'Circulation of *True Manliness*', Australasian White Cross League Annual Report, 1918–19; J. E. Hopkins, *True Manliness*, White Cross Series (London: Hatchards, 1883).

85 SLNSWM, Australasian White Cross League Annual Report, 1885.

86 His biographer wrote that 'Kirby greatly enjoyed his stay in Bombay. He was cordially welcomed and hospitably entertained by Alfred S. Dyer, editor of the *Bombay Guardian* and a zealous member of the Society of Friends. Dyer proved a friend indeed, for he gave Kirby a number of valuable introductions and practically arranged his entire Indian itinerary': E. S. Kiek, *An Apostle in Australia: The Life and Reminiscences of Joseph Coles Kirby* (London: Independent Press, 1927), p. 243.

87 NVA, *A Brief Record of 50 Years' Work*.

88 M. G. Fawcett and E. M. Turner, *Josephine Butler: Her Work and Principles, and Their Meaning for the Twentieth Century* (London: Association for Moral and Social Hygiene, 1927).

89 'A glorious victory!' *The Christian* (15 June 1888) p. 2.

90 Dyer, *Slavery Under the British Flag*, p. 10.

91 Dyer, *Slavery Under the British Flag*, pp. 12–13.

92 Dyer, *Slavery Under the British Flag*, p. 10.

93 'A moral crisis in Calcutta', *Sentinel* (October 1886), p. 1; J. Joyce, 'The legalization of sin in India', *Sentinel* (May 1887), pp. 53–54.

94 'The Gospel Purity Association's work: the cause in India', *Sentinel* (May 1887), p. 60.

95 'Carrying forward the standard of the White Cross in India', *Sentinel* (October 1886), p. 1.

96 'Thanksgiving in India', *Sentinel* (August 1888), p. 106; 'Protest of the Methodist Episcopal Conference on South India', *Sentinel* (May 1887), p. 1.

97 M. Gregory, 'The seventy-one districts in India where impurity is licensed by the British Government', *Sentinel* (May 1887), p. 55.

98 Of course, works attributed to Alfred were not necessarily simply by him. It is sometimes difficult to tease out the contributions of husbands and wives, where both were involved in the writing process, as I have argued in R. Phillips, 'Sexual politics of authorship: rereading the travels and translations of Richard and Isabel Burton', *Gender, Place and Culture*, 6:3 (1999), 241–257. Butler commented on the dynamics between Alfred and Helen Dyer in the production and refinement

of their reports on India. She welcomed Helen's account of Bombay, which she saw as a corrective to her husband, who 'always had a tendency not to make women's work as prominent as it ought to have been. I am therefore glad to read Mrs. Dyer's report': Women's Library, London (hereafter WL), Correspondence of Josephine Butler, letter from Josephine Butler to Mrs Tanner, 12 May 1888, pp. 1–2.

99   A. S. Dyer, 'The black hand in India', *The Christian* (20 January 1888), pp. 11–18.
100 Dyer, 'The black hand in India', p. 17.
101 Dyer, 'The black hand in India', p. 17.
102 Dyer, 'The black hand in India', p. 17.
103 Dyer, 'The black hand in India', p. 17.
104 Fawcett and Turner, *Josephine Butler*.
105 M. Gregory, 'State regulated vice in India', *Sentinel* (September 1895), p. 117.
106 Gregory, 'State regulated vice in India', p. 117.
107 Fawcett and Turner, *Josephine Butler*, p. 129, refer to this unnamed source only as 'another paper', which refers collectively to English opponents of regulation in India as 'Dyer & Co.'.
108 'Regulated vice in India', *Christian* (9 March 1888), p. 22.
109 'A glorious victory', *The Christian* (15 June 1888), p. 2.
110 'A glorious victory', *The Christian* (15 June 1888), p. 2.
111 J. M. Mitchell, *In Western India: Recollections of My Early Missionary Life* (Edinburgh: David Douglas, 1899), p. 173.
112 Butler, *Revival and Extension of the Abolitionist Cause*, p. 6; emphasis added.
113 Butler, *Revival and Extension of the Abolitionist Cause*, p. 15.
114 A. S. Dyer, *Slave Trade in European Girls to British India*, reprinted from *Banner of Asia* (Bombay: Bombay Guardian Printing Works, 1893), p. 1.
115 Wallace Gladwin, Letter from Bombay, *The Christian* (26 August 1887), p. 14.
116 FHL, 10504/3, Leaflet for advertisers, the Bombay Guardian Printers, p. 2.
117 D. Gorham, '"The Maiden Tribute of Modern Babylon" re-examined: child prostitution and the idea of childhood in late-Victorian England', *Victorian Studies*, 21:3 (1978), 357.
118 Maurice Gregory, 'Alfred Dyer', *Friend*, new series, 66 (1926), 1026.
119 SLNSWM, 196D, Purity pamphlet series.
120 George Gillett and Alfred Dyer visited Brussels on behalf of the Society of Friends in 1879; they identified a trade in English girls, and their research and rhetoric formed the core of 1880s' campaigns against the traffic in girls and the differential ages of consent within Europe: Mort, *Dangerous Sexualities*.
121 K. Ballhatchet, *Race, Sex and Class Under the Raj: Imperial Attitudes and Policies and Their Critics* (London: Weidenfeld & Nicolson, 1980), p. 57.
122 David, *Bombay*.
123 *Sentinel* (November 1888), p. 133.
124 Ballhatchet, *Race, Sex and Class Under the Raj*, p. 126. The WL has an incomplete holding of the *Banner of Asia*, copies of which are now rare.
125 FHL, 10504/1, Bombay Guardian Trustees Minutes, December 1896, p. 12.
126 FHL, 10504/3, Leaflet for advertisers, p. 2.
127 FHL, 10504/1, Bombay Guardian Trustees Minutes, October 1890, p. 3.
128 FHL, 10504/6, Bombay Guardian Committee Records, including printing plant and house property pamphlet.
129 For instance, an advertisement for Dyer's *Facts for Men: On Moral Purity and Health* appeared in: *Bombay Guardian* (10 January 1890), p. 12.
130 'Beginning of the end of an infamous traffic', *Bombay Guardian* (8 November 1890), p. 9.
131 'Beginning of the end of an infamous traffic', p. 9.
132 'Alfred Dyer and another of the three editors of the *Banner of Asia*, and two missionaries, were prosecuted by the Government of India. The two editors were sentenced to a month's imprisonment each, with the option of a fine. They chose imprisonment, refusing the fine': Gregory, 'Alfred Dyer', p. 1026.

133 'Alfred Dyer in jail. What next?' *Sentinel* (July 1894), p. 1; Kiek, *Apostle in Australia*, p. 243.
134 Dyer, *Slave Trade in European Girls to British India*, p. 1.
135 Dyer, *Slave Trade in European Girls to British India*, p. 3. Similarly, Wallace Gladwin, writing about a previous campaign in Ceylon, stated: 'I caused the publication of a neat edition of the Criminal Law Amendment Act of England, and had it circulated among the leading men of the Colony. Some time after, a stringent ordinance was passed for the suppression of the brothels, and this has had a marked effect in the improvement of public morals there': W. Gladwin, 'Bombay's hell-gate', *Sentinel* (June 1891), p. 91.
136 'The worst spot in the British Empire', *Sentinel* (March 1894), p. 28; quoted statement attributed to 'the present editor of the *Sentinel*'.
137 'The worst spot in the British Empire', *Sentinel* (March 1894), p. 28.
138 'The worst spot in the British Empire', p. 28.
139 H. S. Dyer, *Revival in India* (London: Morgan & Scott, 1907), pp. 20–21.
140 *Bombay Guardian* (18 January 1890), p. 1.
141 'The new pure literature scheme for India', *Bombay Guardian* (8 March 1890), p. 3.
142 For example, a temperance meeting was announced in the *Bombay Guardian* (4 January 1890), p. 10 and reported the following week: *Bombay Guardian* (11 January 1890), p. 1.
143 'Purity meetings in Bombay', *Sentinel* (June 1892), p. 72.
144 *Bombay Guardian* (14 June 1890), p. 9.
145 *Bombay Guardian* (5 July 1890), p. 9.
146 *Bombay Guardian* (12 July 1890), p. 9.
147 'Women's work in Australia', *Banner of Asia* (June 1889), p. 67.
148 WL, Correspondence of Josephine Butler, letter from Josephine Butler to Miss Priestmans, 27 February 1888, p. 3.
149 Mitchell, *In Western India*, p. 173.
150 Gregory, 'Alfred Dyer', p. 1026.
151 Alfred S. Dyer, 'The opium iniquity: what can the Christian Church do to stop it?' *Banner of Asia* (January 1889), pp. 2–4; 'Christian Churches of Canton respectfully address the Christian Churches of England', *Bombay Guardian* (29 March 1890), p. 9; also see Ballhatchet, *Race, Sex and Class Under the Raj*.
152 'A few of the Indian opinions on Mr Dyer's revelations', *Sentinel* (July 1888), p. 94.
153 'A few of the Indian opinions on Mr Dyer's revelations', p. 94.
154 Helen Dyer, *Revival in India*, p. 22.
155 CERC, Church of England Purity Society, White Cross League Annual Report, 1886, p. 13.
156 H. S. Newman, *Days of Grace in India: A Record of Visits to Indian Missions* (London: Partridge, 1882), p. 12.
157 'Missionaries and licensed vice', letter to the editor, *The Christian* (26 August 1887), p. 14.
158 Mort, *Dangerous Sexualities*, p. 98.
159 WL, Correspondence of Josephine Butler, letter from Josephine Butler to Miss Priestmans, 27 February 1888, p. 3.
160 WL, Correspondence of Josephine Butler, letter from Josephine Butler to Miss Priestmans, 27 February 1888, p. 3.
161 Wallace Gladwin, 'Go forward!' *Banner of Asia* (January 1889), p. 5.
162 H. Janin, *Indo-China Opium Trade in the Nineteenth Century* (London: McFarland, 1999); C. A. Trocki, *Opium, Empire and the Global Political Economy: A Study of the Asian Opium Trade, 1750–1950* (London: Routledge, 1999).
163 H. S. Dyer, *Pandita Ramabai: The Story of Her Life* (London: Morgan & Scott, 1900)
164 'Mr Malabari has returned from his visit to England', *Bombay Guardian* (25 October 1890), p. 1.

165 'In the name of the Lord of Hosts', *Banner of Asia* (January 1889), p. 1; see also FHL, 10504/4, History of the Bombay Guardian, from H. S. Newman's MS, Bombay Guardian Mission Press.
166 H. S. Dyer, 'Letter from Tardeo, Bombay', *Bombay Guardian* (22 March 1890), pp. 11–12.
167 Blaut, *Colonizer's Model of the World*, p. 1.

CHAPTER TWO

Provincialising European sexuality politics: the age of consent in India

Many patterns in the imperial map of regulation and resistance, including changes to laws such as the age of consent, appear to suggest that initiatives spread outwards from England to other parts of the Empire, colonies following precedents through voluntary imitation (by responsible or other forms of semi-autonomous colonial government) or imposition (where more direct systems of government were in place). Recall, for example, that the age was raised from 13 to 16 in England and Wales in 1885, a rise that was matched by South Australia the same year and echoed soon after in other parts of the Empire, including India, where it increased from 10 to 12 in 1891. And if, as Antoinette Burton puts it, '1885 was clearly the *annus mirabilis* of sexual politics in locations beyond London',[1] this seems to have been more than coincidence. Evidence that English developments were originary, their colonial counterparts derivative, is apparently plentiful. The *derivative* hypothesis, which reads colonial sexuality politics as something England did or gave to its colonies, is illustrated and made explicit by the *Indian Spectator*, which seemed simply to accept that India should follow English precedent.

> The Act recently passed, in England, for the protection of young girls has done a great deal for English women. It has been enacted almost in every colony and dependency of Great Britain, except India. But in India a monstrous law is still allowed to have its sway. That law legalizes slavery to lust. That law tramples on the innocence of children. That law holds out immunity to brutal men . . .[2]

Yet the historical and geographical patterns that seem to show that English models of regulation and resistance were more or less replicated in certain colonies, through the sorts of mechanisms identified in chapter 1, do not necessarily demonstrate that English legislators or activists unilaterally forced these events to unfold. This inference of process from pattern would be consistent with the broader Eurocentrism that casts imperialism as something, as Shula Marks put it, *we* did to or for *them*.[3] Marks argues that 'ways have to be found of unifying history from above with history from below, structure with process and individual agency, empire with nation'.[4] This demands sensitivity to the multi-directionality of political influences and relationships, which Burton anticipates in her proposal that disparate sexuality politics be 'brought into the same field of debate'.[5] It calls for sensitivity to the social and spatial dispersal of agency. Alan Hunt, as I have noted, argues that sexuality politics, not simply centralised in any coherent way, formed an interconnected web of discourses stretching across time and place.[6] He limits his exposition of this thesis to the identification of certain forms of agency in England and the US, begging the broader question of how it may be possible to identify more dispersed agency, and to position this within multi-directional patterns of influence in a political field that includes but does not revolve around the metropolitan.

The flow of ideas and information from England to the colonies, which formed just one component of a broader set of multi-directional flows around the British Empire, does not necessarily speak of active sources and passive recipients. Tracing the dissemination of information from England to certain British settler colonies, Alan Lester argues that the recipients of this information were active participants in the process, not simply receiving but actively consuming, interpreting and using the information sent to them.[7] This is a question – central to postcolonial criticism and politics – of how and to what effect culture and politics have been negotiated and produced in colonial locations. Answers to this question, which occupy most of the remaining chapters of this book in some form or other, reflect the diversity and overlapping dimensions of colonialism and colonial experiences. Some people and places have been thoroughly marginalised by colonialism, of course, but for others the experience has been more ambivalent. Great colonial cities such as Sydney and Bombay were ambivalently positioned within the Empire, marginalised by their distance from England, but centres in their own right, hubs of transport, communication and political life, integrated within global networks that facilitated the exchange and, arguably, the generation of ideas. Interested and well-positioned individuals and groups within these cities were therefore able to play particularly active – if often informal – parts in political life.

In this chapter I argue that when individuals and organisations in England exported purity movements, they did not necessarily control the transactions of ideas and information. When their counterparts around the British Empire did import them, they tended to do so actively and creatively. To develop this case, it will first be necessary to elaborate on the relationships between English and colonial agents of sexuality politics, and then to set these relationships within the wider context of English and colonial political geography.

Travelling texts, active readings: Stead's readers

Since sexuality politics revolved so much around the movement of information and ideas, relationships between authors/texts and readers are central to understanding the power dynamics between people and places that exported texts and those that imported them. Power did not rest entirely in the hands of authors; texts did not determine their outcomes; and readers played an active part in producing textual meanings.

In his essay on 'travelling theory', Edward Said qualified the assumption that '[f]irst, there is a point of origin, *or what seems like one*, a set of initial circumstances in which the idea came to birth or entered discourse',[8] by suggesting that ideas are reshaped through the process of travel:

> Cultural and intellectual life are usually nourished and often sustained by this circulation of ideas, and whether it takes the form of acknowledged or unconscious influence, creative borrowing, or wholesale appropriation, the movement of ideas and theories from one place to another is both a fact of life and a usefully enabling condition of intellectual activity.[9]

Said did not discount the point of origin, nor did he suggest that ideas are changed out of recognition as they travel.[10] Dipesh Chakrabarty develops this position by arguing that European texts and ideas have been actively read in the non-European world, their meanings *produced* rather than simply consumed in situated acts of reading. He seeks to provincialise – not to dismiss, but to de-centre – European thought and action, to explore how it 'may be renewed from and for the margins'.[11] One way of provincialising sexuality politics, which addresses 'the problem of getting beyond Eurocentric histories',[12] is to shift attention from European authors and texts to non-European readers, and from textual origins to contexts in which readings take place.

That shift, though ideologically and critically attractive, also makes sense in relation to what is known about reading and about relationships between readers and texts. If, as legal and literary critic Stanley Fish has persuasively argued, a text can be read and used in more than one way, then the text cannot be all-important. Anthony Cohen has shown that texts 'allow those who employ them to supply part of their meaning',[13] Michel de Certeau that the 'presence and circulation of a representation . . . tells us nothing about what it is for its users'.[14] These arguments about the productivity of situated acts of reading can be applied to colonial sexuality politics, as Sally Engle Merry has begun to show in her work on the extension of legal codes from Massachusetts to Hawai'i. She argues that legal 'texts are transferred from one society or nation to another in a process variously called transplantation, reception, or imposition', but that this does not necessary constitute a smooth or uniform extension of the law, since 'texts are more readily transferred than the practices of interpreting and administering them'.[15] The idea that the movement of texts and individuals does not simply relocate ideas but plays an active part in their production and transformation is borne out in biographies and intellectual genealogies. Catherine Hall has shown how highly mobile imperial administrators picked up, discarded and exchanged ideas about race as they moved from place to place, not simply taking these ideas with them but forming and reforming them as they crossed 'the span of colony and metropole'.[16] While it is possible to chart the movements of individuals, it is possible to do the same for texts, showing where they went and how their meanings were produced along the way.

It should be expected that if Stead's readers should have veered away from the readings and uses he intended and asserted, then this should have been particularly pronounced among those further from him, socially and geographically. His most distant readers, with different cultural literacies and different political interests, might interpret and use *his* text in more disparate ways. By considering some of Stead's more distant readers, it should be possible to shift attention away from the author, arguing that the information and ideas he sent around the world were actively received and interpreted by readers who constructed their own meanings.

Before turning to colonial readers, the significance of Stead and the 'Maiden Tribute' can also be qualified with reference to the inflexion in Said's point that there is *'what seems like'* a 'point of origin' in which an 'idea came to birth or entered discourse'.[17] Despite his reputation as a journalistic and political innovator, Stead was not wholly original. Like other English campaigners, he borrowed ideas and strategies from overseas, particularly from continental Europe and the US.[18] Readers, accustomed to ploughing their way through the close print of English papers, were impressed with the innovations he introduced, including illustrations, prominent headlines and engaging formats; they also enjoyed his variously melodramatic, pornographic and allegoric journalistic story-telling.[19] Cultivating his own reputation for innovation in the *Pall Mall Gazette* and then the *Review of Reviews* (which he launched in 1890), Stead portrayed himself as a pioneer of 'new journalism', defined by its use of illustrations, prominent headlines and engaging formats, and including interviews, personalised reports and investigative journalism. He claimed that his influences were, above all, the Bible and the American poet James Russell Lowell.[20] In reality, he was indebted to some more banal influences, including American 'yellow' journalism, which also combined visual and lively presentation with political engagement.[21] In an intensely competitive newspaper industry, everyone copied a good idea, though English journalists probably borrowed more from their American counterparts than vice versa. Robert Pierce argues that Stead's originality lay less in inventing than in being the first to appropriate American inventions.[22] Stead was also indebted, more specifically, to contemporary campaign journalists. The 'Maiden Tribute' borrowed from earlier stories of the abduction and prostitution of juveniles, such as the anonymous *Sins of the Cities of the Plain* (1881), and from earlier campaign polemics, such as Alfred Dyer's *European Slave Trade in English Girls* (1880).

Despite his best efforts, Stead neither caused the 'Maiden Tribute' to be reported as it was around the world nor did he cause those reports to have the effects they did. The media had a dynamic of their own, their concern being not only with intentional individuals but also with market economics. Stead's campaign in the *Pall Mall Gazette* was, among other things, good for sales, rescuing the paper from years of decline. If there was a market as well as a moral logic to the 'Maiden Tribute', this was true of the papers around the world that made decisions about whether and how to run the story. This is not to suggest economic determinism; rather, to begin to contextualise and limit estimations of an individual's ability to determine and control *his own* story, whether in the paper he edited or in others that reproduced it.

Syndicated reports, reproduced without comment or revision, appeared the most neutral, but even these involved decisions about where and how to present. The *Toronto Daily Mail*, for example, decided to give the Maiden Tribute a place on its front page and to present it under the headline 'London's vice'.[23] To speculate for a moment, this might have implied metropolitan sexual decadence, in contrast to Canadian innocence and inexperience.[24] A different sort of contrast may have been implied by the *New York Times* in 'the secret vices of aristocrats in London', which perhaps distanced the events in London from the ostensibly more open and modern American social order.[25] Decisions also had to be made about whether to run a story such as this, of course, as a clash between two Indian news-papers made clear: the *Times of India* accused the *Indian Mirror* of using the 'Maiden Tribute' to spread negative images of London.[26] These examples suggest that the contrasting presentation of Stead's basic story, varying from place to place and from newspaper to news-paper, were linked to the attitudes and sometimes the politics of respective editors and publishers. Journalists used their coverage of the Maiden Tribute as excuses and points of departure for discussing delicate subjects. The *Chicago Daily Tribune* commented 'apropos [sic] of the *Pall Mall Gazette*'s revelations of immoralities of London society' on prostitution in the US, stating that 'London is not alone in that phase of crime'.[27] The active mediation of Stead's story was also – most overtly – evident where the story was not only reprinted and retold, but even restaged, as it was in 'Another Maiden Tribute' – a story of debauchery in Wisconsin lumber camps,[28] and in a publicity stunt by two American missionaries in India, who paid Rs 50 for an 11-year-old girl in an attempt to generate political controversy.[29] It would be possible to find much more evidence to show that Stead's report was actively mediated around the world, but this would dis-tract from the real focus of this chapter: the readers, who not only took ideas from Stead, but took those ideas forward.

Gesturing towards the reader, one of Stead's biographers qualified the claim that the *Pall Mall Gazette* and the 'Maiden Tribute' were read 'everywhere' with the acknowledgement that they were read 'in different moods and with different feelings'.[30] But reading, not simply a function of soft intangibles such as mood and feeling, was socially and politically located. It is important to make and more fully explain this point because I have suggested that the colonial agency examined in this chapter was ambivalently positioned, somewhere between the centres and the margins of colonial power, in this case between the London newspaper editor and the likely illiterate colonial subject. To clarify this position, it is necessary to explain the relationships between reading and power and to distinguish between more and less privileged colonial readers.

Reading can be understood as a social rather than a primarily indi-vidual process, since individuals read according to the rules and literacies handed down to them by what Fish calls their 'interpretive communities'.[31] Different individuals and groups have different forms and degrees of access to the means of producing, advancing and cen-soring readings. This is to say that some 'socially authorised' indi-viduals and groups – journalists, critics and professors, perhaps – have the power to read a text and tell the others what it means and what its more general messages are. Others, including illiterate people and common readers, have much less ability to determine or negotiate the meaning of a text.[32] The power to read a text is, in other words, the power to determine and deploy its meanings and/or to mobilise or more fundamentally to form interpretive communities.[33] Illustrating this point in the arena of sexuality politics, Alan Sinfield has shown how sexual minorities have articulated politicised identities through disruptive readings of key cultural texts. These readers construct and use readings partly, if not wholly, to define their group membership and advance their individual and collective interests. Politicised interpretive communities, not simply competing on even terms, may be identified as variously dominant and subordinate, socially and/or spatially central and marginal. Sinfield finds that 'the centre takes what it wants' from a text, but he insists that the margins should do the same.[34] But, as his analysis of contrasting dominant readings of cultural texts makes clear (he finds radically different readings of a certain text within the mainstream media), 'the centre' encompasses multiple voices and interests. This complicates any expectation of clear, or singular, central and marginal, dominant and subordinate positions, pointing instead to fractured, plural readings in each of these social locations. Sinfield's own ambivalent position – a queer-identified, white, male professor, he combines a degree of marginality with sufficient social power to read and to advance a politicised textual reading – can be loosely likened to the elite colonial subject who shared the subjection of colonised peoples and countries but was nevertheless privileged within their own societies.[35] This gives rise to questions about how such privilege was used, questions about whether and how colonial readers actively read the 'Maiden Tribute', using it to advance their own projects.

Prominent among the ambivalently positioned active readers of Stead, and indeed of English social purity discourse more generally, was the Bombay journalist, editor and 'chief campaigner' for a bill to raise the age of consent in India, Behramji Malabari (1853–1912; figure 2.1).[36] The sections following unpack Antoinette Burton's claim that 'historians of late-Victorian Britain will recognize Malabari's use of the urban press corps to reflect and produce anxiety about the sexual activities of women and girls as strikingly parallel to W. T. Stead's agitation in the *Pall Mall Gazette*',[37] tracing similarities to Malabari's active reading of Stead. I suggest that Malabari's reading of Stead played an important part in his campaign on the Indian age of consent, and that this was an active reading, determined less by Stead's text than by Malabari's active response to it.

[63]

2.1 Behramji Malabari

Politics of reading: Behramji Malabari's power to read

Before tracing Malabari's reading of Stead, it is important to locate him as a *reader*, applying the general principles outlined in the previous section regarding inequalities in access to textual interpretation, in particular to the propagation and use of certain readings.

Malabari was positioned within a political arena in which reading and the media had a heightened significance. There were no formal channels linking public opinion with legislative process in India, as there were in some other parts of the British Empire, and this meant that many Indian people had little or no formal political voice, but not that *no* Indians had a voice. The power of some Indian people to influence the English authorities that governed them through the formal political channels must be set in the context of an overview of the structures of British rule in India. Crown rule, established after the rebellion of 1857, operated on multiple levels, important tiers of which governed India as a whole (under the viceroy), the presidencies (each with a governor) and municipalities (in cities where municipal governments existed). The age of consent legislation discussed in this chapter was determined by the Viceroy's Council and applied to India as a whole, with the exception of the semi-autonomous princely states, where the adoption of English laws was discretionary.[38] Though non-elected, the Government of India answered to the demands of the home Government, and thus to English public opinion, as well as to (English assessments of) Indian public opinion. It was therefore possible, in principle, to influence the imperial Government of India through English public opinion, direct appeals to the English Government, and through Indian public opinion. With respect to the age of consent, for example, the viceroy (then Lord Ripon) responded to Malabari's first call for change with a qualified refusal, which stated that his policy was to uphold 'customs [that] are sanctioned by the general opinion of the society in which they prevail',[39] but expressing a willingness to reconsider if and when 'the sentiment and opinion of the community' favoured a change in the law.[40] Given the English interest in public opinion, founded on its policy of avoiding controversial initiatives except where imperial objectives were clearly at stake, lobbyists knew that they must try to lead public opinion, and/or to convince government that public opinion was favourable to their proposals, and/or that imperial interests would be advanced by them.

An important way of leading and claiming to report Indian public opinion was through the press. Indeed, in the words of one prominent contemporary editor (Kristodas Pal, of the *Hindu Patriot*), the press was 'the only channel for the communication of the views and wishes of the people'.[41] A critical and multilingual press flourished in the second half of the nineteenth century, despite some attempts at censorship by the British authorities (a bill for the better control of publications in oriental languages was passed by Lord Lytton in 1878 but repealed by his successor, Lord Ripon), and despite limited markets, in which low levels of both literacy and material wealth kept circulations relatively low. As Robert Knight, the editor of the *Times of India*, put it in a letter to Lord Lytton, the press in India occupied a 'position not dissimilar from that of Her Majesty's Opposition'.[42] Mountstuart Elphinstone, once governor of Bombay, expressed the power of the media in even stronger terms, as 'more than a match for the Indian Government', and he asserted that the 'public opinion' it reflected and commanded should not be under-estimated.[43]

[65]

One in four British Indian newspapers was published in Bombay Presidency (123 out of 548 in 1877), the majority of these in the city of Bombay.[44] Given the tendency of Indian journalists to become politically active and the tendency of activists to become involved in journalism, the centres of India's newspaper industry were also centres of political influence.[45] Bombay, in particular, has been described as 'the citadel from where the Indian press launched its social reform movement'.[46] National titles, and with them national politics, were launched in Bombay. Knight changed the title of the *Bombay Times*, which he edited and owned, to the *Times of India*, explaining that as Bombay was already the capital of India, the press in Bombay should cease to be provincial.[47] The city provided journalists with a strong vantage point Particularly after the opening of the Suez Canal in 1869, it was the country's main port of arrival and departure for British mails,[48] and this enhanced its status as an information gateway, through which a 'continual stream of European thought and action' was imported.[49] Bombay was therefore an important node within a national and international information network.[50] Despite its relative marginalisation by British imperialism, which pushed it from the centre of one ocean system to the position of a subordinated or dependent region within a wider system,[51] Bombay remained both an important point through which information and ideas flowed and one in which they were actively generated.

The power of reading was rarely more evident than in colonial Bombay. This power was structured, in the first instance, by the extent of literacy, which was estimated at not more than 4 per cent of men and 1 per cent of women, in India as a whole.[52] Literate people played an important role in channelling the contents of newspapers to others. As one contemporary English observer reported, 'people were called together', when a copy was received, to hear 'its contents read, explained, and discussed'.[53] The illiterate majority thereby participated in the media culture, leading Basu to conclude that 'from the petty shopkeeper to the princely merchant and from the simple village folk to the landed aristocracy – all were permeated with the spirit of this Press'.[54] To the English observer William Digby, the 'free discussion of public events' in newspapers was a blessing of British rule, a 'liberty' of the 'subject races'.[55] Digby may have been an imperial apologist, but there was some truth in his assertion that newspaper readers – those who read, listened while others read, or more actively read and retold stories from the world's press – retained a form of agency, access to the limited yet potentially effective political channels of the day.

A journalist and editor in a colonial political environment dominated by the media, a member of an elite religious and social group that identified with progressive social causes, Behramji Malabari was well placed to participate in contemporary political life. Following the publication of a volume of his poetry, Malabari was approached and employed by the editor of the *Times of India*.[56] Training in journalism and editorial work, he also acquired an impressive address book, which included many of 'the leading citizens of Bombay',[57] and more impressive and useful contacts elsewhere in India and in England.[58] As a Parsi, Malabari occupied a social, economic and political niche somewhere between the English and many other Indian subjects:[59] 'More westernised than most other Indian elites',[60] Parsis (or Parsees) sometimes assumed the role of mediators between the English and the Hindus,[61] challenging Hindu traditions and endorsing English alternatives.[62] Politically engaged, identifying with and claiming to defer to England, particularly within progressive causes, Parsis played an important part in negotiating English precedents and perspectives. Sometimes they directly appealed to English public opinion and lobbied the home Government, as Malabari did in London in 1890.[63] At other times they responded to English politics, *reading* political developments and key texts, actively interpreting, mediating and using them within their own political agendas.

Before interpreting Malabari's agency as a reader and leader of the age of consent campaign, it is necessary to summarise this campaign, albeit briefly since it is chronicled in detail elsewhere.[64] Malabari launched the main phase of his age of consent campaign with two sets of notes, published in August and October 1884, entitled *Infant Marriage in India* and *Enforced Widowhood in India*, which he sent to government officials and influential private persons in India and England.[65] The first blamed the legally tolerated custom of 'infant marriage in India' for a wide range of personal and social problems, from 'the ushering in of disease' to 'the necessity of feeding many mouths, poverty and dependence',[66] and, finally, 'enforced widowhood', which exacerbated women's status as 'the inferior of man as a social unit'.[67] It proposed a range of measures to counteract early marriage, among them an increase in the age of consent. The second note amplified the first, and also reviewed and responded to the various endorsements and criticisms it had received. Both notes were reprinted in 1887, with a digest of responses, as *Infant Marriage and Enforced Widowhood in India, Being a Collection of Opinions, For and Against, Received by Mr. Behramji M. Malabari*.[68] These interventions were widely noticed in both the English-language and native papers, where they were translated into vernacular languages.[69] Malabari used his editorship of the weekly *Indian Spectator* and later the monthly *Voice of India*, a review of the Indian press that merged with his own title in 1890,[70] to develop the agenda he had set in the notes, in the context of a wider political engagement.

Stead–Malabari

Malabari's age of consent campaign did not simply echo Stead's, and in many respects the two interventions were quite different, though the Indian activist did draw on the specific ideas and tactics of his English counterpart, reading and appropriating the 'Maiden Tribute' within what Burton has called his 'strikingly parallel' media campaign.[71]

Malabari's appropriation of certain elements of English campaign journalism took place in the context of a wider adoption by the Bombay media of English (and American) models. Some historians argue that the British Indian news media was essentially derivative. Smith argues simply and broadly: 'The patterns of the English press were stamped on new newspaper industries throughout the Anglo-Saxon and imperial world.'[72] Rangaswami Parthasarathy claims that 'the newspaper came to India as an alien product, as one of the benefits of British rule',[73] and that 'the newspaper as we know it today is of European origin'.[74] Histories of the transplantation of English journalism to India emphasise the significance of English editors and writers and other English-language titles in the 'diffusion of western methods of criticism'.[75] In this context, Malabari was seen by some of his contemporaries as an Anglophile, an 'admirer of everything English',[76] who chose to work in the medium of English and within the new journalism associated with figures such as Stead.

This derivative reading of Indian journalism has been challenged and qualified by critics who emphasise Indian agency in the process. David Finkelstein and Douglas Peers argue that Indian print culture did not merely mimic its English counterpart, that it assumed a hybrid form of its own.[77] Javed Majeed develops this point by showing that while the Urdu periodical press incorporated translations from English, its mistranslations and appropriations were often not only untidy and inaccurate, but – as original meanings were lost or mutated – potentially subversive.[78] Finkelstein and Peers argue, further, that 'subversion was also present in the press's frequent juxtaposition of news items with each other, irrespective of whether they referred to events in India or Europe'.[79] Thus, as I have argued in relation to the active manner in which the 'Maiden Tribute' was reported around the world, Indian journalists borrowed freely but also selectively and critically from others, particularly their English counterparts. Although it might be easy to position Malabari within a derivative history of

Indian campaign journalism, it may be more insightful to draw out the selective, autonomous and critical elements of his appropriation.

Similarities

Both Malabari and Stead were media personalities whose journalistic, political and moral reputations underpinned their campaigns, which focused on a few key issues, above all the protection of women and the age of consent. As Malabari's biographer put it, he 'championed the cause of Indian womanhood with the same fervour and chivalry with which the late Mr. W. T. Stead espoused the dignity of the daughters of Eve'.[80] Whereas Stead demanded that the English age of consent be raised to 18 or 21 from its current level of 13,[81] Malabari wanted its Indian counterparts for girls and boys raised to 12 and 16 respectively, through an amendment to the Indian Majority Act of 1875.[82] He cited the English developments, first the arguments for change and then the legislative change itself, which set the age of consent at 16, as the precedent for his actions (figure 2.2.).[83]

There are many similarities between the content and style of Stead's and Malabari's journalism. Stead publicised the 'bitter cry of outcast London',[84] Malabari the 'outcry of outcast' people.[85] Both appealed to the melodramatic tastes of their readers, Stead in descriptions of young prostitutes, Malabari of young widows, each to blame a range of miseries on low ages of consent. Stead asked his readers to pity a young prostitute, 'helpless as a sparrow when caught by the falling brick of the schoolboy's trap',[86] whereas Malabari asked his to come to the rescue of a widow, whose condition he blamed on the custom of marrying young girls to older men, with a drawn-out *suttee*, 'a perpetual agony, a burning to death by slow fire'.[87] Both used emotive case histories and interviews to personalise their more general points. Stead's 'revelations' about child prostitution centred around the story of one girl's abduction, an event that he staged – illegally as it turned out – to highlight the more general case. Malabari printed the 'sad tale of a Hindu girl who only the other day went to a premature grave, apparently under the evil concomitant of early marriage'.[88] Both journalists published sensationalist articles under eye-catching headlines that stood out from the conservatism and small print that dominated the news-stands. Whereas Stead attracted readers' attention with headings such as 'Confessions of a brothel keeper' and 'Strapping girls down', Malabari – a little more restrained – did so with promises of information about 'More harrowing cases!!!'[89] Both journalists evoked the youthful vulnerability of figures who, they asserted, needed the protection of the law in the form of a higher age of consent. In Stead's account, a typical 'child was about fourteen, dark, with long black

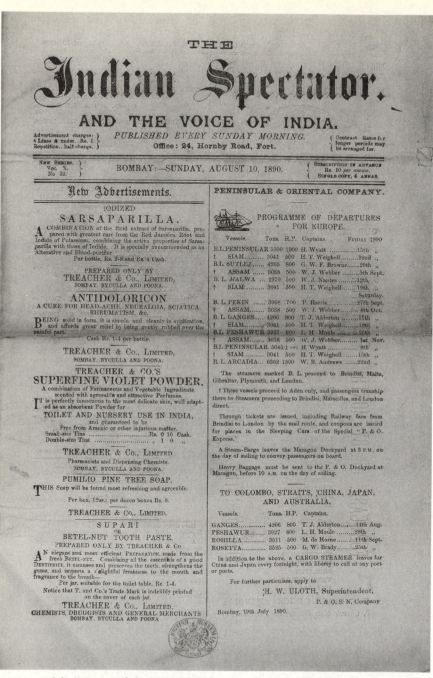

2.2 Typical front cover of the *Indian Spectator* (10 August 1890) during Malabari's age of consent campaign

hair and dark eyes. She was not fully grown, and might develop into a woman of somewhat striking appearance.'[90] If not 'well cared for' in youth, however, she would descend into something quite different. 'The child – she is seldom more than fifteen or sixteen – comes up from her country village with her box, and is installed in service.' Child-like at 14 or 15, cast as pre-sexual, vulnerable, dependent figures, these girls or young women demanded the protection of the law in the form of an increased age of consent. Malabari, arguing a similar case, also portrayed vulnerable, child-like victims of current legislation that 'tramples upon the innocence of children'.[91]

Of course, few of these devices were unique to either Stead or Malabari, or even to journalism. Speaking out against 'brutal slavery',[92] Malabari adopted strategies favoured not only by Stead but by purity campaigners around the world. Like Stead, but also Hopkins and Butler in England and their counterparts in other countries, he identified his cause with the struggle against the Atlantic slave trade and the institution of slavery. Like purity campaigners around the world – including those in Canada, for instance[93] – he adopted a conventional rhetoric to make his specific case, speaking for example of purity and impurity, light and darkness.[94] Malabari's journalism can be located more widely still if, as David Spurr argues, there was much continuity and exchange between journalistic and more literary forms of writing in the British imperial context.[95] It was, for instance, Charles Dickens rather than Stead who most forcefully explored social questions through individual figures, whose often sentimental, caricatured characters engaged readers in a way that generalisations could not have done.[96] Dickens's social realism was influential in India, not only among writers but, on another level, journalists who shared his concern with the 'passionate espousal of the cause of the dispossessed and the down-trodden'.[97] It is, however, beyond the scope of this discussion to consider all of Stead's and Malabari's literary influences; the point is that, whatever their ultimate influences may have been, there was considerable overlap between these two figures and within their political journalism.

Both Malabari and Stead juxtaposed dramatic stories with political demands and advice to activists, with specific suggestions on how to form campaign groups; both followed up their initial stories with lengthy digests of reactions from journalists and correspondents, and both claimed to have stirred and to represent public opinion. Stead followed his initial demands by working with fellow-activists Benjamin Scott, William Coote and Ellice Hopkins to organise a demonstration and launch the NVA, which campaigned for the age of consent legislation.[98] Malabari concluded his first note, *Infant Marriage in India*, by proposing 'the establishment of a national association for social reform, with the existing societies as branches' and with the support and involvement of members of the Government, governors and the viceroy.[99] He also printed supportive reports about public meetings that 'discussed the evils of child marriage'.[100] He maintained the campaign – which took much longer than its English counterpart to achieve its goals – by printing a steady stream of (increasingly repetitive) editorials and articles. These reflected the political strategy used by Stead and also that suggested by Auckland Colvin, a powerful member of the Government of India, who advised Malabari to find test cases that might reveal the workings of the existing laws and show whether legislation were needed to improve women's position.[101] Through the publication of numerous such cases and histories, Malabari claimed both to provoke and to represent public opinion, asserting that 'there is a very large and intelligent portion of the community in favour of reform'.[102] Since both the customs he attacked and the majority who were seen to endorse existing laws in India were identified as Hindu, Malabari attached particular significance to Hindu expressions of support for his proposals. He stated, for example: 'I am glad to have a general concurrence with some of my suggestions from the more important Hindu papers.'[103] In addition to these *ad hoc* reactions and reviews, both Stead and Malabari edited media digests – Malabari the *Voice of India*, Stead the *Review of Reviews* – which were sympathetic towards the purity agenda but broader in scope. Finally, they were similar in other ways, both, for example, being extremely well connected and prolific correspondents; they not only shared acquaintances, but knew and corresponded with each other.

Appropriation

Parallels between events in London and Bombay, however striking, do not simply demonstrate the export of metropolitan models of journalism and campaigning. Indeed, the detailed timeline undermines this explanation, showing that developments did not always take place first in London and that sometimes the opposite was true. Malabari's age of consent campaign was initiated in 1884, some time after its English counterpart, which had begun in earnest with Dyer's interventions in 1880, but a year before the 'Maiden Tribute' and thus before many of Stead's campaign tricks were seen in print. Some of Malabari's journalistic activities predated Stead's. His editorship of a progressive media review (the *Voice of India*) began in 1883, seven years before Stead began at the ostensibly groundbreaking *Review of Reviews*.[104] And Malabari's style at the *Indian Spectator* – a newspaper that he made in his own image – borrowed less from Stead than it did from the Indian media, where relatively low levels of capitalisation made it more common than in England for individual titles to be dominated by the personality and will of a single figure.[105]

When Malabari borrowed from English counterparts, he did so actively and selectively. I have explained that decisions about whether and how to cover the 'Maiden Tribute' forced editors around the world to take positive decisions on the subject or, rather, gave them the opportunity to take such decisions. Malabari took positive decisions to cover the scandal, in the face of complaints from some quarters in India that it contravened 'common decency',[106] and also to tone down the coverage, leaving out some of Stead's more sensational claims. More generally, he distanced himself from what he considered the excesses of certain Western journalists, who seemed to him (according to a biographer) to be sinking to low levels, 'courting moral bankruptcy in [their] thirst for gold and popularity'.[107] Malabari also distanced himself from the actions of certain English purity activists, commenting for example that while 'Dyer's zeal and earnestness in all philanthropic works is highly commendable', he did 'not think he at all showed discrimination or judgement in his recent agitation' against a moral test case in court.[108] Butler made similar criticisms of Dyer, as I mentioned in chapter 1. Tensions and disagreements within English sexuality politics serve as a reminder that even if Malabari had wanted to import 'the English agenda' wholesale, he could not have done so, for there was no unified or stable English agenda. Like English activists, he picked, chose and came to his own conclusions. And, like those activists, he assumed positions that brought him into conflict with areas of English law and the imperial establishment. Contrary to Sudhir Chandra's argument that battle lines on the issue were fundamentally drawn around a colonial divide – 'a war between the rulers and the ruled in which . . . the two sought to distinguish their respective institutions, ideals and values with regard to women, marriage and family in order to claim superiority over the other[109] – Malabari's position on the age of consent does not collapse into an expression either of Indian anti-colonialism or of blind colonial loyalty. Malabari, much like English counterparts such as Butler, placed moral questions above imperial ones when the two came into conflict. He was particularly critical of the existing marriage law and of the imperial authority's inconsistently enforced principle of non-interference with the cultural traditions of Indian subjects,[110] which led the British regime in India to respect Hindu customs relating to marriage and obstructed Malabari's reform agenda.[111] Once again, the evidence points to a figure who drew on the ideas and strategies of his day, and did so actively and selectively.

   Selective in his attention to the purity agenda, Malabari expressed 'deep sympathy with the Purity Movement' in England and the desire 'to have a similar movement set on foot in this country',[112] but argued that Indians must establish their own priorities. Concentrating on marriage and the age of consent, he variously postponed and ignored certain other issues that preoccupied his English counterparts. Whereas the English purity movements and many individual English activists began by fighting regulation and moved on to other issues such as the age of consent, Malabari launched straight into the latter, showing a different set of priorities. Nor did he join his English colleagues, including those in India, in presenting any sustained resistance to the opium trade. This particular selectivity might have been strategic, given the involvement of fellow-Parsis in the opium economy. Intervention on his part might not only have been difficult, it might have damaged the support he was gathering among fellow-Parsis for a change in the age of consent. Malabari's selective approach to purity activism – his focus on social reform and on what he portrayed as the modernisation of certain social relations – was also shaped by his pretension towards certain values which have been linked to his Parsi religion and culture, including tolerance, liberalism and acceptance of modern, reformist and progressive attitudes.[113] By asserting those values, Malabari was able to selectively draw on purity movements that in England were closely identified with Christianity, recasting and formulating a focused, ostensibly secular, Indian purity agenda. He pitted this against the religion in general and Hinduism in particular, arguing that in India 'every custom that is unintelligible, or actually indefensible, becomes a religious question',[114] and singling out Hindu marriage customs for particular criticism and reformist energy.

   Malabari's relationship with English purity activism and activists was reciprocal in some respects, rather than simply – if selectively – appropriative. An active participant in campaign networks, he contributed, as well as received, information and ideas. He used his extensive contacts in the English media, sending periodical telegrams to publicise the latest developments in his campaign and to elicit support,[115] exploiting 'the liberality of the English press' to promote awareness of conditions in India.[116] He used his contacts in India, which granted him access to Lord Ripon, the viceroy and many other members of the Supreme Government, to launch his campaign, in 1884, and then to sustain it. He not only supported Stead, but found support from him, for example in Stead's *Review of Reviews*, which talked up Malabari's campaign, stating that 'Indian marriage reform . . . is discussed in nearly all the leading Reviews'.[117] Malabari published arguments in favour of reciprocity rather than deference to English reformers, for example in the publication of a letter calling for 'a free exchange of ideas and a little genuine fellow-feeling' rather than yet more 'lectures and articles' delivered or penned by patronising English people.[118] Malabari's expression of desire for an equal footing with English purity campaigners might appear at odds with his frequent assertions of loyalty and subservience to English campaigners, but for the context and strategy behind those assertions.

Impact

Malabari appears to have been instrumental in securing positive outcomes both for individuals whose case histories he publicised in support of his broader campaign and for that broader campaign on the age of consent. The former are well documented in the secondary literature. For instance, a cause that Malabari championed to mutually beneficial effect was that of Rukhmabai, a 22-year-old who had been married at the age of 11, and who contested in court her husband's claim to conjugal rights with her. In letters to the *Times of India*, Rukhmabai allied herself with Malabari's call for legislative change. Burton argues that she did so in a voice and with an agenda of her own, and that her relationship with Malabari was reciprocal.[119] She was encouraged by his published 'notes', while he supported and covered her case, portraying her as a martyr to the cause of Indian women, and defended Rukhmabai against critics who portrayed her as a dangerously subversive modern woman. (It must be emphasised that Rukhmabai herself was not simply a vehicle for Malabari or any other third-party reformist, but was a reformer and publicist in her own right, not only in her court case but in her letters to newspapers, including the *Times of India* and the London *Times*, on infant marriage.[120]) The case dragged on from 1884 to 1888 and reached the Bombay High Court, ending when Rukhmabai's husband agreed out of court to relinquish his claims on her.[121] Another case that Malabari championed related to the prosecution of a Calcutta man, Hari Mohan Moitee (or Maiti) for the death of Phulmani (or Phulmony), his 11-year-old wife, in an act of forcible intercourse.[122] Responding to the man's sentence to 'one year's rigorous imprisonment', the *Indian Spectator* argued that the consequences of the man's lawful behaviour had been predictable, and thus called for stronger legislation to prevent and more comprehensively punish such behaviour.[123]

Historians tend to agree that Malabari's work in Bombay and his visit to London played some part in persuading the Government of India to pass the Act of 1891 that raised the age of consent for girls from 10 to 12.[124] This did not achieve the intended outcome, however, as opponents found a new and more effective way to block the new law.[125] They obstructed its enforcement for a number of cultural and political reasons, such as a resistance on the part of women and their relatives to make complaints against men, then to submit to the medical examinations that were required as evidence.[126] Though it entered the statute books, the Age of Consent Act arguably 'left behind a trail of bitterness among the leaders of the Orthodox Hindus, particularly in Bengal and Maharashtra', and it 'opened the eyes of the Orthodox Hindus to the value of organised agitation'.[127] The outcome of Malabari's intervention was therefore mixed.

Conclusions

Malabari's intervention was structured by his active engagement within campaign networks, and to some extent this enabled him to import ideas from other places, including England. This analysis of Malabari's activism has challenged the idea that regulation and resistance were simply exported from metropolitan to non-metropolitan spheres. Doing so, it has challenged the self-effacing manner in which Malabari portrayed himself and was content to be seen by contemporaries. It was, of course, easier to sell Indian social reform to English politicians, editors and members of the public if he portrayed it as derivative, a copy and extension of their own initiatives. Put on their terms, the English would be able not only to understand his project, but to support it, for it respected and legitimated the imperial order as they understood it. The appropriation of selected Western laws and values that could be portrayed as modern and progressive may be seen not simply as a form of deference to imperialism but rather as a strategy for self-empowerment, through which colonial subjects (or people threatened with colonisation) declare loyalty towards and affinity for the powers that be, as they seek for themselves 'a new place in the global order'.[128] It has long been recognised that Parsi 'loyalty' to the imperial establishment, and to British policies including 'progressive' social reform, empowered Parsis, while they disempowered or alien-ated those Hindus who could not accommodate such reforms.[129] I would therefore concur with, but extend to India, Burton's assess-ment that the rise of reform in England was the result, not of 'unilat-eral' English activism, but of 'spirited exchanges among a variety of actors'.[130]

My intention in rethinking relationships between Malabari and his English counterparts has been to reassess the balance of power between metropolitan and non-metropolitan journalists and cam-paigners, rather than to assert the significance of Malabari in any absolute sense. On the contrary, I would defer to other critics who have argued that within India the significance of Malabari has perhaps been overstated and that the role of others within the reform movement is due for reassessment. For example, Burton argues that while Rukhmabai defended Malabari's call for legislation, her letters to *The Times* 'were not merely imitative or repetitive of his aims'.[131] Burton de-centres Malabari, not only in relation to Rukhmabai but to others involved in the women's rights movements in India. A full account of the politics of Indian social reform must acknowledge the multiple origins of support for and opposition to the process.

By recognising the active role of the reader, and thereby de-centring authors and texts, it has been possible to begin to think beyond binary – 'we did or gave this to them' – histories and geographies.[132] More specifically, by clarifying the ways in which an Indian journalist read his English counterpart, actively imported and appropriated the techniques of English campaign journalism, it has been possible to trace processes by which developments in India were linked to wider developments, while not being simply derivative of them. This complements the work of historians who identify internal causes of the Indian age of consent controversy, notably Charles Heimsath who attributes this movement to an emerging national social reform movement.[133] Recognising the existence of a wider political field in which English players loomed large, but arguing that Indian campaigners and activists were not necessarily derivative, and showing how they actively read the broader political landscape and its key ideas and texts, this chapter also complements the body of postcolonial criticism which in this field seeks to de-centre English humanitarians in the Indian reform movement.[134] Chandra demonstrates the value of turning from canonised English activists and texts, and indeed from their closest Indian allies. I have tried to move in a similar direction, but through different methods, by provincialising the English within this equation. This may appear a very tentative critical step, though I would argue that subtle departures from English precedent, which delicately negotiated specific and general forms of English authority, played a politically pragmatic part in shaping textured relationships between metropolitan and non-metropolitan texts and readers.

The political terrain suggested by this critique was organised not simply around a dominant centre but by 'the connections between things'.[135] By tracing the productivity of these connections, for example within transactions between authors, texts and readers, it is possible to transcend the sort of hierarchical space suggested in the flows of information and ideas from England to other parts of the Empire, which were considered in the previous chapter. Lester challenges the idea of hierarchical imperial space, structured around a productive originary centre, with the concept of network space consisting of productive nodes 'knitted together within a global cultural and political fabric'.[136] He argues that colonial projects and discourses were forged locally, but also through interactions with other colonies and 'across a network linking these sites together'.[137] This network space, locating productivity at points of contact, resonates with broader ideas about contact zones between metropolitan and non-metropolitan spheres, and, in Alan Lester's and Elleke Boehmer's reworkings, between colonies. As Boehmer puts it, 'the entire imperial framework becomes from this perspective at once decentred and multiply centred, a network, one might say, of interrelating margins'.[138] To exchange hierarchical for multiply centred 'geographies of connection'[139] is not, as this chapter has shown, necessarily to exchange power-structured geographies for their egalitarian opposites. Indeed, the dispersal of agency within formal sexuality politics has proved, in the first instance, to be quite limited. Malabari's active part in sexuality politics, as I have shown, was a function of his 'power to read' and in broader terms of his elite social position within colonial Bombay. More generally, the nodes in geographies of connection each represent local concentrations of power, and individuals with privileged access to the connective infrastructure of imperialism – the material networks of transport and communication.[140] These geographies of connection therefore represented geographically but not always socially dispersed power. This gives rise to further questions about how others, who occupied less privileged roles in these networks, might nevertheless have reclaimed some political agency and spoken to sexuality politics.

This chapter represents a first and tentative step in provincialising English sexuality politics. Chapter 3 moves beyond such subtle negotiations of English texts and precedents, drawing out the productivity of the margins not only in ostensibly reproducing English models of regulation and resistance but even in resisting and rejecting them. Like this chapter, it considers the interventions of locally powerful individuals, groups and organisations, but it examines more assertive interventions, framed by a different kind of colonial political context. Specifically, it examines the selective use and refusal of English precedent in colonial Australia.

Notes

1 Burton, *At the Heart of Empire*, pp. 160–161.
2 *Indian Spectator* (10 August, 1890), p. 633.
3 Marks, 'History, the nation and empire', p. 112.
4 Marks, 'History, the nation and empire', p. 116.

5   Burton, *At the Heart of Empire*, pp. 160–161.
6   Hunt, *Governing Morals*, p. 9.
7   Lester, *Imperial Networks*.
8   Said, 'Travelling theory', pp. 226–227; emphasis added.
9   Said, 'Travelling theory', p. 226.
10 Said, 'Travelling theory', p. 226.
11 D. Chakrabarty, *Provincialising Europe: Postcolonial Thought and Historical Difference* (Princeton, NJ: Princeton University Press, 2000), p. 16.
12 Chakrabarty, *Provincialising Europe*, p. 17.
13 A. P. Cohen, *Symbolic Construction of Community* (London: Tavistock, 1985), p. 14.
14 M. de Certeau, *The Practice of Everyday Life*, trans. S. Rendall (Berkeley: University of California Press, 1984), p. xiii.
15 S. Engle Merry, *Colonizing Hawai'i: The Cultural Power of Law* (Princeton, NJ: Princeton University Press, 2000), p. 261.
16 C. Hall, *Civilising Subjects: Metropole and Colony in the English Imagination 1830–1867* (Cambridge: Polity, 2002), p. 27.
17 Said, 'Travelling theory', pp. 226–227; emphasis added.
18 Fawcett and Turner, *Josephine Butler*.
19 Valverde, *Age of Light*.
20 Whyte, *Life of W. T. Stead*.
21 A. Smith, *Newspaper: An International History* (London: Thames & Hudson, 1979), p. 152.
22 R. N. Pierce, *Lord Northcliffe: Trans-Atlantic Influences*, Journalism Monographs No. 40 (Lexington, KY: Association for Education in Journalism, 1975).
23 *Toronto Daily Mail* (10 August 1885), p. 1.
24 Valverde, *Age of Light*.
25 *New York Times* (9 July 1885), p. 3.
26 'The Indian mirror', *Times of India* (7 September 1885), p. 5.
27 *Chicago Daily Tribune* (8 July 1885), p. 1.
28 'The Wisconsin lumber dens', *Sentinel* (March 1889), p. 32; Pivar, *Purity Crusade*, p. 136.
29 Ballhatchet, *Race, Sex and Class Under the Raj*, p. 13.
30 Whyte, *Life of W. T. Stead*, p. 166.
31 S. Fish, *Is There a Text in This Class?* (Cambridge, MA: Harvard University Press, 1980), p. 320; R. Phillips, 'Politics of reading; decolonising children's geographies', *Ecumene: A Journal of Cultural Geographies*, 8:2 (2001), 125–150.
32 De Certeau, *Practice of Everyday Life*, p. 171; see also: Z. Bauman, *Legislators and Interpreters: Modernity, Postmodernity and Intellectuals* (Ithaca, NY: Cornell University Press, 1987); M. Foucault, 'The order of discourse', in R. Young (ed.), *Untying the Text: A Post-Structuralist Reader* (London: Routledge, 1981).
33 B. Stock, *Implications of Literacy: Written Language and Models of Interpretation in the 11th and 12th Centuries* (Princeton, NJ: Princeton University Press, 1983).
34 A. Sinfield, *Cultural Politics: Queer Reading* (London: Routledge, 1994), p. 82.
35 Sinfield, *Cultural Politics*, p. 82.
36 R. Parthasarathy, *Journalism in India from the Earliest Times to the Present Day* (New Delhi: Sterling, 1989), p. 56.
37 Burton, *At the Heart of Empire*, p. 160.
38 J. A. Bernard, *From Raj to the Republic: A Political History of India* (New Delhi: Har-Anand, 2001).
39 B. M. Malabari, *Infant Marriage and Enforced Widowhood in India, Being a Collection of Opinions, For and Against, Received by Mr. Behramji M. Malabari, from Representative Hindu Gentlemen and Official Other Authorities* (Bombay: Voice of India Press, 1887), p. 11.
40 Malabari, *Infant Marriage and Enforced Widowhood in India*, p. 11.
41 Parthasarathy, *Journalism in India*, p. 59.

42 J. N. Basu, *Romance of Indian Journalism* (Calcutta: Calcutta University, 1979), p. 236.
43 J. Wilson, 'Short memorial of the Honourable Mountstuart Elphinstone, and of his contributions to Oriental geography and history', *Journal of the Bombay Branch of the Royal Asiatic Society*, 6 (1861), 97–111, at 105.
44 W. Digby, 'Native newspapers of India and Ceylon', *Calcutta Review*, 65 (1877), 356–394.
45 Smith, *Newspaper*.
46 Parthasarathy, *Journalism in India*, p. 52.
47 Basu, *Romance of Indian Journalism*, p. 200.
48 E. C. Cox, *Short History of the Bombay Presidency* (Bombay: Thacker, 1887).
49 Digby, 'Native newspapers of India and Ceylon', p. 373.
50 K. N. Chaudhuri, *Trade and Civilisation in the Indian Ocean: An Economic History from the Rise of Islam to 1750* (Cambridge: Cambridge University Press, 1985), p. 1.
51 K. McPherson, *Indian Ocean: History of People and the Sea* (Delhi: Oxford University Press, 1993).
52 'An appeal from the daughters of India', *Indian Spectator* (28 September 1890), p. 775.
53 Digby, 'Native newspapers of India and Ceylon', p. 363.
54 Basu, *Romance of Indian Journalism*, p. 218.
55 Digby, 'Native newspapers of India and Ceylon', p. 358.
56 D. Gidumal, *Behramji M. Malabari: A Biographical Sketch* (Bombay: Education Society's Press, 1888).
57 S. J. Singh, *B. M. Malabari: Rambles with the Pilgrim Reformer* (London: G. Bell, 1914), p. 42.
58 Anonymous, *Behramji M. Malabari: A Sketch of His Life and Appreciation of His Works* (Madras: Natesan, 1914), pp. 31–32.
59 P. P. Balsara, *Highlights of Parsi History*, 3rd edn, rev. and enlarged (Bombay: C. B. Trikannad for K. & J. Cooper, 1964); D. L. White, *Competition and Collaboration: Parsi Merchants and the English East India Company in 18th Century India* (New Delhi: Munshiram Manoharlal, 1995).
60 T. M. Luhrmann, *Good Parsi: The Fate of a Colonial Elite in a Postcolonial Society* (Cambridge, MA: Harvard University Press, 1996), p. 1.
61 Burton, *At the Heart of Empire*, p. 157.
62 Burton, *At the Heart of Empire*, p. 157.
63 Burton, *At the Heart of Empire*.
64 Burton, *At the Heart of Empire*; S. Chandra, *Enslaved Daughters: Colonialism, Law and Women's Rights* (Delhi: Oxford University Press, 1998); Gidumal, *Behramji M. Malabari*.
65 Malabari, *Infant Marriage and Enforced Widowhood in India*.
66 Malabari, *Infant Marriage and Enforced Widowhood in India*, p. 1.
67 Malabari, *Infant Marriage and Enforced Widowhood in India*, p. 4.
68 Malabari, *Infant Marriage and Enforced Widowhood in India*.
69 A. Burton, 'Institutionalising imperial reform: the Indian magazine and late-Victorian colonial politics', in D. Finkelstein and D. M. Peers (eds), *Negotiating India in the Nineteenth-Century Media* (Basingstoke: Macmillan, 2000), pp. 23–50.
70 Parthasarathy, *Journalism in India*, pp. 55–56.
71 Burton, *At the Heart of Empire*, p. 160.
72 Smith, *Newspaper*, p. 130.
73 Parthasarathy, *Journalism in India*, p. 23.
74 Parthasarathy, *Journalism in India*, p. 3.
75 Basu, *Romance of Indian Journalism*, p. 218.
76 Parthasarathy, *Journalism in India*, p. 54.
77 Finkelstein and Peers, *Negotiating India in the Nineteenth-Century Media*, p. 13.

78   J. Majeed, 'Narratives of progress and idioms of community: two Urdu period-
     icals of the 1870s', in D. Finkelstein and D. M. Peers, *Negotiating India in the
     Nineteenth-Century Media* (Basingstoke, England: Macmillan, 2000), pp. 135–163.
79   Finkelstein and Peers, *Negotiating India in the Nineteenth-Century Media*, p. 13.
80   Anonymous, *Behramji M. Malabari*, p. 45.
81   E. J. Bristow, *Vice and Vigilance: Purity Movements in Britain since 1700*
     (Dublin: Gill & Macmillan, 1977), p. 111.
82   B. Malabari, 'Infant marriage and enforced widowhood', *Indian Spectator* (23
     November 1884), pp. 934–935.
83   For example: 'Cruelty to child wives', *Indian Spectator* (13 July 1890), p. 553.
84   R. L. Schults, *Crusader in Babylon: W. T. Stead and the Pall Mall Gazette*
     (Lincoln: University of Nebraska Press, 1972).
85   'An appeal from the daughters of India', *Indian Spectator* (5 October 1890),
     p. 793.
86   *Pall Mall Gazette* (8 July 1885), p. 4.
87   Malabari, *Infant Marriage and Enforced Widowhood in India*, p. 4.
88   'An orthodox Hindu', letter to the editor, *Indian Spectator* (31 July 1890), p. 694.
89   *Indian Spectator* (26 October 1890), p. 852.
90   *Pall Mall Gazette* (7 July 1885), p. 4.
91   *Indian Spectator* (10 August 1890), p. 633.
92   *Indian Spectator* (20 July 1890), p. 569.
93   Valverde, *Age of Light*.
94   'An appeal from the daughters of India', *Indian Spectator* (28 September 1890),
     p. 774.
95   D. Spurr, *Rhetoric of Empire: Colonial Discourse in Journalism, Travel Writing
     and Imperial Administration* (Durham, NC: Duke University Press, 1992).
96   N. Philip and V. Neuburg, *Charles Dickens, a December Vision: Social Journal-
     ism* (London: Collins, 1986), pp. 12–13.
97   V. Singh, *Social Realism in the Fiction of Dickens and Mulk Raj Anand* (New
     Delhi: Commonwealth, 1997), p. vii.
98   'The protection of girls: demonstration in Hyde Park', *South London Press*
     (29 August 1885), p. 3; Bristow, *Vice and Vigilance*, p. 112.
99   Malabari, *Infant Marriage and Enforced Widowhood in India*, p. 6.
100 Malabari, B., 'Editorial notes', *Indian Spectator* (15 July 1888), p. 565.
101 Chandra, *Enslaved Daughters*, p. 27.
102 Malabari, B., 'Reformers and reform', *Indian Spectator* (23 November 1884), p. 933.
103 Malabari, B., 'Infant marriage and enforced widowhood', *Indian Spectator* (14
     September 1884), p. 733.
104 Gidumal, *Behramji M. Malabari*, p. xcv.
105 Digby, 'Native newspapers of India and Ceylon'.
106 *Times of India* (5 August 1885), p. 3.
107 Singh, *B. M. Malabari*, p. 57.
108 *Indian Spectator* (6 January 1889), p. 14.
109 Chandra, *Enslaved Daughters*, pp. 2–3.
110 C. H. Heimsath, 'Origin and enactment of the Indian Age of Consent Bill, 1891',
     Journal of Asian Studies, 21 (1962), 491–504; M. Kosambi, *Pandita Ramabai's
     Feminist and Christian Conversions* (Bombay: Research Centre for Women's
     Studies, 1995); M. Sinha, *Colonial Masculinity: The 'Manly Englishman' and the
     'Effeminate Bengali' in the Late Nineteenth Century* (Manchester: Manchester
     University Press, 1995).
111 B. Malabari, 'Editorial', *Indian Spectator* (18 May 1890), p. 387; B. Malabari, 'An
     unnatural *parens patriae*', *Indian Spectator* (27 July 1890), p. 593.
112 'Indian social reform', letter to the editor, *Indian Spectator* (5 April 1885), p. 274.
113 D. F. Karaka, *History of the Parsis* (London: Macmillan, 1884), p. 107; Luhrmann,
     Good Parsi.
114 Malabari, *Infant Marriage and Enforced Widowhood in India*, p. 2.
115 Gidumal, *Behramji M. Malabari*.

116 B. Malabari, 'Some problems of British Indian government', *Indian Spectator* (20 April 1890), p. 313.
117 *Review of Reviews* (November 1890), p. 448.
118 N. S. Ginwalla, 'Infant marriage and enforced widowhood', letter to the editor, *Indian Spectator* (7 September 1890), p. 716.
119 Burton, 'Institutionalising imperial reform'.
120 Chandra, *Enslaved Daughters.*
121 M. Kosambi, *Pandita Ramabai Through Her Own Words: Selected Works* (New Delhi: Oxford University Press, 2000).
122 Burton, 'Institutionalising imperial reform'.
123 *Indian Spectator* (3 August 1890), p. 607.
124 Burton, *At the Heart of Empire.*
125 Heimsath, 'Origin and enactment of the Indian Age of Consent Bill, 1891'; D. Engels, 'The Age of Consent Act of 1891: colonial ideology in Bengal', *South Asia Research*, 3 (1983), 107–131.
126 M. Kosambi, 'Girl-brides and socio-legal change: Age of Consent Bill (1891) controversy', *Economic and Political Weekly* (3 August 1991), pp. 1857–1868, at 1866.
127 Basu, *Romance of Indian Journalism*, p. 271.
128 Engle Merry, *Colonizing Hawai'i*, p. 260.
129 J. Gunther, *The Facets of Asia*, 2 vols (Delhi: Shubhi, 1999), vol. 2, p. 449; Burton, *At the Heart of Empire.*
130 Burton, 'Institutionalising imperial reform', p. 33.
131 Burton, 'Institutionalising imperial reform', p. 37.
132 Marks, 'History, the nation and empire', p. 112.
133 Heimsath, 'Origin and enactment of the Indian Age of Consent Bill, 1891'.
134 Chandra, *Enslaved Daughters.*
135 Marks, 'History, the nation and empire', p. 116.
136 Lester, *Imperial Networks*, p. 5.
137 Lester, *Imperial Networks*, p. 5.
138 Boehmer, *Empire, the National, and the Postcolonial*, p. 6.
139 Ogborn, *Spaces of Modernity*, p. 19.
140 Lester, *Imperial Networks*, p. 6.

CHAPTER THREE

Colonial departures: Australian activists on the age of consent and prostitution

Two of the central claims of this book are that in the field of sexuality politics there was life beyond England, and that geographical perspectives can throw light on this by illuminating non-metropolitan sites of political action. Beginning with Malabari, I have suggested that people in colonies exercised some control over legal and political transplantation and transformation, and that this control was site specific, shaped (but not determined) by local conditions. To more fully develop this case, it helps to turn from Bombay to a different kind of colonial environment, one which facilitated different kinds of colonial agency. Compared with the Indian city, where formal political channels were closed and exclusive, Australia was a relatively inclusive society, politically speaking. Responsible government gave local electorates a more formal say and influence over the adoption or rejection of legal and governmental precedents. Sites of political action are not defined by forms of government alone, however, so it will also be necessary to ask questions about the other conditions that enabled and constrained political action there: the power of the media and the churches, for instance. It will also be possible to think about these sites on a more abstract level, not only as the settings for political action, but somehow as vehicles for it, active agents. Elleke Boehmer is not being wholly metaphorical when she reads the central question addressed by subaltern studies as how resistance emerged 'from the *place* of otherness'.[1] The settlers whose interventions are explored in this chapter were more colonial agents than they were subjects, though their positions and interventions were non-metropolitan, and as such they illuminate some of the political life that existed beyond England.

The negotiation of metropolitan precedent – the selective transplantation of European society, culture and politics – was fundamental to the colonial experience. As Louis Hartz has generalised, certain strands of European life were discarded while others were amplified in processes of settlement and colonisation.[2] Consequently, European traits variously shrivelled and flourished, mutated, hybridised and creolised in non-European colonial fields and contact zones. According to Cole Harris, this led to the 'simplification of Europe overseas',[3] as much of the old world was left behind. He explains, for example, that migrants abandoned many of their class distinctions but took the nuclear family with them when they moved to New England, the Antipodes or Southern Africa. These are plausible but apolitical arguments. The botanical source of Harris's preferred metaphor – transplantation – gives the impression that the selective transfer of European traits – including socio-sexual institutions and arrangements – was somehow natural. The reality was anything but. The power of the nuclear family – its transfer from Europe, departure from European models and situated reconfiguration – was an outcome of colonial sexuality politics. Colonists produced and reproduced families, both biologically and legally, as the building blocks of their colonial social order. To politicise the Hartzian thesis, it helps to reflect on Edward Said's argument that the 'idea' does not travel intact but shifts according to 'conditions of acceptance or, as an inevitable part of acceptance, resistances – which then confronts the transplanted theory or idea, making possible its introduction or toleration, however alien it might appear to be'.[4] Colonists did not just select, they negotiated, resisted and invented.

The recognition that English precedents within the arena of sexuality politics were transplanted unevenly, and that this was in part a function of situated colonial negotiations and sometimes refusals of them, is to raise further questions about the consequences of all this. Should the failure of metropolitan models to universally, neatly relocate be interpreted as a failure – an effect of the limits – of imperial power? Or should it be seen as an effect of the flexibility of imperialism, its ability to assume different forms in different contexts? Conversely, how should the (partial) extension of metropolitan models be interpreted? Should it be regarded as an effect of (qualified) imperial hegemony, or another consequence of colonial agency?

These questions are explored in the body of this chapter through case studies of colonial agency in sexuality politics, but it is possible to speculate on some possible answers at this stage. The extension of metropolitan models of regulation and resistance may be read as a symbol of imperial authority and/or as a substantive means of reproducing and exercising that power; conversely, the failure to effect such an extension may be read as a symbolic and/or substantive limitation of imperial power. The former argument is qualified by the consideration that imperialism was overtly flexible, assuming different forms in different contexts without necessarily undermining its fundamental power relations. The latter is complicated by the difficulty – perhaps impossibility – of identifying certain events and processes as either simply for or simply against imperialism, given the lack of any universally accepted, essential or stable definition of or vision for imperialism. Both complications conspire to render sexuality politics politically ambiguous. For example, some would say the increased age of consent in India or Australia buttressed and legitimated English hegemony by universalising English laws and ethics and by variously drawing people away from pre-colonial affiliations and producing the socio-sexual building-blocks of a new colonial order. Others, however, would say that the increased age of consent weakened Britain's imperial presence by meddling unnecessarily and gaining enemies, and that its consequences were unpredictable and ambivalent, variously serving and hindering a mixture of contested imperial imperatives and projects, which were themselves contested and contradictory. It was not clear what effects the laws would have, or whether supporting or opposing specific laws meant supporting or opposing, or simply reforming or negotiating, imperialism.

The question of whether colonial negotiations of metropolitan precedent could be understood as hegemonic, ultimately subservient to imperial hegemony, or whether they represented some form of resistance to this, is largely an empirical one. Before turning to case histories, however, it is important to be clear about the key term: hegemony. Imperialism was hegemonic where the imperial order and specific imperial practices were not crudely forced on colonists and colonial subjects, but maintained with their tacit acceptance and negotiated with their involvement. The mechanisms of this varied, ranging from establishing responsible governments that enfranchised many of the residents in certain white-dominated settler societies, reducing the chance that they would follow the American colonists and rebel against the Empire, to calculating and considering the attitudes of colonial subjects when forming legislation.[5] Though such calculations were unfair and imperfect, Richard Rathbone argues that they did help to win a measure of consent for many colonial laws, which were 'domesticated' rather than hated or resisted.[6] Engels and Marks develop this point, arguing that many aspects of imperial government courted and won tacit acceptance:

> Over the past couple of decades history 'from below' has focused on colonial resistance and protest. Scholars have tried to compensate for generations of Eurocentric and elite-oriented historiography, which

[85]

initially described the benevolent impact of colonialism and later portrayed the nationalist struggle mainly through the eyes of the Indian and African middle classes. More recently, historians of the oppressed have placed the exploitative character of colonial rule, the outbreak of peasant protest and insurrection, and the development of a growing rural and urban proletariat at the centre of their analysis. Revisionist scholars of African, especially East and southern African, history, and the *Subaltern Studies* group of Indian historians have paid some attention to the colonial state, although in general they have stressed its coercive capacity rather than the ways in which its political strategies were directed at creating consent among the colonized. The emphasis has thus been on what has been regarded as the inevitable resistance and protest of the oppressed, rather than on their strategies of accommodation and survival.[7]

The recognition that political action cannot always be located simply for or against the dominant power – as either hegemonic or resistant – points to the need for research that does not simply seek out clear cases of empire-building or resistance to it, but traces more subtle negotiations of imperial power, which nevertheless politicise Hartz's and Harris's observations about the negotiations of European precedent that were so important to and commonplace in colonial life.

Negotiating precedent: the age of consent in South Australia

Colonial legislators and activists looked to, and often appeared to copy, English (and other metropolitan) models of regulation and resistance. In her book about Canadian social purity movements, Mariana Valverde comments that it 'would be impossible here to detail all the forms and channels of English and American influence on Canadian ideas about social and moral reform'.[8] In Australia, similarly, much of the content of social purity movements could be traced to English and American sources. Regulation Bills, put before and sometimes passed by responsible colonial governments, were generally modelled directly or indirectly on their English counterparts. English campaign strategies were also transplanted and adopted, as the preceding discussions of Dyer and Malabari have made clear. The career of South Australian social purity campaigner Reverend Joseph Coles Kirby (1837–1924) was equally derivative, at least on the surface. This section examines Kirby's interventions, locating his political agency and tracing the strategies through which he exercised it, before assessing the extent to which these interventions either underpinned or resisted imperial hegemony.

[86]

To consider the agency that facilitated Kirby's intervention, it is necessary to position him (and other South Australian activists) within a broader political context. The agency of South Australian activists was structured by the particular form of colonialism there, and by a range of historical, cultural and geographical contextual factors, which revolved around self government, a tradition of political independence, a politically active nonconformist religious culture, and a free press. Responsible government had been secured in 1857, barely a generation after the formal foundation of the colony. A tradition of political independence was present from the start, according to contemporary observers and also historians. In *Paradise of Dissent: South*

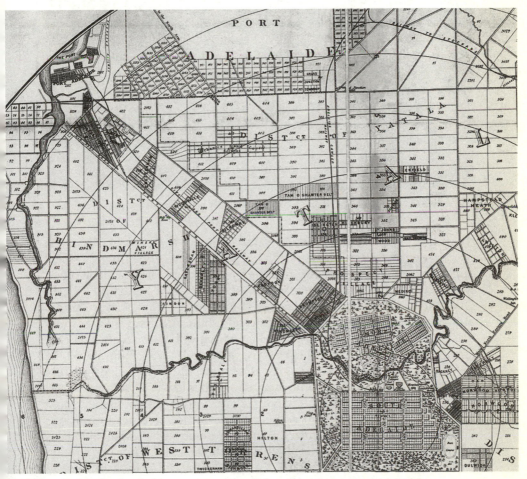

3.1 Map of Adelaide, detail showing proximity of the city and port (Port Adelaide)

3.2 Colonial democracy: Parliament House, Adelaide (c.1879)

Australia, 1829–1857, Douglas Pike claimed that South Australia was settled by 'men whose professed ideals were civil liberty, social opportunity and equality for all religions. Though each of these ideas was moulded in Britain, each was a protest against British practice.'[9] Over the years many of the ideals of the original colonists were gradually off-loaded or compromised, though some idealism and willingness to depart from English precedent remained. One result was that for its first century, the Legislative Assembly was 'dominated by independents' who 'knew no party allegiance, but followed alternately the whims of themselves and their constituents'.[10]

The system of responsible government, which distinguished most white-majority resettlement societies from other colonial formations in the Victorian period, requires some introduction.[11] Responsible government formally enfranchised white adult men and, later on, women (South Australia was one of the first places in the British Empire to enfranchise women, a move it made in 1894).[12] Australian colonial

3.3 A predominantly rural colony: rural landscape of South Australia, with Adelaide in the distance (c.1890)

governments, the first of which was established in the 1850s, were modelled on the English Upper and Lower Houses of Parliament, translated (as closely as circumstances allowed) to colonial legislative councils and assemblies, respectively.[13] Australian colonial governments assumed responsibility for many areas of legislation, including the regulation of prostitution and the determination of ages of consent. After the Australian colonies federated to form the Australian Commonwealth in 1901, their governments retained these powers. The agenda for legislation on the regulation of sexuality in any given Australian colony (state, post-federation) was influenced by developments elsewhere, notably but not only in England and in other Australian colonies (states). The ways in which individual colonial (state) governments raised and addressed legislation of this nature were also influenced by contextual colonial conditions and by the actions of local agents, the latter including activists and pressure groups which sought to influence public opinion (voters) and to lobby members of the legislative assemblies and councils.

As Pike showed, South Australian legislators sometimes refused to follow party lines or legislative precedents, whether set in other Australian colonies or in the imperial Parliament. Their willingness to follow their consciences was linked both to their politicised nonconformity and to that of their electorate. Of all the Australian colonies, South Australia had the lowest degrees of affiliation to the Church of England and the Roman Catholic Church, and the highest to Methodist, Baptist, Congregational and Lutheran denominations.[14] Nonconformists, in general contrast to their Anglican and Catholic counterparts (considered below with reference to New South Wales [NSW]), were politically engaged and effective, particularly within purity politics. As the leading opponent of purity legislation argued: 'The whole agitation from the first had been priestly.'[15] The devolved structure of certain nonconformist churches left individuals free to invent, debate and advance political ideas.[16] It also provided individuals with affiliations, which served to strengthen their political projects in the legislature and in other spheres of public life.[17] Thus, the prominent Methodist Sir John Colton held office both as Premier of South Australia and as president of the South Australian Social Purity Society; and it was a Congregationalist who led the South Australian purity movement in the 1880s. Kirby was for twenty-eight years minister of the Port Adelaide Congregational Church, and was twice elected as chair of the Congregational Union of South Australia (1886 and 1906). He used his position within the church to secure support for the purity movement he initiated.[18] Finally, another source of local relative autonomy, linked to the responsible government (variously as a voice of its support, opposition and analysis) and to the nonconformist political culture, was the South Australian press, a political force that intervened also in purity politics. The leading daily newspaper, the *South Australian Register*, made this explicit, commenting for example that 'we think it is the duty of the secular press to inculcate morality'.[19] Collectively, these sources of social and political power established the context in which activists such as Kirby were able to operate, with some independence from metropolitan texts and authors, political discourses and leaders.

It might have appeared that South Australia closely followed English precedent, in the sense that the colony passed legislation very similar to that enacted in the mother country the same year. I argue, however, that the colony did not simply follow England, nor could it have done so, for the successful passage of this legislation depended in both places on high levels of public interest and political momentum. South Australian legislation on social purity was not simply an imperial imposition or an action of colonial deference. When Kirby campaigned for an increase in the age of consent, he did so actively and with some autonomy.

In 1885 the South Australian parliament passed legislation, similar to England's Criminal Law Amendment Act, which raised the age of consent from 13 to 16 and introduced a series of other restrictions and regulations on sexual conduct. The events leading up to the enactment of this legislation had begun five years earlier. A paper entitled 'Our duty as to public morals' was read at the Annual Meeting of the Congregational Union (April 22, 1880), which appointed a committee to examine the state of public morality in the colony. The investigation did not get off the ground, but the committee's failure had the effect of setting an agenda and producing a vacuum that another member of the Congregational Union was to fill. In July 1882 Kirby delivered three public lectures on the subject of social purity in an Adelaide church hall. The lectures concentrated on reviewing the wider struggle against regulation (lecture one) and arguments about moral double standards, which provided a point of departure for proposing a positive agenda for legislative change, including an increase in the South Australian age of consent, ideally to 18. At the close of his third lecture, a social purity committee was formed, and the lectures were printed and distributed to public figures and opinion leaders.[20] Kirby campaigned actively in the months that followed, organising the first of thirty-nine petitions that were sent to the legislature before the end of 1884. Bills along lines proposed by Kirby were considered in 1883 (the Young Person's Protection Bill), 1884 (the Protection of Young Women Bill) and 1885 (the Criminal Law Consolidation Bill). Legislation was stalled in 1884 by the resignation of the government, but public opinion and the support of religious bodies, the police force and various corporations and district councils helped to ensure that the Bill passed swiftly the following year.[21] The Act did much that Kirby and other social purity activists demanded, including raising the age of consent to 16 (a subsequent Act raised it to 17).

From the start of his campaign, Kirby depended heavily on arguments imported from England, accurately prefaced with 'no pretence to originality'.[22] That said, general arguments were actively appropriated and deployed in the creation of local, colonial and national social purity movements, which were conceived as more than variants on an English model. Kirby concluded his three lectures on social purity with a call to action: 'Let South Australia show a lead resolute and effective', which might be an example 'to Australasia and to the whole British Empire'.[23] To that end, and not simply to execute essentially English politics, he worked within campaign networks to promote the South Australian and the wider purity cause. His regular correspondents included Benjamin Scott (a leading purity activist in London) and Dyer, who he visited in India. Kirby was also a prolific correspondent of the *Sentinel*, which published his regular letters and articles, and chronicled the progress of the South Australian Purity Society (the three lectures were reported by the *Sentinel* in September, November and December 1882). In this manner Kirby was able to inform English campaigners of his projects and to win their support, and also to influence public opinion in South Australia itself, where the *Sentinel* was read. The mutual rather than subservient nature of Kirby's relationship with English campaigners was demonstrated when, in England in 1891, he shared a platform with Josephine Butler and W. T. Stead, and 'was asked to say a few words as representing the social reformers of Australia'.[24] As the *Sentinel* put it: 'If action in Great Britain has been an encouragement to our friends in Australasia, they may be assured that their action is in return an encouragement to us here.'[25] Kirby acknowledged the assistance of his English and international colleagues for the information and advice they had sent,[26] but he ultimately attributed success in South Australia – largely in relation to blocking regulatonist Bills and securing positive legislation – to the efforts of South Australians.

English arguments and tactics helped to bring about change in South Australia, but only because they were actively mobilised by South Australians, and supplemented with contextual arguments and tactics. As in debates on regulation, many arguments were simply borrowed from England, as Kirby admitted.[27] He made no mention of Adelaide or South Australia until the final page of his forty-five-page script (in booklet form), which concentrated on general issues and comparative solutions, and applied an established campaign debate to South Australia. General arguments were, however, appropriated and deployed in the creation of a social purity society in South Australia, which was conceived as more than a mere variant of an English model.[28] Arguments previously voiced in England were also employed in legislative debates. Premier Colton, for example, reviewed English arguments and experiences, and quoted authorities such as Lord Shaftesbury on the subject.[29] Similarly, opponents of the purity movements rehearsed arguments that had also been used in England. Rees quoted Lord Beaconsfield, for example, who had warned that legislation would reduce English men and women to 'children', only 'to gratify the prigs and pedants'.[30]

English arguments and evidence were deployed selectively. For example, when the Social Purity Society of South Australia circulated in pamphlet form a copy of extracts from the Criminal Law Amendment Act (1885),[31] it reproduced only those elements of the English

Act that served its immediate purposes, which were focused on ages of consent and protection of young women. It did not, for example, include the section on male homosexuality, which was prominent in the English legislation. The tendency of South Australians to actively interpret and deploy English arguments is illustrated by the variety of ways in which they cited English texts and authorities. Butler, whose work revolved around the defence of personal rights, was ambivalent about the repressive second-wave purity movements, and consequently she provided some encouragement – and quotable statements – to both the purity campaigners and their opponents.[32] The Ladies' Branch of the South Australian Purity Society stated that it followed 'the example of such women as Miss Nightingale, Mrs Josephine Butler, and Miss Ellice Hopkins in England'.[33] On the other hand, the leading opponent of South Australian purity movements quoted Butler's advice not to 'go in for constructive legislation'.[34] Similarly, a member of the Legislative Assemby (MLA) who opposed the Bill noted:

> When the Bill was introduced into the House of Commons it met the strenuous, loyal, strong opposition of nearly all English philanthropists and of those who were lovers of liberty, notably of those very persons most frequently quoted by the Rev. Mr. Kirby in his astounding crusade – Mrs. Josephine Butler included.[35]

Never simply imposed or transplanted, English purity discourse was actively applied, modified and adapted to the South Australian context. South Australian purity campaigners thus took possession of and transformed arguments that had been used in England. It was by no means obvious that the sexual life of London, the world's largest city and the metropolitan centre of the British Empire, compared with that of South Australia – a small and mostly rural colony. Purity campaigners had to *make* the connection. Thus, one MLA 'presumed most hon. members had read the remarks in the *Pall Mall Gazette*' and argued that 'if a tithe of them was well founded it might be true on a smaller scale in a smaller city like Adelaide, and the necessity for the Bill [would then be] more apparent than ever'.[36] Opponents could only ask the perennial question: why were colonists 'so susceptible in regard to matters 14,000 miles away'?[37]

Arguments were adapted to South Australian moral geography. Purity campaigners (some of whom had downplayed claims about prostitution and syphilis in the colony when opposing CD Bills) made sometimes-extravagant claims about immorality in the colony. Addressing the Congregational Union of South Australia, the Rev. O. Copland estimated that 'there are in Adelaide at least 1,000 young girls and women living in known sin, while 500 of them are recognised by the police as regular prostitutes'.[38] Opponents of social purity legislation claimed the opposite. Rowland Rees 'protested against the aspersions cast on happy and moral South Australia by Mr. Kirby and his followers'.[39] In England, it had been argued that the low age of consent, juxtaposed to higher ages of consent in France and Belgium, made it attractive for brothel-keepers on the Continent to recruit young prostitutes in England. This argument was adapted to the Australian context by substituting French possessions in the South Pacific, and arguing (with little or no evidence, as critics pointed out) that girls and young women were recruited in Australia for the brothels of New Caledonia.[40] General arguments about the significance of English and international purity movements in the Australian context – which some purity activists saw as a 'young society' marked by 'rampant larrikinism' and 'capable of forms of brutal vice and crime which make the blood run cold'[41] – were borrowed and endorsed in the South Australian legislature.[42] Finally, legislative developments in England were cited as suitable precedents for South Australians to follow – by many of the same politicians and activists who had argued that English precedents on regulation should be resisted. For example, one supporter of the purity legislation told MLAs: 'Hon. members would have observed by a recent telegram that a similar measure had just passed the House of Commons, thus showing that the people in the old country were alive to the importance of the subject.'[43] By advocating that some English precedents should be followed and others resisted, South Australians made clear their priorities and strategies: they were prepared to deploy their links, with an apparent deference to England, in a manner that suited them.

This discussion has shown that, despite their appearance of following closely and quickly the example set in England, South Australians determined to a considerable degree the course of legislation in the colony. South Australian campaigners and legislators were, of course, aware of events in England, and were to some extent influenced by them, but nevertheless possessed and exercised considerable degrees of agency. It was through their very awareness of events in England that they fashioned their own politics – by actively interpreting and deploying metropolitan texts and discourses, and by doing so through their situated positions within networks of activism, networks that linked them into a dispersed movement, but did not simply marginalise them or render them passive. The question remains, however, whether South Australians were really making their own choices and thereby potentially working against imperial hegemony, or whether they were merely endorsing it, finding ways to adapt imperial systems to local conditions – just as, for instance, Arthur adapted English purity texts to Australian conditions (as discussed in chapter 1). This question should not be oversimplified, since actions can rarely be categorically identified either with domination or resistance. These are rarely unambiguous fields of action, and the distinctions between them can be fuzzy, complex and contested. A minority of political actions appear to be easily classified in this way – as Said pointed out, 'there are evidently still acts of brutal domination occurring, and also instances of spirited resistance'[44] – but many more do not. Critics have found resistance in actions from 'foot dragging' and 'feigned ignorance'[45] to 'anti-colonial dance',[46] but not everyone would agree with these interpretations. The difficulty of identifying certain political actions with either domination or resistance has led some critics to fundamentally question the usefulness of these terms.[47] Doreen Massey has argued against a simplified reiteration of dualisms that pitted big structures against little people,[48] Philip Howell against a 'static pairing of a dominant bourgeois repressive culture and heroic resistance of individuals, groups or bodies'.[49] The difference between domination and resistance comes not in black and white, but shades of grey, a continuum.[50] Kirby's negotiations of English precedent can be located somewhere along that continuum, since they were neither entirely subservient to the hegemonic order nor unambiguously resistant to it. Though politically ambivalent, Kirby's interventions did at least speak of active, situated, colonial agency in imperial sexuality politics.

Refusing precedent: regulation Bills defeated in South Australia

Despite the insistence of Rathbone, and of Engels and Marks, that attention might profitably be shifted from resistance to consent, the two were – and are – never far apart. On the continuum of resistance, colonial responses to the English precedents and laws examined in this chapter, and the book as a whole, appear towards the weaker end of the spectrum. This does not make them wishy-washy gestures so much as realistic ones according to Jean and John Comaroff, who argue that 'for the most part ... the ripostes of the colonized hover in the space between the tacit and the articulate, the direct and the indirect'.[51] I have stated that these subtle gestures are not always clearly distinguishable from compliance with domination, and that the two tend to intermingle, spatially and temporally. Engels and Marks explain that in colonial states, as in the metropole, hegemony is 'always subject to contestation and manipulation'.[52] Resistance may, in certain circumstances, be understood as part of the contextual process of negotiating hegemony, not simply as opposition to crude forms of domination. This understanding of (consent and) resistance as a series of subtle and complex negotiations, rather than self-evident and simplistic (impositions or) refusals, resonates with the preceding accounts of Malabari's and Kirby's interventions, and with other sexuality politics in South Australia and NSW, which are examined in this section and the next.

If South Australians appeared to follow England's lead with respect to the age of consent, their position on CD legislation was different. By actively blocking the passage of CD legislation, they departed from imperial precedent and reshaped the agenda for sexuality and gender politics in their colony. This section situates this move with further reference to the South Australian political context and the agency of those involved, before asking more fundamental questions about relationships between these political departures and the broader imperial order.

A CD Bill was introduced by the government of South Australia in 1869, one year after a similar Act had been passed in Queensland.[53] Female prostitution had been officially acknowledged and therefore admitted to the political agenda from early in the colony's European history. In 1842 an advisor to Governor George Grey made reference to 'the large number of females who are living by a life of prostitution in the city of Adelaide, out of all proportion to the respectable population'.[54] In the decades that followed, part- and full-time prostitutes lived and worked throughout the colony, and were most concentrated in Adelaide and Port Adelaide.[55] The 1869 Bill was to provide for the registration and regular medical examination of prostitutes. It was produced in response to the South Australian parliamentary *Report on the Committee of the Contagious Diseases Act* (23 June 1868)[56] and modelled most directly on Acts passed by the imperial and Queensland parliaments. The Bill was introduced in the House of Assembly by the attorney-general (12 August 1869), was passed and sent to the Legislative Council (12 October 1869), but was finally allowed to lapse.[57] A similar Bill was introduced to the Legislative Assembly six years later as a private member's bill, but after debate within the Assembly and criticism without (notably in the nonconformist[58] press),[59] the Bill was withdrawn. The MLA concerned explained that he had been persuaded that the matter should be dealt with by doctors rather than by the police, and he said he would introduce a suitably modified bill at a later date (he never did).[60]

The failure of CD Bills in the South Australian parliament might be explained, in part, by reference to the political will of South Australians. Arguably, the agency and independent political culture, discussed in the preceding section, led the colony's responsible government to deviate from imperial and other Australian precedent.

Opponents and proponents of the 1869 CD Bill each borrowed general arguments from their English counterparts. Proponents pointed out that the Bill followed English precedent, and noted that a copy of the English Act had been used in drafting it;[61] and in 1875 they explained that the new CD Bill incorporated amendments to the laws in England.[62] A supporter of the Bill informed members of the Legislative Council that 'an Act of similar nature had been passed in England . . . and it had the effect of decreasing the ravages of the disease as much as 60 or 70 per cent among the soldiers and sailors'.[63] The attorney-general pointed to support for the Acts in England, notably among religious leaders (including Anglican bishops) and in the media.[64] Introducing the 1875 Bill, John Ingleby, who admitted to having no specialist knowledge of the subject, cited arguments presented in the *Westminster Review* and read from a speech previously delivered in the House of Commons.[65] But if supporters of the CD Bill could borrow arguments, so could opponents. South Australians reiterated Butler's well-known argument that the Acts institutionalised a moral double standard. Carr, who led opposition to the Bill in the Legislative Assembly, criticised the 'measure which so greatly interfered with the rights and liberties of so many members of the community'.[66] He seconded a motion to amend the Bill to apply equally to both sexes, by asserting: 'What is sauce for the goose is sauce for the gander.'[67] Opponents also described the degradation and suffering that the Acts allegedly caused in England and in other places where they applied. Carr argued: 'On the Continent and in England women had been had been driven to death by persecution under the Act, and under the dread of exposure and false accusation they had been driven into wrong-doing.'[68] South Australian legislative debates on CD Bills were therefore second-hand; they were, however, deployed actively rather than passively by South Australians, whose projects and voices did more than echo those of their English counterparts.

South Australians also actively drew on some of the tactics of their English counterparts. Supporters of the Bill tried to exploit the embarrassment associated with open discussion of prostitution and sexuality, thus minimising discussion and opposition, and ushering the Bill quietly through parliament. This had been simplest in England when the first CD Act was passed, but had become increasingly difficult as campaigners and MPs spoke out in public against the Act and its successors. The member who introduced the Bill to the Legislative Assembly stated that 'if hon. Members felt it was a question which they would like not like to discuss with the publicity which attached to their so doing, he should be prepared to consent to its being referred to a Special Committee'.[69] The chief secretary said that 'in his experience he generally found that those who assumed the greatest ignorance very frequently were the best informed'.[70] But by the time this CD Bill reached the South Australian parliament, the anti-regulationist tactic of forcing debate into the open, and thereby slowing its progress and potentially embarrassing its supporters, had become established. Thus, one MLA insisted, in a speech on moral double standards, that no 'good would be gained by referring the Bill to a Committee'.[71] Discussed in the open, the Bill would stand less chance of successful passage through parliament.

In addition to general arguments and tactics, opponents of regulation also used a number of arguments that were more specific to South Australia. A number of contextual factors that discouraged CD legislation in the colony have been introduced, though in doing so no explanation was provided of the mechanisms linking contextual factors to legislative outcomes. One such mechanism was the mobilisation of contextual arguments by opponents of the Bill, in public and in parliament. A number of MLAs and MLCs argued that the Bill had little relevance in their own 'small community of less than 200,000 people'.[72] The Hon. H. Mildred, who moved successfully to suspend the Bill, argued that 'a measure of this kind might be suitable for large towns in England, such as Chatham, Deptford, and Portsmouth, where there were large bodies of troops, but it would not be required here'.[73] Another opponent of the Bill told the Assembly: 'There might be some excuse or argument in favour of the Bill if we had soldiers stationed here, who were debarred from marriage except with the consent of their officers . . . but here we had no such cause for legislation'.[74]

Contextual arguments against regulation in South Australia revolved also around estimations of the specific moral geography of the colony. Those who supported the Bill felt obliged to argue that the colony had related problems with syphilis and prostitution. One MLA made the extravagant claim that one-twelfth of the population of Adelaide and its suburbs was affected with syphilis;[75] another argued that 'Adelaide of a Sunday night was like one vast brothel'.[76] Such claims were contested by opponents of the Bill. Rejecting Ingleby's claim, Carr argued that 'Adelaide was reported as one of the best-conducted cities in the world as far as police supervision, good order, and general morality were concerned, and he thought a great injustice to our foster land was done by the statements made.'[77] He claimed to have 'seen more immorality in certain streets of Liverpool in half an hour than he had seen or heard of during the whole of his sojourn in Adelaide; but it appeared to be the fashion to traduce everything colonial'.[78] Another opponent of the Bill reassured members that their adopted home was morally 'in advance of the other colonies, and it was not wise to try to blacken South Australia'.[79]

South Australians thereby used the agency of responsible government to bring about a significant political outcome. They determined South Australian policies on prostitution (nominal criminalisation rather than regulation) which were to survive until the end of the twentieth century.[80] They did not manage to prevent prostitutes (and women suspected of being prostitutes) from being regulated informally and often bullied by the police, who maintained a general policy of 'surveillance and segregation'[81] and, like their colleagues in other Australian colonies, arrested and charged many prostitutes with public order offences.[82] They did, however, circumvent the passage of repressive legislation that Butler and others dedicated nearly two decades to opposing in England and elsewhere, and as a result they freed up critical energy to address other issues including the related enfranchisement of women and advancement of a positive purity agenda.

So, to return to the broader themes of this chapter, does South Australian resistance to regulation Bills constitute ongoing domination or resistance to it? Contemporary purity campaigners in both South Australia and England would have no doubt that their action was resistant – triumphantly so – though, once again, the reality was more complex. South Australians certainly resisted certain strands of English precedent and imperial practice, but in doing so they embraced others, including ascendant anti-regulationism and a longer tradition of imperial humanitarianism. Neither was the colony's resistance to regulation politically transparent: did this mean resistance to imperial precedent *per se* or to a substantively imperial law, or both? Once again it is impossible to position this political move in any simple way, such as in relation to a distinction between domination and resistance. Once again, however, it is possible to conclude that patterns of regulation and resistance were not simply imposed on colonies but negotiated there, through situated expressions of colonial agency.

Cultural resistance? Age of consent legislation delayed in NSW

One reason that many political actions and historical situations are, as the Comaroffs put it, 'extremely murky' is that they mean different things to different people, and 'domination' is rarely self-evident.[83] In other words, actions and situations cannot be understood or classified simply on the basis of the intentions of some or all of those involved in their execution and interpretation. If, as Homi Bhabha argues, 'resistance is not necessarily an oppositional act of political intention',[84] then histories of resistance and political action more generally need not be written in terms recognisable to their protagonists. This section examines resistance to English legislative precedent, which may not have been intended as such, and which – perhaps like most historical situations – was intended and understood differently by the different people involved. A second study of Australian resistance to English precedent, the section explains the repeated failure of age of consent legislation in NSW with reference to informal – indirect and/ or unintentional – cultural opposition. Though they devoted less time and energy than their South Australian counterparts to campaigning for or against purity movements and legislative change, people in NSW stood *culturally* in the way of moral reform. It would be an oversimplification to characterise South Australian resistance as intentional, New South Walean as cultural, since both intentional and cultural factors applied in each colony. Whereas intentional resistance may have decided the fate of South Australian moral politics, however, this does not appear to have been the case in NSW, where the purity agenda was impeded, in the context of some apathy on the part of the general public, by a broader raft of cultural contextual factors.

Like South Australia, NSW had diverged from English precedent when it failed to introduce CD legislation. It went its own way once again when it failed to enact positive purity legislation.[85] Like their South Australian counterparts, purity activists and groups in NSW campaigned for age of consent and other positive legislation, doing so in partnership with English and international contacts. Purity Bills were put before the colonial legislature in 1892 and 1893, containing clauses to raise the age of consent from 14 (where it had stood since 1883) to 17, but these Bills made little progress, and positive purity legislation slipped down the political agenda. The failure of these private member's Bills was partly due to the limited political competence of the MLA who introduced them. Mr Nield introduced the sweeping and negatively entitled Vice Suppression Bill in summary and evasive fashion, and failed to persuade his colleagues.[86] Arguably, however, the Bill was defeated primarily by contextual factors and by formal and informal opposition which militated against the efforts of purity campaigners. Further defeats followed between 1903 and 1909, and it was not until 1910 that the age of consent was finally raised from 14 to 16 (by the Crimes [Girls' Protection] Act).

The failure of positive purity legislation in NSW was not for want of trying, if only on the part of a moral minority. Purity activists there followed campaign strategies similar to those that had worked for their South Australian counterparts. These consisted of local initiatives by activists such as Dr Richard Arthur (perhaps the best-known purity campaigner in the colony), backed up by cooperation with English and other individuals and groups (see chapter 1). Arthur arrived from England shortly before the first of Nield's Bills was introduced in the legislature, and almost immediately began to campaign on its behalf, partly by drawing on the arguments, tactics and resources of the contemporary campaign network. Attributing the failure of Nield's Bill to public apathy and ignorance on the subject,[87] Arthur circulated petitions, addressed public meetings and wrote to newspapers.[88] In 1904 he was elected to the Legislative Assembly, where he continued to campaign.[89] Like his counterparts in South Australia, Arthur felt the need for external support, and wrote to the *Sentinel*, declaring: 'What we need is some earnest and eloquent speaker to come among us, and rouse us to the awfulness of the conditions around us. Is there no such one in England who could devote a year to stirring up a holy crusade in Australia against the sins of impurity?'[90] No one of any standing responded directly, and it remained up to Arthur and his colleagues to take the initiative. Arthur sought the advice of English and American campaigners and groups, including Ellice Hopkins, the White Cross League and the Woman's Christian Temperance Union.[91] He formed a NSW, then an Australasian, branch of the Church of England's purity society – the White Cross League – (in 1896 and 1901 respectively)[92] and used his links with the organisation and his correspondence with its leader, Ellice Hopkins, to bolster his purity work, including his demand for legislative change. As explained in more detail in chapter 1, Arthur imported, distributed, endorsed and produced White Cross books and tracts, which he adapted to the Australian context and/or reprinted. The impacts of Arthur and the Australasian White Cross League are difficult to measure. The *Australian Christian World* could only speculate that their 'influence though quiet is far reaching'.[93] However, Arthur and the White Cross League did little to help secure an increase in the age of consent, and that failure highlights the limited ability of English movements to replicate or even to be replicated through local agency in colonies.

A range of contextual factors militated against and/or marginalised purity agendas. An allegedly relaxed sexual culture in Sydney might explain disinterest in or hostility to purity politics there – some in Australia and England identified Sydney as a city of morally, specifically sexually, low standards, while others enjoyed its permissiveness. In 1873, a detailed survey, *Vice and its Victims in Sydney*, argued that 'the youth and manhood of Sydney are rapidly being corrupted'

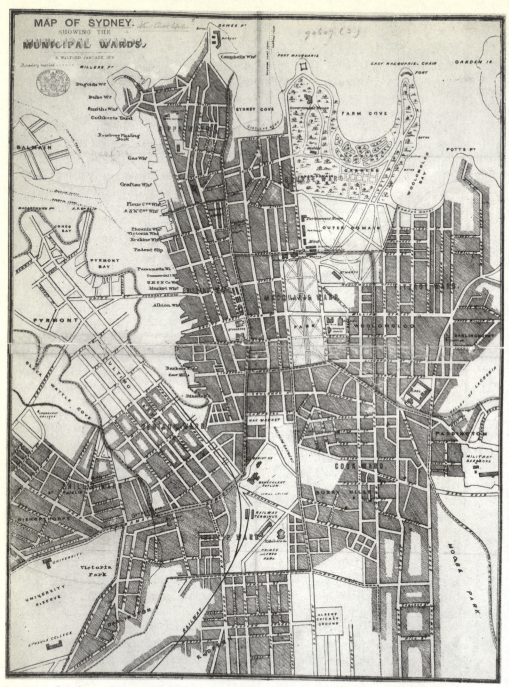

3.4 Map of Sydney, showing proximity of city to wharves, naval docks and military barracks. Hyde Park, shown in figure 3.5, appears near the centre of the map

3.5 Men standing near the statue of Prince Albert in Hyde Park (c.1885), a popular cruising area

by sexually permissive attitudes prevalent in the city.[94] In 1899 the London *Church Times* portrayed Sydney as a city with casual attitudes to sex:

> Sydney is a seaport, with all the usual vices and temptations of seaport towns. Here, all the great European and American passenger steamers spend their spare time, vessels of ten thousand tons and upwards finding good anchorage within a few hundred yards of the General Post Office. It is also the Naval Station of Australia, the squadron being located here for the greater proportion of the year.

The paper went on to suggest that 'A visitor to Sydney cannot fail to be struck by the fact of shameless immorality displayed in the streets of the city at nightfall'.[95] Sydney's allegedly relaxed attitudes to sex can be contextualised with reference to its demographic profile, in which one in four mature men was unmarried (compared to one in six in South Australia), and in which men who did marry did not generally do so until their late twenties. The large numbers of unmarried young men who lived in the central and dockside areas of Sydney, and throughout the colony (particularly in outback regions), enjoyed sex, with each other[96] and with women, outside the bounds of marriage.[97] This situation inspired a number of projects, ranging from inner-city church extensions to missions among prostitutes, to urban 'purification' (regeneration) schemes.[98] These efforts, though somewhat successful, were not widely supported.

Without mass support for the purity movements, the failure of Nield's Bill could be attributed partly to the state of public opinion and partly to opinion in the legislature. As one MLA argued, 'if Parliament stretches the law beyond the consciences of the people [and] attempts to go beyond the average moral sense of humanity in a manner of this kind, juries will take the law into their own hands and refuse to administer it'.[99] Purity campaigners met with outspoken criticism, which they had generally been spared in places such as South Australia. In the Assembly, Nield was dismissed as 'an hysterical enthusiast or fanatic',[100] other purity campaigners as 'old maids'.[101] Those who promoted age of consent legislation in the 1900s generally found it necessary to distance themselves from those who were known pejoratively as 'wowsers'. The arguments of purity campaigners were also caricatured as equally out of touch and out of place. For example, it was argued that NSW should not follow England in raising the age of consent, because moral, economic, climatic and other geographical conditions in the Australian colony were different from those in the mother country, one MLA arguing that 'females in this country are often women before they would be women in other countries to which we look for guidance in legislation'.[102] Other opponents of age of consent Bills drew attention to cultural differences between England and NSW, arguing for example that warmth and prosperity brought early maturity in the colony, which necessitated lower ages of consent there.[103]

Outside of the legislature, the broader political (or apolitical) culture of NSW failed to nurture purity movements in the way that South Australia had done. This was partly because, in contrast to the politically motivated and organised nonconformist culture of that colony, NSW was dominated by nominal Anglicanism (with low levels of church attendance, particularly in urban areas) and by a Church (then called the Church of England) that showed relatively little interest in social and political questions. A strand of moralistic evangelicalism had stood since the convict era against what its members saw as the immoral majority, but constituted little more than a counter-current to the dominant moral political climate, and after some embarrassing defeats (over divorce law, in the 1890s) Anglican leaders abandoned serious attempts at political intervention.[104] Arthur argued in 1894 that 'little is being done to try and stem the tide of impurity which threatens the very basis of our existence as a community. The churches have not yet attempted to grapple with the problem.'[105] Similarly, the *Church Times* claimed: 'No Sydney clergyman has publicly raised his voice against [child prostitution]',[106] and the *Australian Christian World* regretted that the 'church has buried its head in the sand' on matters of social purity.[107] Walter Phillips argues that, in the 1880s and 1890s, Christians in NSW were less effectual than their counterparts elsewhere in Australia with respect to social purity politics.[108] This might be attributed to the general fact that in Australia, as in England, nonconformists tended to lead purity movements, most Anglicans either following (as they were persuaded to do in South Australia) or abstaining/opposing.[109] Evangelical Anglicans persisted as a vocal interest group rather than a broad-based social movement,[110] and the nominally Anglican majority in NSW helps to explain the general lack of support for purity movements there.

Some Sydneysiders spoke out against the Christian morality professed by some of their contemporaries. Among the more articulate and explicit of these were Freethinkers. Freethought movements flourished in Australia, with a particular concentration in Sydney – in 1891, 5,900 people in NSW identified Freethought as their primary 'religious' affiliation, and many others identified with the movement[111] – and this vocal group added an outspoken and critical dimension to the social and moral politics of the colony.[112] Freethinkers attacked Christian morals in general and purity campaigns in particular.[113] Others who criticised and opposed purity movements in NSW included feminists, who positioned debates about prostitution and age of consent in relation to the broader material position of women and girls. One member of the Women's Suffrage League, for example, countered Arthur's call for an increased age of consent with arguments that women should be able to vote to decide on their own protection and/or freedom.[114]

Others opposed the purity movements through their actions rather than their words. So-called 'quack' doctors had been targeted for special criticism by English purity campaigners, who found their advertisements obscene and were concerned that their promises of easy abortions and cures for sexually transmitted diseases might foster a more permissive sexual culture.[115] Similarly, a high-profile contingent of quack doctors in Sydney presented an informal opposition to official medicine and to the practices and legislation regarding regulation of sexuality, which it sanctioned. Doctors such as Arthur frequently came to blows with the popular quacks, who performed abortions and were generally seen to sanction sexual licence, in a manner that generally offended purity campaigners and Christians. The *Australian Christian World* complained about the 'existence of a large number of men whose advertisements disgrace the columns of our press' and who 'make large incomes by trading on the fears of those who at some time or other have fallen into the sin against their own body'.[116] The paper called for the prosecution of such 'men who wickedly call themselves doctors'.[117]

Fearful of quack doctors, as of the countless other forces of secularism in NSW, these Christians implicitly recognised the strength of informal opposition to their agenda, including the purity agenda that they supported. Ultimately, they proved unable to sell this agenda to their fellow-colonists, whose refusal represented a departure from precedents that had been set in England and elsewhere in Australia.

This section has suggested – albeit speculatively – that the long delays in enactment of legislation to raise the age of consent in NSW can be attributed to weak campaigning and to the presence of contextual factors and local opposition that militated against the successful passage of purity measures. The failure of NSW to follow either the imperial or other Australian parliaments in raising the age of consent, and the failure of engagement with English and other Australian purity activists and organisations to intervene effectively in this respect, reveals the limited extent to which systems for the regulation of sexuality could be and/or were imposed on or copied in self-governing regions of the British Empire. The result was far from utopian, for moral politics in NSW in the period took a different and arguably more repressive form. Allen argues that moral politics in NSW at this time was oriented more towards suppressing moral minorities than in legislating for the population as a whole. She interprets contemporary provisions for the suppression of liquor, tobacco, drugs, gambling, abortion, usury and firearms as systems for penalising, scapegoating and oppressing the 'small fry', while reinforcing the status quo of male power and freedom.[118] Thus, the system in NSW should not be seen as necessarily more liberated than that in South Australia or England; still, for better or worse, the colony/state had steered its own political course, powered in the process by a mixture of agency and contextual determinants. But did it endorse or resist imperial hegemony? This case study certainly demonstrates reluctance to follow an imperial precedent, therefore perhaps a form of resistance, albeit one qualified, like the South Australian resistance to regulation

Bills, in its mixture of attraction and repulsion to the contrasting strands of English precedents in sexuality politics, and in the ambiguity of its political outcomes. It extends the general and spatial debate about domination and resistance through its exploration of unintentional and unconscious resistance, and its identification of places that foster such resistance. This poses questions about the spatiality of domination and resistance, and suggestions about the possibility that geographies might not only contextualise political agency but actually constitute agents in their own right. Those questions are addressed more fully in chapter 4.

Conclusion

This chapter has shown how metropolitan models of regulation were filtered and mutated as they travelled to colonies, where they were actively received and resisted rather then passively adopted. These active engagements were structured by contextual factors such as systems of colonial government, which influenced political agendas and determined the sorts of interventions that were or were not possible. Their consequences were subtle, impossible to categorise as vehicles of either domination or resistance. I have been careful to distinguish selective refusals of English precedent from wholesale resistance to British imperialism, and to avoid simplistic answers to questions of whether colonial agency went with or against the deeper grain of imperialism, though I have concluded that colonial engagements with imperial sexuality politics were not simply subservient to imperial hegemony, but were located instead along a continuum of domination and resistance. That resistance, though framed in shades of grey and not so much distinct from colonial domination as 'mutually imbricated' with it,[119] was directed at the symbolic authority of England – its ability to impose its laws on colonies or to set precedents – and/or elements of its substantive power over the colonial society. The range of interventions in sexuality politics, some of which have been examined in this chapter, helped to produce an uneven geography of regulation, which contradicted the universalist claims and ambitions of certain campaigners and legislators.

Chapter 4 explains this variable geography from a different perspective, turning from debatably resistant acts to what I call resistant spaces. Developing the argument, introduced with respect to cultural resistance in NSW, that specific forms of resistance need be neither intentional nor fundamentally anti-imperial, chapter 4 examines site-specific resistance to metropolitan innovations. Shifting attention from spaces of resistance to resistant spaces, it traces another set of processes behind the heterogeneity of imperial sexuality politics, another set of generative colonial geographies. More overtly than in this chapter, the *resistance* described in chapter 4 was productive: refusing one imperial strategy, it adopted another.

Notes

1 Boehmer, *Empire, the National and the Postcolonial*, p. 2.
2 L. Hartz, *Founding of New Societies* (New York: Harcourt, Brace & World, 1946).
3 Harris, 'The simplification of Europe overseas', *Annals of the Association of American Geographers*, 67 (1977), 469–483.
4 Said, 'Travelling theory', p. 227.
5 R. Rathbone, 'Law, lawyers and politics in Ghana in the 1940s', in D. Engels and S. Marks (eds), *Contesting Colonial Hegemony: State and Society in Africa and India* (London: British Academic Press, 1994), pp. 227–247.
6 Rathbone, 'Law, lawyers and politics in Ghana in the 1940s', pp. 228–229.
7 Engels and Marks, *Contesting Colonial Hegemony*, p. 2.
8 Valverde, *Age of Light*, p. 16.
9 D. Pike, *Paradise of Dissent: South Australia 1829–1857* (Melbourne: Cambridge University Press, 1967 [1957]), p. 3.
10 Pike, *Paradise of Dissent*, p. 481.
11 J. M. Ward, *Colonial Self-Government: The British Experience, 1759–1856* (London: Macmillan, 1976).
12 R. Teale (ed.), *Colonial Eve: Sources of Women in Australia, 1788–1914* (Melbourne: Oxford University Press, 1978).
13 Ward, *Colonial Self-Government*.
14 Pike, *Paradise of Dissent*, p. 493; D. Hilliard and A. R. Hunt, 'Religion', in E. Richards (ed.), *Flinders History of South Australia: Social History* (Adelaide: Wakefield Press, 1986), pp. 194–234.
15 South Australian Parliamentary Debates (SAPD) (8 December 1885), p. 1811.
16 R. Walker, 'Congregationalism in South Australia, 1837–1900,' *Royal Geographical Society of Australasia, South Australia Branch*, 69 (1967), 13–28.
17 W. Phillips, Influence of Congregationalism in South Australia, 1837–1915, BA dissertation, University of Adelaide, 1957.
18 For example, at the half-yearly meeting of the Congregational Union in October 1882, Kirby proposed the motion that the Union should support the new Social Purity Society; the motion was carried: F. Cox (ed.), *South Australian Congregational Year Book* (Adelaide: Congregational Union, 1882), p. 99; Kiek, *An Apostle in Australia*.
19 *South Australian Register* (4 October 1881), p. 4.
20 J. C. Kirby, *Three Lectures Concerning the Social Evil: Its Causes, Effects and Remedies* (Port Adelaide: privately printed, 1882).
21 Phillips, Influence of Congregationalism; J. Jose, 'Legislating for social purity, 1883–1885: the Reverend Joseph Coles Kirby and the Social Purity Society', *Journal of the Historical Society of South Australia*, 25 (1996), 45–57.
22 Kirby, *Three Lectures*, p. 3.
23 Kirby, *Three Lectures*, p. 45.
24 Kiek, *An Apostle in Australia*, p. 232.
25 *Sentinel* (February 1886), p. 24.
26 *Sentinel* (February 1886), p. 24.
27 Kirby, *Three Lectures*, p. 3.
28 Kirby, *Three Lectures*, p. 45.
29 SAPD (10 October 1883), p. 1282.
30 SAPD (10 October 1883), p. 1283.

31 SLNSWM, 196.5 S, *Copy of Part of the British Criminal Law Amendment Act* (Adelaide: Social Purity Society of South Australia, undated).

32 L. Bland, *Banishing the Beast: English Feminism and Sexual Morality 1885–1914* (London: Penguin, 1995).

33 *South Australian Register* (4 December 1883).

34 SAPD (10 October 1883), p. 1287.

35 SAPD (4 August 1885), p. 433.

36 SAPD (20 August 1885), p. 604.

37 SAPD (8 December 1885), p. 1813.

38 Cox, *South Australian Congregational Year Book*, p. 84.

39 SAPD (10 October 1883).

40 For example, the minister of justice and education argued that claims about 'the entrapping of young women for Noumea, in New Caledonia [had] been greatly exaggerated': SAPD (30 September 1884), p. 1122.

41 *South Australian Register* (11 October 1884), p. 7.

42 SAPD (10 November 1884), p. 1693; J. Moorehouse (Bishop of Melbourne), *Personal Purity, Home Life and National Greatness*, Knight of Purity Series No. 1 (London, 1885).

43 SAPD (13 August 1885), p. 539.

44 J. P. Sharp, P. Routledge, C. Philo and R. Paddison (eds), *Entanglements of Power: Geographies of Domination/Resistance* (London: Routledge, 2000), p. 21.

45 J. C. Scott, *Weapons of the Weak: Everyday Forms of Peasant Resistance* (New Haven, CT, and London: Yale University Press, 1985), p. xvi.

46 N. Lazarus, *Resistance in Postcolonial African Fiction* (New Haven, CT: Yale University Press, 1990); L. Chrisman, *Rereading the Imperial Romance: British Imperialism and South African Resistance in Haggard, Schreiner and Plaatje* (Oxford: Clarendon Press, 2000); C. C. Ahmed, 'God, anti-colonialism and dance: Sheekh Uways and the Uwaysiaayya', in G. Maddox (ed.), *Conquest and Resistance to Colonialism in Africa* (New York: Garland, 1993), pp. 145–167.

47 G. Pratt, 'Resistance', in Johnston, Gregory, Pratt and Watts, *Dictionary of Human Geography*, pp. 705–706, at 705.

48 D. Massey, 'Entanglements of power: reflections?' in Sharp, Routledge, Philo and Paddison, *Entanglements of Power*, pp. 279–286, at 280.

49 P. Howell, 'Victorian sexuality and the moralisation of Cremorne Gardens', in Sharp, Routledge, Philo and Paddison, *Entanglements of Power*, pp. 43–66, at 45.

50 Sharp, Routledge, Philo and Paddison, *Entanglements of Power*, p. 21; S. W. Mintz, *Caribbean Transformations* (New York: Columbia University Press, 1989).

51 J. Comaroff and J. L. Comaroff, *Of Revelation and Revolution: Christianity, Colonialism, and Consciousness in South Africa* (Chicago, IL: University of Chicago Press, 1991), vol. 1, p. 31.

52 Engels and Marks, *Contesting Colonial Hegemony*, p. 3.

53 Mr Strangway, the attorney-general, described the Bill as 'nearly a copy of an Act which had been in force in England for some time, the main provisions of which had been successfully adopted in Queensland': SAPD (12 August 1869), p. 66.

54 Quoted by S. Horan, 'More sinned against than sinning? Prostitution in South Australia, 1836–1914', in K. Daniels (ed.), *So Much Hard Work: Women and Prostitution in Australian History* (Sydney: Fontana, 1984), pp. 87–126, at 87; see also C. Nance, 'Women, morality and prostitution in early South Australia', *The Push from the Bush*, 3 (1979), 33–43.

55 Based on 1881 police statistics: Horan, 'More sinned against than sinning?', p. 89.

56 SAPD (8 September 1875), p. 979.

57 *South Australian Register* (10 November 1869), p. 2.

58 The term 'nonconformist' is not strictly applicable in colonial Australia, where there was no established Church, though it is useful to describe religious bodies there that had their roots in English dissent.

59 A. Hunt, *This Side of Heaven: A History of Methodism in Australia* (Adelaide: Lutheran Publishing, 1985).

60 SAPD (13 October 1875), p. 1367.
61 SAPD (26 October 1869), p. 714.
62 SAPD (8 September 1875), p. 980.
63 J. T. Bagot, SAPD (19 October 1869), p. 602.
64 SAPD (30 September 1869), p. 488.
65 SAPD (8 September 1875), p. 979.
66 SAPD (12 August 1869), p. 66.
67 SAPD (7 October 1869), p. 538.
68 SAPD (8 September 1875), p. 981.
69 SAPD (12 August 1869), p. 66.
70 Bagot, SAPD (19 October 1869), p. 603.
71 SAPD (30 September 1869), p. 486.
72 J. Crozier: SAPD (19 October 1869), p. 603.
73 SAPD (19 October 1869), p. 603.
74 SAPD (8 September 1875), p. 982.
75 SAPD (8 September 1875), p. 980.
76 SAPD (5 October 1869), p. 519.
77 SAPD (8 September 1875), p. 980.
78 SAPD (7 October 1869), p. 538.
79 SAPD (5 October 1869), p. 525.
80 P. Krupka, 'Reform in the air for prostitutes', *Nation* (Melbourne) (20 January 2000), p. 3.
81 Horan, 'More sinned against than sinning?', p. 114.
82 J. Allen, 'The making of a prostitute in early twentieth-century New South Wales', in Daniels, *So Much Hard Work*, p. 198.
83 Comaroff and Comaroff, *Of Revelation and Revolution*, p. 31.
84 H. K. Bhabha, 'Signs taken for wonders: questions of ambivalence and authority under a tree outside Delhi, May 1817', *Critical Inquiry*, 12 (1985), 153.
85 Allen, 'The making of a prostitute', p. 207.
86 Nield: New South Wales Parliamentary Debates (NSWPD) (25 October 1892), p. 1389; Frank Farnell, MLA, commented on the unrealistic ambitiousness of Nield's Bill, claiming: 'In attempting all this the hon. member has set himself a big task': NSWPD (25 October 1892), p. 1370.
87 R. Arthur, Letter to the editor, *Sentinel* (July 1894), p. 122.
88 SLNSWM, MSS 473, Box 1, Papers of Richard Arthur, cuttings of letters sent by Arthur and published in: *Sydney Morning Herald* (18 November 1892), p. 2; *Australian Christian World* (Sydney) (13 October 1892), p. 7; *Sentinel* (July 1894), p. 122; *Daily Telegraph* (Sydney) (21 November 1893).
89 Later he concentrated on venereal disease and drafted the Act, passed in 1918, which provided for notification and treatment: M. Roe, 'Richard Arthur', in B. Nairn and N. Serle (eds), *Australian Dictionary of Biography*, vol. 7: *1891–1939* (Melbourne: Melbourne University Press, 1979), p. 3.
90 Arthur, Letter to the editor, *Sentinel* (July 1894), p. 122.
91 SLNSWM, MSS 473, Box 1, Papers of Richard Arthur, pamphlet by Arthur: *The Needed Change in the Age of Consent: An Appeal for the Better Protection of Our Girls* (Sydney: privately printed, 1901 [1896]), p. 11.
92 *Australian Christian World* (19 June 1896), p. 15.
93 *Australian Christian World* (22 January 1904), p. 6.
94 'Pupil of the late John Woolley', *Vice and its Victims in Sydney* (Sydney, 1873).
95 *Church Times* (5 May 1899), p. 527.
96 R. Hughes, *Fatal Shore: The Epic of Australia's Founding* (New York: Vintage, 1986); R. French, *Camping by a Billabong: Gay and Lesbian Stories from Australian History* (Sydney: Black Wattle Press, 1993).
97 G. Davison, J. W. McCarty and A. McLeary (eds), *Australians: A Historical Library*, vol. 3: *Australians, 1888* (Cambridge: Cambridge University Press, 1987), pp. 203, 309.

98   A. J. C. Mayne, *Fever, Squalor and Vice: Sensation and Social Policy in Victorian Sydney* (Brisbane: Queensland University Press, 1982).
99   Wise, NSWPD (25 October 1892), p. 1376.
100 Mackellar, NSWPD (30 July 1903), p. 1154.
101 Wood, NSWPD (28 November 1905), p. 4201.
102 Barton, NSWPD (25 October 1892), p. 1382.
103 Scobie, NSWPD (19 September 1905), p. 2250.
104 W. J. Lawton, *The Better Time to Be: Utopian Attitudes to Society Among Sydney Anglicans, 1885–1914* (Kensington: New South Wales University Press, 1990).
105 Arthur, Letter to the editor, *Sentinel* (July 1894), p. 122.
106 *Church Times* (5 May 1899), p. 527.
107 *Australian Christian World* (Sydney) (1 February 1895), p. 3.
108 W. Phillips, *Defending a Christian Country: Churchmen and Society in New South Wales in the 1880s and After* (Brisbane: University of Queensland Press, 1981).
109 F. B. Smith, 'CD Acts reconsidered', *Social History of Medicine*, 3 (1990), 197–215.
110 D. Hilliard, 'Sydney Anglicans and homosexuality', *Journal of Homosexuality*, 33:2 (1997), 101–123.
111 *Australian Christian World* (25 April 1902).
112 E. Royle, *Radicals, Secularists and Republicans: Popular Freethought in Britain, 1866–1815* (Manchester: Manchester University Press, 1980).
113 Phillips, *Defending a Christian Country*.
114 SLNSWM, MSS 473, Box 1, Papers of Richard Arthur, newspaper cutting: *Daily Telegraph* (Sydney) (22 November 1893).
115 W. A. Coote and A. Baker, *Romance of Philanthropy: Being a Record of Work of the NVA* (London: National Vigilance Association, 1916).
116 *Australian Christian World* (19 June 1896), p. 15.
117 *Australian Christian World* (13 September 1895), p. 7.
118 Allen, 'The making of a prostitute', p. 207.
119 D. S. Moore, 'Remapping resistance: ground for struggle and the politics of place', in S. Pile and M. Keith (eds), *Geographies of Resistance* (London: Routledge, 1997), pp. 87–106, at 92.

CHAPTER FOUR

Heterogeneous imperialism: deciding against regulation in West Africa

I have suggested that, while some political ideas travelled smoothly, arriving intact or even strengthened, others were changed by the journey or stopped in their tracks. Consequently, despite the universal claims and preoccupations of many activists and historians, historical geographies of regulation and resistance were differentiated: uneven and broken. Despite Butler's generalisation that 'annexation or conquest' was 'habitually accompanied by the forcible or deceitful introduction'[1] of regulation, a large proportion of colonial governments never introduced CD laws, and those that did introduced them to relatively small areas. Contrary to Levine's generalisation that, 'though different in detail from colony to colony, [regulation] was in place by the mid-1870s throughout most of Britain's empire'[2] – in 'almost all of Britain's overseas possessions'[3] – regulation was actually the exception rather than the norm. Of great symbolic importance, its application was geographically localised and historically limited, applying to relatively few places for brief periods. While, as figure 4.1 shows, approximately half of all British possessions had some form of CD legislation on their statute books in 1886, when the system generally peaked *half did not*. Furthermore, those laws applied to very restrictive geographical areas. The domestic Acts applied to just 11 (later 13) dock and garrison towns,[4] their Canadian counterparts to an equally small area, as the map of regulation in the Dominion of Canada illustrates (figure 4.2). Even in these small parts of Canada the system remained in operation for as few as five years, and was not generally enforced even before it lapsed in 1870.[5] The Dominion opted, as it would again in the wake of the Criminal Law Amendment Act, for what Canadian historian John McLaren calls a 'pale shadow' of the metropolitan legislation, one that was historically and geographically limited.[6]

The imperial region that escaped regulation most comprehensively – if not completely – was British Africa. CD laws were introduced in

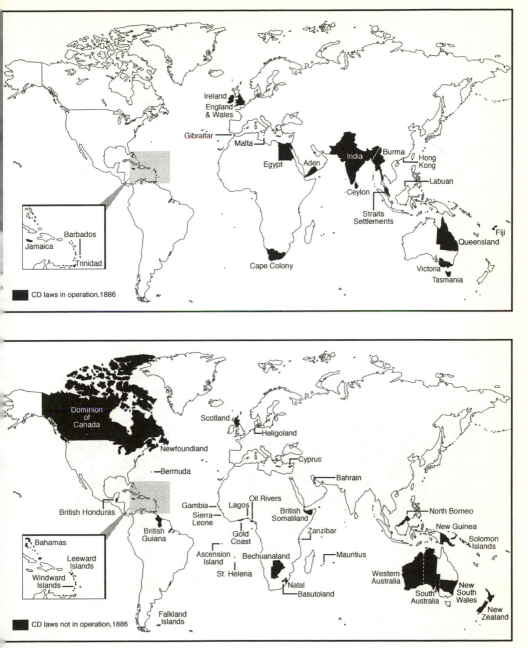

.1 British possessions, with and without some form of CD legislation, on 1 January 1886

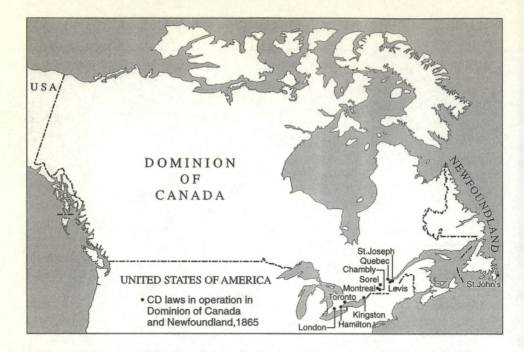

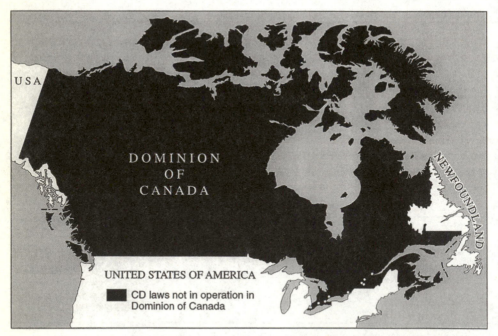

4.2 Regulation in the Dominion of Canada, 1865. Note the small area affected by CD laws, which lapsed in 1870, after just 5 years in operation

a few places for a few years – including the Cape Colony – but they remained a rarity in the continent as a whole.[7] English purity movements made an equally weak impression in Africa, despite pretensions to world-wide, or at least empire-wide, significance. This was due in part to the reactive nature of early purity movements. The pages of the *Sentinel* reflect this pattern of opposition to regulation wherever it existed – notably, in England and in India, Hong Kong, Australia, Gibraltar, and Jamaica – and, by corollary, a tendency to ignore areas where regulation had not been introduced or seriously proposed. Since regulation made little impression in British Africa, reactive purity campaigners did not pay much attention to the continent. But neither did their pro-active counterparts.[8] The CEPS, for instance, concentrated on North America, Australia and India, and only slowly moved to consider Africa, then mainly through its work among British military personnel posted in the region or off its coast.[9] Neither did English missionaries in Africa generally engage in social purity politics, as some of their colleagues did elsewhere. For example, whereas many Wesleyan Methodists in England and Australia supported purity campaigns,[10] their counterparts in Africa concentrated on what they regarded as more fundamental projects, concerned with basic evangelism, education and cultural reform – attempting to divert Africans from many of their traditional practices and customary 'vices'.[11] English and American missionaries and temperance activists visited from time to time, attempting to spark movements, but with less success than they enjoyed in many other parts of the world.[12]

If, much like English people, metropolitan sexuality politics did not generally travel smoothly to Africa, this gives rise to questions about why this was the case and what, if anything, took their place. The previous chapter began to address these questions by showing how people in colonies used and forged agency with which to actively negotiate imperial precedents, not necessarily to oppose imperial fundamentals but certainly to reconfigure their situated expressions and mechanisms. This chapter explores the heterogeneity of imperial sexuality politics and more generally of imperialism from a different angle. I suggest that regulation travelled poorly to Africa, in part because it was impeded by colonial environments, as seen and experienced by those who inhabited and governed them. Exploring an illuminating if not, of course, generally representative component of the 'unregulated Empire' – colonies that proved resistant to CD laws – the chapter traces the deliberations on the possibility of introducing CD laws on the part of key figures in Sierra Leone's colonial establishment. Doing so, it focuses on their perceptions of the particular colonial environment and their judgements about whether CD laws would work there and, if not, what else might. This study of situated colonial governance builds on chapters 2 and 3 by elaborating further on the spatiality of imperialism – on the multiple, de-centred geographies in which power was forged and contested – and does so with reference to elite colonial figures, deferring further consideration of more democratic and everyday cultural political life to later chapters, particularly chapter 7, which revisits Sierra Leone.

Proposals for regulation rejected in Sierra Leone: environmental obstacles?

On several occasions, proposals for regulation were put before the colony's Legislative and Executive Councils (the workings of which are explained in due course), and followed up in official correspondence and despatches. Each time, the proposals were summarily rejected, ostensibly for financial reasons. The most sustained exchanges occurred in 1876 and 1877, when a senior army doctor submitted detailed proposals to the governor and the Legislative Council. In a letter dated February 15, 1876,[13] Surgeon Major Gray alerted the Council to 'the ravages that Venereal is making in the colony', and proposed the adoption of CD legislation, which would improve the health and efficiency of the military, and bring 'great benefit to the Civil population, as well as to the unfortunates themselves'. The ordinance he proposed, much like the English and colonial Acts on which it was based, would have provided for the detention and treatment of 'any common prostitute' alleged to have transmitted venereal disease to a soldier; also for the imprisonment of a prostitute who 'knowingly having a contagious disease' continues to work; similarly for the imprisonment of brothel-keepers who knowingly permit infected prostitutes to work on their premises; and for the similar punishment of prostitutes who refuse treatment or leave the lock hospital. Anticipating financial and practical objections to his proposals, Gray argued that such a CD ordinance could be introduced within existing budgets and medical and police infrastructure. He argued:

> The colony will not be put to one shilling in working the Act. Let a ward be set apart in the Female Hospital for Venereal, say 12 beds and let the colonial surgeons look after them, with the assistance of a Military Medical Officer if necessary, so that these creatures be detained till cured. [Ultimately] there will be a great saving annually to the Estimates [for the colonial budget].[14]

Advising the governor on how best to respond to Gray's proposals, Colonial Surgeon Francis Lovell pointed out that 'this matter has been brought before the notice of the Executive on several occasions – the last time it was proposed by Dr Elliot the P.M.O. in December 1874 when no further steps were taken by the Acting Governor in Chief'.[15] When the Council considered Gray's proposals, on 24 November 1876, it quickly came to a similar conclusion. Item 7 on the agenda was reported as follows:

> A letter from the Principal Medical Officer dated 15 February 1876, enclosing a draft of the proposed Contagious Diseases Act, taken from the British Act, together with a report thereon by the Colonial Surgeon dated 19 February 1876, was read. The Council were of opinion that they could take no initiative in the matter.[16]

The surgeon major asked for further explanation, and the answers he received – as well as those he did not – provide insights into the colonial government's departure from imperial precedent. They suggest, most generally, that different places were seen to demand distinct policies. Governor C. H. Kortright[17] had been instrumental in introducing a CD ordinance in Trinidad, in 1868, when he served as governor there[18], so his track record suggests that he was not opposed to the system as such, but that he considered regulation unsuitable or unnecessary for Sierra Leone (figures 4.3 and 4.4).

One explanation for the absence of CD laws in Africa is that the system would have been prohibitively expensive to implement there.[19] The evidence suggests that cost was indeed a factor in Sierra Leone. In his advice to the governor, Lovell explained that previous proposals had been rejected 'because it was considered that the financial state of the colony would not permit of the necessary expenditure in carrying out the Act in question. I am at a loss to see in what way the Contagious Diseases Act can be brought into force and efficiently carried out without a considerable expenditure of money.'[20] Financial arguments for inaction were reiterated by Kortright in 1877 when, in a despatch to the Colonial Office,[21] he asserted simply: 'The Colony cannot afford luxuries.' He explained, in a letter to the Earl of Carnarvon at the Colonial Office, that the Council had decided to 'take no initiative in the matter' because it 'would not feel itself justified in saddling the colony with the construction of a new building for a hospital, and with a large increase to the medical staff, for an object of very doubtful benefit to the settlement'.[22] Certainly, Sierra Leone was not a wealthy colony: the poor state of public finances was reflected in official government returns (reported in 'Blue Books', the annual reports on each colony) and in the colonial media, which acknowledged financial impediments to many otherwise desirable areas of public spending. One local paper, the *West African Reporter*, illustrated a more general feeling in the colony when it complained of 'an exhausted exchequer', rooted partly in the 'stagnation of trade' and the depressed colonial economy.[23]

It might be argued that spending priorities in Sierra Leone were dictated by necessity, and that the necessities of mitigating the worst of a permanent health crisis pushed venereal diseases down the agenda. Venereal disease was recognised as a problem in the colony. Long before CD laws were introduced in many parts of the British Empire, and proposed in Sierra Leone, a colonial doctor had noted that 'syphilitic disorders are of frequent occurrence' and reported that in his five years' service 'very many cases of syphilis fell under my observation at Kissy Hospital', in Freetown.[24] More recently, Richard Burton – an English traveller and writer who visited and wrote about the colony – had implied that sexually transmitted diseases were still prevalent, suggesting: 'What the state of morality at Sierra Leone is they who are connected with the hospitals best know.'[25] Medical statistics returned by the Colonial Hospital, Freetown, testify to the prevalence of venereal diseases: in 1874, for example, ninety-six cases were treated; Gray cited similar figures in his letter to the clerk of Council, in which he referred to 'the marked prevalence of Syphilis and Gonorrhoea at this station' and to 'the ravages that Venereal is making

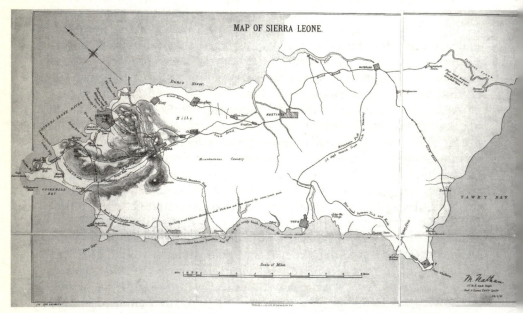

4.3 Map of Freetown and Sierra Leone

amongst the troops'.[26] Official correspondence acknowledged the extent of this disease among soldiers: one return estimated that 10 per cent of the men were sick in hospital at any one time, 'mostly from venereal'.[27] Yet patients suffering from venereal disease were few compared to those with other complaints: in 1874, for example, hospital admissions and deaths for venereal disease were dwarfed by conditions such as coast fever (150 admissions, of whom 6 died), abdominal conditions (85, 10) and surgical infections (184, 4).[28] Travellers to the colony added to this picture, embroidering the colony's reputation in England as 'the white man's grave' with detailed descriptions of the effects of sleeping sickness, smallpox, bilharzia, dysentery, malaria and yellow fever.[29] Sickness and death rates were also high among the non-white populations. Healthcare in Sierra Leone amounted to little more than fire-fighting, serving Europeans poorly and Africans barely at all. The year that Grey proposed a CD ordinance, the government of Sierra Leone admitted that it could not afford to pay even for existing public health measures. The governor regretted that 'it has not been found possible to carry out any comprehensive plan for the sanitary improvement of Freetown, but the matter is kept in sight by the colonial authorities and dealt with in detail so far as the resources at their disposal will allow'.[30]

4.4 Freetown street scene (c.1890) showing pedestrians on the roadway and the Tower Hill Barracks on the skyline in the background

Of course, priorities are a function not simply of objectively defined environmental necessities, but also of politics and perceptions. Sierra Leone did suffer 'financial derangements',[31] but its spending decisions were still a function of priorities and interests, As Levine has convincingly established, although it was not a narrowly military system, regulation became a priority in many militarised areas. There, military spokesmen and lobbyists either introduced systems of their own or asserted the need to combat venereal disease, as chapter 5 explains in more detail. Dyer pointed to a correlation between imperial militarism and regulation at different geographical scales – in the British Empire as a whole, in India and in localities within India (see figures 0.2, 0.3 and 1.1). Others condemned what the *Sentinel* called 'the moral evils of expanded militarism'.[32] Purity campaigners disagreed about the strength of this correlation. Some asserted that the military could be reformed, persuaded both institutionally and personally to abandon regulation and the culture of which it was a part. They lobbied the military authorities and worked among soldiers, distributing pamphlets on manly purity, with stories of military role models who 'provide inspiration and positive models of discipline and restraint and purity'.[33] Others felt the military was irredeemably impure, committed to vice and institutionalised prostitution, and that the road to purity lay in demilitarisation and, where necessary, decolonisation. One commentator argued in the *Sentinel*: 'No more effective means for promoting the growth of social vice exists, than the enormous fighting establishments, which are the bane of modern civilisation.'[34]

Polemics aside, there is evidence of some correlation between militarism and regulation in Africa. The few regions of British Africa that were subjected to regulation were, indeed, highly militarised. One purity correspondent in Cairo observed that 'the C.D. Acts are in full force, in the most shameless way in Egypt, wherever our troops are stationed'.[35] This was not mere coincidence, since certain military authorities both operated their own form of regulation and covertly and overtly lobbied for civilian CD laws. Though the military was by no means the only or necessarily the leading force behind regulation, the surgeon major's initiative in Sierra Leone echoed military initiatives around the Empire, from India to Africa.[36] Conversely, attempts to extend CD legislation to purely civilian spaces without much military presence were neither particularly common nor usually successful. This was sometimes made explicit, as for example in South Australia where there was little military presence.[37] An opponent of the system told the South Australian Legislative Assembly: 'There might be some excuse or argument in favour of the [CD] Bill if we had soldiers stationed here, who were debarred from marriage except with the consent of their officers . . . but here we had no such cause for legislation'.[38]

The fact that Sierra Leone was militarised by land and sea but not subjected to regulation is consistent with Levine's argument that regulation was neither simply nor universally a military system. If the military in this part of West Africa could survive without CD laws, as officials insisted it could, this was not because men were less likely to suffer from venereal disease. In other parts of the British Empire, particularly India, regulation was introduced among a number of health and sanitation investments that were intended not simply to improve the general health of personnel but as a targeted means of boosting morale among British soldiers.[39] The West African military commanders, with fewer British soldiers to maintain, did not feel the same needs. They suffered similar rates of venereal disease.[40] And yet Kortright asserted that 'the rate of admissions to the Military Hospital for Venereal for five years, furnished by Major Gray, in a garrison of 400 men is not excessive or alarming'.[41] This more relaxed attitude to the health of soldiers was arguably linked to their racial profile. Sierra Leone was garrisoned by Africans. The West Indian Regiment recruited largely from slave ships intercepted by the British.[42] The decline in slave traffic reduced the recruitment pool, but also the military requirement. Freetown remained the most valuable British base on the West Coast of Africa, but the overall naval presence was shrinking.[43] Demilitarisation affected land forces, too: the Sierra Leone militia (composed of irregulars – called up occasionally) was disbanded after a mutiny in 1862. Numbers of imperial troops in Sierra Leone were reduced less dramatically than in other parts of British West Africa – the Gambia, Gold Coast and Lagos – but nevertheless declined from 551 in 1867 to 375 in 1869, and the number of regular troops in Sierra Leone and West Africa remained relatively low through the 1870s.[44] A period of remilitarisation eventually followed, with British participation in the scramble for Africa.[45] The assertion of territorial claims, against challenges from the French and resistance by Africans, led to the establishment of the inter-territorial West African Frontier Force, in Nigeria in 1897 and the West African Regiment, in Sierra Leone in 1898. However, without significant needs for recruitment and retention during the period in which regulation was high on the agenda, the military was less vulnerable to the inefficiencies associated with the sickness (rarely death) concomitant with diseases such as syphilis.

On the other hand, the decision not to introduce CD laws in Sierra Leone may speak not simply of a reality or perception that such laws were not needed, or that they could not be afforded or prioritised, but rather that they might not have been applicable or workable there. Since regulation revolved around a model of prostitution recognisable to the English, it could be argued that the system could be introduced only where British officials found the kind of prostitution they understood, identified with what were loosely defined as 'common prostitutes' – full-time female sex workers who walked the streets or worked in brothels.[46] Studies have identified many culturally, geographically and historically specific forms of prostitution in Africa, only some of which correspond to the notoriously vague Western stereotype.[47] Europeans did not find what, to them, were recognisable forms of prostitution in large parts of sub-Saharan Africa. Sexologist Havelock Ellis generalised that 'among unspoilt savages customs that can properly be called prostitution rarely prevail'.[48] Some Africans endorsed this view, attributing to Europe the conditions that gave rise to prostitution. Edward Blyden, whose interventions in sexuality politics are considered more fully in chapter 7, asserted that 'in no part of Africa is there the melancholy state of things' that exist in England and Europe; there are no 'women of the under world'.[49] Nevertheless, forms of prostitution did exist in the colony.[50] Visitors alluded, if not always to prostitutes, then to their clients – including an 'inferior class of British merchant seamen [who] keep up their debaucheries to a late hour'.[51] They commented that sailors and soldiers carried 'into the new community, the vices and crimes of an old country',[52] and wrote elliptically about their 'looseness of morals' and 'brutal indecency'.[53] Evidence of prostitution is more readily available for more recent times. An English worker, posted to the colony in the 1940s, reminisced: 'You could hardly walk the streets at that time without the girls accosting you from across the street.'[54] A 1957 survey identified prostitutes in Freetown who conformed to the European model.[55] If the British colonial officials did not always recognise prostitution,[56] they were not blind to all of its forms or to its prevalence. Indeed, Kortright asserted that prostitution was 'common'[57] in the colony, and thus potentially a subject for regulation.

The governor added, however, that prostitution was 'so common' and was 'adopted at so early an age, that it would be impossible to carry out the measures recommended by Surgeon Major Gray'.[58] He may simply have meant that there were too many prostitutes to consider regulating, but this allusion to an ungovernable sexual world also betrays deeper European beliefs about Africa and Africans, as Luise White argues:

It is possible that Contagious Diseases laws, or the regulation of prostitutes, raised questions about gender, race, class, and their relationship to conceptualisations of male and female lust that would have complicated the business of colonial rule, which consistently saw African sexual behaviour as something beyond legislation.[59]

She continues with reference to her research on East Africa:

In Kenya, unrestrained female sexuality was not seen to have the same causal relationship to venereal disease that it was seen to have elsewhere. This was probably due to ideas about African sexuality in general, and those ideas had the overall effect of making officials believe that English legislation was inappropriate for Africa.[60]

Kortright's attitude to the possibility of regulation in Sierra Leone might therefore be located within a broader European view of African sexuality as overwhelming, excessive, beyond conventional forms of regulation. Of course, such records and attitudes say more about the colonial government and colonial ways of seeing than they do about prostitution or sexuality in Sierra Leone. They also underline the limits to objectivity in questions about whether or not given laws could be introduced to a particular place. No colony was either intrinsically receptive or resistant to regulation, and decisions about regulation were never simply matters of environmental perception or pragmatic decision-making.

Perhaps, if Sierra Leone proved inhospitable to CD laws, this was less a function of the real or perceived colonial environment – the exchequer, the military, the sexual culture – than of the political environment, which rendered certain laws conceivable and others inconceivable, and gave voice to some people but not others. The process by which proposals for regulation in Sierra Leone were submitted, considered and rejected was also a function of its political and governmental structures.[61] The colonial administration consisted of an appointed governor, formally answerable only to London. The imperial Parliament occasionally passed legislation that directly impacted on Sierra Leone, such as when it established the colony and outlawed the slave trade, but mostly it devolved decision-making and law-making authority to governors, themselves formally constrained only by superiors in London, who generally expected them to follow English precedent and work within small budgets. Locally, governors had a relatively free hand and were advised but not formally checked by legislative and executive councils.

The people of Sierra Leone were left with few if any formal channels through which to participate in colonial politics. Not surprisingly, then, exchanges on the subject of regulation, which I have quoted, were cursory and undemocratic compared to those that took place in many other – less summarily governed – parts of the Empire. Indeed, this colonial administration was criticised for its failure to respond to the wishes of the people. As one local journalist put it, the infrequent and summary sittings of the Legislative Council reflected 'a disposition either to be despotic or to be idle'.[62] The colonial regime in Sierra Leone did receive petitions and proposals from the public and, more commonly, from colonial civil and military officials (such as Gray), but it was not directly responsive to the views of an electorate, nor therefore to public opinion. Most legislation in Sierra Leone (all but the few laws passed directly by the imperial Parliament in London) was simply originated by the governor and rubber stamped by the Legislative Council, which for most of the nineteenth century is said to have functioned mainly as a 'committee room' rather than a 'political assembly',[63] before being dispatched to the authorities in London, and generally – not always – returned with royal assent. The unresponsive nature of the government of Sierra Leone may help to explain why, when the Legislative Council considered proposals for regulation, it was not lobbied by the kind of campaigners and pressure groups that had sprung up in or campaigned with great effect on behalf of many other parts of the British Empire. Elsewhere, for example in South Australia and the Cape Colony, the failure of CD Bills and the suspension and repeal of CD Acts could be attributed in part to the interventions of purity campaigners.

In discussing the political system of Sierra Leone, and in recognising the centralisation of power in the hands of the governor and the Colonial Office, it should also be recognised that though the authority of the governor and his officials was considerable, and though there were few formal channels for opposition, colonial hegemony was subject ultimately to some form of legitimation among and compliance on the part of local people (as argued in the previous chapter). Colonised peoples not only represented themselves through formal and informal channels but shaped the parameters of imperial rule. When the British attempted to overreach their limited authority in West Africa, they were opposed. Conversely, they calculated what they could do largely on the basis of what they thought colonial subjects would accept. The formula for effective hegemony – balancing British interests against perceived public opinion – informed all areas of colonial government,[64] including legislation, as Rathbone explains:

> Legislation followed an uncomfortable route which was neither concessive enough to create widespread support nor repressive enough to be able to be unconcerned about opposition. At the same time it is clear that legislators often attempted to carry those they deemed to be

politically significant, rather than the majority, with them. In the largely unrepresentative political systems which survived in West Africa until the mid-1940s, the majority had almost no way in which to make themselves known or felt. Colonial political calculations were rarely accurate and more often profoundly flawed. But it is worth remembering that a historiography which for decades has concentrated on the roots of resistance and nationalism has highlighted the legislation which provoked opposition but has seldom touched the infinitely larger volume of legislation to be found in the Gazettes which became law without serious contestation.[65]

There were constant reminders of the limits to British authority. One, still fresh in the minds of the authorities in the 1870s, was the British defeat in the second Ashanti War (1863). The British commissioner who had investigated the defeat reported that 'our policy should be to encourage in the natives the exercise of those qualities which may render it possible for us more and more to transfer to them the administration of all the governments with a view to our ultimate withdrawal' from the region[66] – in other words, there could and should be less, not more, colonial government. In the light of such resistance, it was clear that British rule in West Africa was limited, and that the British may have doubted their ability to introduce the intrusive measures that had been adopted elsewhere.

I have suggested that the colonial authorities introduced CD Acts only where they believed they were necessary, workable and acceptable to their colonial subjects, and that they did not introduce them in African colonies such as Sierra Leone because they did not expect all those conditions to be met. This gives rise to further questions about how to interpret the uneven geography of regulation and more generally the heterogeneity of empire: about whether this spoke of the fractures and failures of imperial power or, rather, its flexibility.

Flexible imperialism? Responding to local conditions

Anthony Padgen argues that imperialism assumed different forms not because it was stronger in some places than others, but because imperial governments found different ways of doing the same things, fulfilling the same fundamental imperatives.[67] From this perspective, the uneven geography of regulation might therefore be interpreted as a reflection of flexible imperialism, the variable form of which was not determined by local conditions, but nevertheless responded to them.

The emphasis of this chapter reflects and perhaps reproduces a preoccupation within historical and geographical research on imperialism and sexuality with CD laws. And yet CD laws existed alongside a raft of measures, ranging from criminal law on interracial rape to urban planning and social segregation (excluding suspected prostitutes from markets, for example), which were concerned with or had the effect of producing and maintaining the sexual and/or moral systems that helped to underpin colonial political economies.[68] It has been possible to move from the preoccupation with CD laws, and from the points of departure they provide, by addressing more positively some of the contexts beyond their reach and asking what filled those apparent regulatory voids.

British colonial authorities in African colonies such as Sierra Leone may have held back on CD laws because they approached the regulation of sexuality in other ways and focused on other, perhaps more basic, problems in the moral economy. Different forms of moral and sexual regulation jostled for position, questions about prostitution competing with others, revolving around the management of the body and the definition of the family. Missionaries promoted what they considered civilised practices, from the use of knives and forks to the wearing of clothes. They tried to divert Africans from other social and sexual customs, such as clitoridectomy and polygamy.[69] Marriage emerged as the main issue in colonial moral politics, as missionaries, legislators and others recognised its preeminent significance in relation to sexual and gender relations. Indeed, it has been argued that 'no question aroused greater passion' in late nineteenth-century British West Africa, where marriage was 'a virtual obsession'.[70] When adherence to recognisable models of marriage was not strong or was threatened, colonial authorities devoted considerable attention to reinforcing and introducing it, and purity campaigners and missionaries turned their attention away from other issues and towards marriage. Marriage rates in the region and the colony were high – women in most places had little choice but to marry[71] – but marriage practices were diverse and, to the British, both slippery and casual.[72] Identifying priorities, an Anglican bishop proclaimed:

> The great desideratum in the social life of the colony is the sanctity of the marriage relationship, and the creation and maintenance of home and family life. There are plain signs here and there of the beginning of this; but the comparative absence of the ideas of love and fellowship from the marriage tie, utterly wrong views about the relative duties of husband and wife, tend to encourage concubinage, and this degrades woman from her true place, becomes the fruitful source of strife and disunion, and children dragged up under these circumstances are apt to see and hear much that is most unfortunate.[73]

Acting on these priorities, missionaries actively promoted Christian marriage, and the colonial courts worked to standardise and define marriage, transforming it from a 'fluid, dialogical process' to a formal institution recognisable by the law.[74] In the last decades of the nineteenth century and the first of the twentieth a legal framework for marriage was devised under the dual legal system.[75] English and African courts in Sierra Leone recognised customary marriage for Africans alongside civil, Christian and Islamic marriage.[76] Yet the preoccupation with marriage does not necessarily explain the neglect of more peripheral subjects such as prostitution. Formalised marriage rates were also very low in some other colonies, notably in the West Indies, where CD laws were nevertheless introduced. In Jamaica, for instance, rates of illegitimate births – indicators of low formal marriage rates – were reported at 59.8 in Jamaica and 71.3 in St Lucia.[77] So, if both the government of Sierra Leone and those that lobbied it concentrated on marriage rather than prostitution, on the sexual centre rather than the margins, that was a matter of strategy and priority.

It might equally be argued that the government of Sierra Leone did not introduce CD laws because it had found other ways of regulating prostitution. In particular, the Police Ordinance of 1851 sought 'to improve public morals' and legislated on a series of sexual and other broadly moral practices.[78] It imposed penalties for public drunkenness and/or fighting; for indecent exposure; for swearing, verbal obscenity or other forms of verbal disturbance of the peace; and for betting and playing in public places. It also targeted African and Creole customs and practices, ranging from public nudity to dancing and drumming (after 8 p.m.) to practising traditional religion. Forty shillings was the penalty for the public worship of 'thunder, alligators, snakes, or other reptiles' and/or for those who 'pretend or profess to discover by means of any subtle art, craft, fetish, or greegree or country custom or device, lost or stolen goods' and/or for those who 'profess by any tricks, device, or preparations to exercise any undue influence over the mind of any other person or persons'.[79] In addition to these provisions, the Police Ordinance set a forty shilling fine for 'every common prostitute or night-walker loitering or being in any thoroughfare, or public place, for the purposes of prostitution or solicitation, to the annoyance of the inhabitants or passengers'.[80] Until the enactment of laws for the protection of women and children and the regulation of prostitution in 1926 and 1927, the Police Act largely defined the position of prostitutes in Sierra Leone.[81] It is not clear what impacts these technical provisions had on prostitutes in the colony.[82] Contemporary observers noted that some other aspects of the Police Ordinance, such as a prohibition against drumming at night, were 'seldom enforced'.[83] Convictions at the Police Magistrates Court and the Supreme Court, reported in the colonial media, show that other aspects of the Ordinance, such as the provisions against abusive and obscene language, were regularly enforced.[84] There is also some patchy evidence of the enforcement of laws on prostitution. For example, the *Sierra Leone Weekly News*[85] reported that a woman named Christiana Bull was charged with loitering unlawfully in the Commissariat Buildings, having an unlawful purpose and an intent to commit an unspecified felony (prostitutes were convicted for loitering with intent, rather than for actual sex acts). Fragments such as this serve as a reminder that prostitution was regulated and policed in many ways – not just by CD legislation – in the British Empire.

Paradoxically, though the introduction of CD laws advanced imperial projects in some places and in some ways, decisions not to introduce or to repeal them could be equally productive. To the extent that it was a pillar of the imperial order, regulation was both ambivalent and debatable. It seemed, though this was always a matter for debate, to serve some imperial imperatives but to hamper others; and, of course, questions remained open about which of the series of competing and in some cases contradictory imperial objectives should be prioritised and how each could best be fulfilled. Sally Engle Merry contrasts the priorities of Christians and capitalists, finding the first of these overlapping groups interested in the eating habits, cleanliness, sleep and sexuality of colonial subjects, the latter in their punctuality and discipline.[86] Similarly, purity campaigners asserted one set of imperial objectives (for example, the requirements of the British military in India) over another (the moral legitimacy of the British Empire), and came down in favour of the latter. By resisting one set of imperial interests, the government of Sierra Leone effectively served another. For instance, it may have strengthened the unity and hierarchy of the British Empire to follow changing imperial precedents on the regulation of prostitution, regardless of their substantive implications for colonialism at the local level. Jeremy Martens has shown how a CD Bill, forwarded in 1890 by the governor of Natal to the secretary of state for the colonies, was refused royal assent on the grounds that in England the system had been condemned and abandoned, and that similar laws had been repealed in the colonies and in India.[87] The late timing of this Bill, in relation to the wider history of regulation in the British Empire and the expectation of the British authorities that colonies would follow its example, points towards a more general reason for the failure of the system in sub-Saharan Africa – if not in Sierra Leone, one of the few crown colonies to have been established in the continent before the last few years of the nineteenth century, when CD laws were repealed rather than extended.

Another imperial imperative that clashed with regulation was that of minimising the overheads of an already sprawling empire. It is perhaps no coincidence that the art of minimalist colonial government was refined in this region – by the first governor of Nigeria, Lord Frederick Lugard, in the form of 'Indirect Rule'. British governors in West Africa, Kortright included, spent and did as little as possible.[88] If Kortright refused the demands of military and medical lobbyists, this was because he thought they and the colony could manage without such 'luxuries', and with a more modest system of government. There was nothing new about this. The British presence in this part of Africa had traditionally been minimal, its infrastructure consisting of small European enclaves perched tenuously on the coastal fringes of African kingdoms, whose sovereignty they had no real need to challenge and whose governments they had no desire to replace.[89] Inaction on regulation can be linked to inaction on most other fronts. With few British colonists, travellers, soldiers or missionaries, either in Sierra Leone itself or in the surrounding areas, the British had maintained a minimal presence and a *laissez-faire* regime throughout the period in which CD laws were being introduced in other parts.[90] The British invested little in medical infrastructure, on which regulation would have depended,[91] despite the demands and protests of colonial officials[92] and journalists,[93] and despite technical commitments to act (including an 1874 Public Health Ordinance and a Board of Health, established in 1876). As the Freetown *Independent* put it, the under-staffed sanitary authorities were unable to do their job, and 'the sanitary by-laws are becoming dead letters',[94] and that remained the case until well into the twentieth century.[95] But if, as Soma Hewa suggests, imperial medicine was developed primarily 'to protect the economic and political interests of the empire',[96] rather than to improve the health of colonial subjects, then it makes sense that the British authorities in Sierra Leone would have turned a blind eye to certain levels of illness – and to a colonial infrastructure unequal to changing this through measures such as CD legislation. Though the colonial infrastructure was thin, particularly in relation to the health crisis, this did not prevent the colony from functioning, which suggests that in some sense the *needs* of the colonial power were being met, without the sort of expense and inconvenience associated with some other colonies.

Another imperative of British imperialism which conflicted with calls for regulation stemmed from the special significance of Sierra Leone with respect to the practical and symbolic movement against slavery and towards a more ethical, humanitarian imperialism. Pivotal in the fight against slavery, Sierra Leone was historically a symbolic and strategic rather than an economically lucrative colony. Elsewhere within the British Empire, as I have explained, purity campaigners argued that regulation undermined the moral basis of imperialism. If, in India and many colonies, the practical benefits of the system to the local military and the economy were judged to outweigh the moral objections, the scales were tipped differently in Sierra Leone. Sensitivity to the ethical dimensions of regulation was particularly keen in this colony, defined as it was by humanitarianism and the fight against anti-slavery, given Butler's influential argument that regulation was the new slavery, anti-regulation the new abolitionism.

The decision to reject regulation could also be identified with a different sort of new imperialism, defined less by humanitarianism than by aggressive expansionism. Having lost its *raison d'être* with the final decline of the slave trade in the 1860s, Sierra Leone started to find a new role in the late 1870s and 1880s, providing a foothold for British economic and military penetration of the African interior in the face of French competition in the region and the wider scramble for Africa. Before the end of the century, this expansion saw a twenty-fold growth of Sierra Leone, with the designation of 'Protectorate' and an assertion of British interests in the region as a whole. When the governor contended that prostitution would be 'impossible' to regulate,[97] when he implied that African sexualities were somehow beyond regulation, he reproduced and extended a form of colonial discourse that sexualised non-Europeans, marking them out for colonial subjection. He echoed a wider European representation of Africans as degenerate, over-sexed, lazy, dirty and intellectually inferior.[98] As chapter 6 explains, Burton exemplified a tendency to portray black Africans as deeply, even bestially, sexual and sub-Saharan Africa as a region of sexual excess and extreme otherness.[99] Europeans were particularly preoccupied with – attracted to and repulsed by – the sexuality they attributed to African men.[100] Consequently, British colonial governments in Africa devoted disproportionate time and energy to policing the sexuality of black men, designating racially specific laws for sexual offences.[101] They also, however, channelled those sexual attitudes in other areas. Helen Callaway argues that sexual anxieties, which existed at a largely ideological rather than an experiential level (she finds little evidence that white women were actually afraid of black men), were embedded within the 'political tensions and ideological structures of imperial power'.[102] The sexualisation of Africans legitimated rapid and absolutist European incursions into Africa in the final years of the nineteenth century. As in other parts of the world, the sexualisation of would-be colonial subjects was used to legitimate their conquest and ostensibly their civilisation.[103] Burton applied this logic to Sierra Leone, concluding an unsympathetic account of the colony with the suggestion that it could be changed and, 'with good management', turned from 'the mere ruin of an emporium' into 'a flourishing portion of the empire'.[104] Apparently, if the scramble for Africa and the incursion into Sierra Leone's hinterland needed legitimation, this was it. Again, the decision not to introduce CD laws in Sierra Leone need not be regarded as a weak point in British imperial power, but can be seen as an active extension of that power.

Conclusion

While it initially seemed that the failure of metropolitan models of regulation and resistance to make their mark in African colonies such as Sierra Leone could be put down to an inhospitable environment, one that held back the course of empire, this chapter has ultimately suggested something quite different. Places, never intrinsically resistant, were always mediated by people, particularly the powerful. When Kortright and his colleagues in the government of Sierra Leone refused to follow English precedents on regulation, they also found different and more locally effective means of fulfilling the same specific and fundamental objectives, which involved some negotiation between conflicting demands and interests. Their situated pragmatism throws some light on the genesis and significance of imperial heterogeneity, on the ability of empires to accommodate difference in their systems of government, and moreover on their need to do so, to find local solutions to common – yet contested and changing – imperatives. Though ultimately more an analysis of domination than resistance, this chapter has contributed to the postcolonial geographical project identified by Blunt and McEwan, and developed in this book as a whole: 'understanding the spatial dynamics of power, identity and knowledge'.[105] It has done this by mapping an element of the de-centred spatiality of colonial rule.

The rejection of proposals for CD laws in Sierra Leone was linked to the forging of a new kind of colonialism, generated not simply through dictates from the Colonial Office, but through local action, both from within the colonial establishment (the subject of this chapter) and from without. Developing the latter, chapter 7 explores Creole engagements with sexuality politics in Sierra Leone. First, however, there is more to say about the ways in which colonial environments proved fertile grounds for innovation with respect to the regulation of sexuality. This chapter has examined creativity in a small colony, one that existed on a shoestring budget, and that lacked either the capacity or the need to function like a modern state.[106] The same could not be said of certain other colonies, in which pretensions to modernity extended to innovation in certain areas of statecraft, including the regulation of sexuality. There, precedents in sexuality politics were not simply resisted or negotiated: they were set.

Notes

1   J. E. Butler, 'A grave question that needs answering by the churches of Great Britain', reprinted from the *Sentinel* (London: Sentinel, 1886), p. 1.
2   P. Levine, *Prostitution, Race and Politics: Policing Venereal Disease in the British Empire* (London: Routledge, 2003), p. 1.
3   Levine, *Prostitution, Race and Politics*, p. 25.
4   The first domestic CD Act (1864) applied to Portsmouth, Plymouth (including Devonport and Stonehouse), Woolwich, Chatham, Sheerness, Aldershot, Colchester, Shorncliffe, the Curragh, Cork and Queenstown; the Act of 1866 included also Windsor. The modified Act of 1869 was extended, applying to Canterbury, Dover, Gravesend, Maidstone, Winchester and Southampton (total of eighteen stations); source: J. R. Walkowitz, *Prostitution and Victorian Society: Women, Class and the State* (Cambridge: Cambridge University Press, 1980).
5   Valverde, *Age of Light*, p. 82; C. Backhouse, 'Nineteenth century Canadian prostitution law: reflection of a discriminatory society', *Histoire Sociale/Social History*, 18 (1986), 387–423.
6   J. P. S. McLaren, 'Chasing the social evil: moral fervour and the evolution of Canada's prostitution laws, 1867–1917', *Canadian Journal of Law and Society*, 1 (1986), 135.
7   E. B. van Heyningen, 'The social evil in the Cape Colony 1868–1902: prostitution and the Contagious Diseases Acts', *Journal of Southern African Studies*, 10:2 (1984), 170–197.
8   M. Leavitt, 'West coast of Africa', *Sentinel* (June 1890), p. 65.
9   CERC, *Church of England Purity Society Annual Report* (1902), p. 11.
10 R. Phillips, 'Imperialism and the regulation of sexuality: colonial legislation on contagious diseases and ages of consent', *Journal of Historical Geography*, 28:3 (2002), 339–362.
11 Church Missionary Society (CMS), *Church Missionary Society's African Missions: Sierra Leone*, 2nd edn (London: CMS, 1899 [1863]).
12 Correspondence, *Sierra Leone Church Times* (17 February 17 1886), p. 4.
13 Public Record Office, London (hereafter PRO), CO 267/331, Gray to the Clerk of Council (15 February 1876).
14 PRO, CO 267/331, Gray to the Clerk of Council (15 February 1876).
15 PRO, CO 267/332, Minutes of Legislative Council, 1874. There are no records of this proposal or of the colonial government's reactions to it. The Minutes of the Executive Council do not record any meetings at all for December 1874, and those for the Legislative Council do not record any reference to CDs.
16 PRO, CO 270/332, Minutes of Legislative Council (24 November 1876).
17 Sir Cornelius Hendrichsen Kortright (1817–1897) was governor of the West African settlements from 1875 to 1877: *Who Was Who* (London: A. & C. Black, 1920), vol. 1, p. 295.
18 Kortright's name appeared on the statute books for Trinidad, in relation to Ordinance 19 (2 August 1868): 'An Ordinance enacted by the Governor of Trinidad, with the Advice and Consent of the Legislative Council thereof, for the better prevention of Contagious Diseases, C. H. Kortright.'
19 L. White, *Comforts of Home: Prostitution and Colonial Nairobi* (Chicago, IL: University of Chicago Press 1990), p. 176.
20 PRO, CO 267/332, Lovell to Governor Rowe (19 February 1876).
21 PRO, CO 267/332, Despatch 44 (24 February 1877).

22 PRO, CO 267/331, Kortright to the Earl of Carnarvon, Colonial Office (24 February 1877).
23 West African Reporter (19 September 1876), p. 2.
24 R. Clarke, *Description of the Manners and Customs of the Liberated Africans* (London, James Ridgway, 1843), p. 92.
25 R. F. Burton, *Wanderings in West Africa*, 2 vols (London: Tinsley, 1863), vol. 1, p. 267.
26 PRO, CO 267/331, Gray to Clerk of Council (15 February 1876).
27 PRO, CO 267/333, War Office to Under Secretary of State, Colonial Office (7 July 1877).
28 *Sierra Leone Blue Book* (Freetown: Government Printing Office, 1874).
29 S. Hewa, *Colonialism, Tropical Disease and Imperial Medicine* (Lanham, MD: University Press of America, 1995); R. Macleod and M. Lewis (eds), *Disease, Medicine and Empire: Perspectives on Western Medicine and the Experience of European Expansion* (London: Routledge, 1988).
30 PRO, CO 267/333, Despatch on Sanitary Condition of Freetown (26 May 1877).
31 *West African Reporter* (19 September 1876), p. 2.
32 'The moral dangers of militarism in America', *Sentinel* (July 1899), p. 89.
33 J. Morris, *Our Sin and Our Shame* (London: J. S. Amoore, 1885), p. 3.
34 W. Catchpool, 'The war system and immorality', *Sentinel* (December 1887), p. 144.
35 Dyer, *Slavery Under the British Flag*, pp. 44, 95.
36 J. C. Martens, '"Almost a public calamity": prostitutes, "nurseboys" and attempts to control venereal diseases in colonial Natal, 1886–1890', *South African Historical Journal*, 45 (2001), 27–52.
37 In 1841, the governor remarked on the 'total absence of any armed force in the colony', a condition that did not change significantly until the next century: R. Clyne, *Colonial Blue: A History of the South Australian Police Force, 1836–1916* (Adelaide: Wakefield Press, 1987), p. 67.
38 SAPD (8 September 1875), p. 982.
39 R. Ramasubban, 'Imperial health in British India, 1857–1900', in Macleod and Lewis, *Disease, Medicine and Empire*, pp. 38–60. In post-mutiny India, investments in health and sanitation (living quarters, water supply and drainage, hospitals) were designed to improve the efficiency, retention and recruitment of British soldiers.
40 T. Gale, 'The struggle against disease in Sierra Leone: early sanitary reforms in Freetown', *Africana Research Bulletin*, 6:2 (1976), 29–44.
41 PRO, CO 267/331, Kortright to Carnarvon (24 February 1877).
42 Hewa, *Colonialism, Tropical Disease.*
43 P. M. Mbaeyi, *British Military and Naval Forces in West African History, 1807–1874* (London: NOK Publishers, 1978), p. 62.
44 Mbaeyi, *British Military and Naval Forces in West African History*, p. 176.
45 A. Clayton and D. Killingray, *Khaki and Blue: Military and Police in British Colonial Africa* (Athens: Ohio University Press, 1989).
46 F. Henriques, *Prostitution and Society*, vol. 1: *Primitive, Classical and Oriental* (London, Macgibbon & Kee, 1962).
47 White, *Comforts of Home.*
48 H. Ellis, *Studies in the Psychology of Sex* (Philadelphia, PA: F. A. Davis, 1910), vol. 3, p. 260.
49 E. W. Blyden, 'African life and customs', *Sierra Leone Weekly News* (Freetown, 1908), p. 24.
50 White, *Comforts of Home.*
51 Clarke, *Description of the Manners and Customs of the Liberated Africans*, p. 76.
52 J. Holman, *Travels in Madeira, Sierra Leone, Tenerife . . .* (London: Routledge, 1840), p. 123.
53 T. E. Poole, *Life, Scenery and Customs in Sierra Leone and the Gambia* (London, Richard Bentley, 1850), p. i.296.

54 Quoted by A. Gill, *Ruling Passions: Sex, Race and Empire* (London, BBC Books, 1995), p. 33.
55 M. Banton, *West African City: A Study of Tribal Life in Freetown* (London: Oxford University Press, 1957); E. Muga, *Studies in Prostitution* (Nairobi: Kenya Literature Bureau, 1980).
56 K. Little, *African Women in Towns* (Cambridge: Cambridge University Press, 1973); White, *Comforts of Home*.
57 PRO, CO 267/331, Kortright to Carnarvon (24 February 1877).
58 PRO, CO 267/331, Kortright to Carnarvon (24 February 1877); emphasis added.
59 White, *Comforts of Home*, p. 176.
60 White, *Comforts of Home*, p. 176.
61 T. O. Elias, *Ghana and Sierra Leone: The Development of Their Laws and Constitutions* (London: Stevens, 1962).
62 *West African Reporter* (19 September 1876), p. 2.
63 Elias, *Ghana and Sierra Leone*.
64 Engels and Marks, *Contesting Colonial Hegemony*.
65 Rathbone, 'Law, lawyers and politics in Ghana in the 1940s', p. 228.
66 Cited by Elias, *Ghana and Sierra Leone*, p. 240.
67 A. Pagden, *Lords of All the World: Ideologies of Empire in Spain, Britain and France c.1500–1800* (New Haven, CT, and London: Yale University Press, 1995).
68 P. Scully, 'Rape, race and colonial culture: the sexual politics of identity in nineteenth-century Cape Colony, South Africa', *American Historical Review*, 100 (1995), 335–359; B. Bush, *Imperialism, Race and Resistance: Africa and Britain, 1919–1945* (London: Routledge, 1999); S. Klausen, ' "For the sake of the race": eugenic discourses of feeblemindedness and motherhood in the South African medical record, 1903–1926', *Journal of Southern African Studies*, 23:1 (1997), 27–50.
69 L. M. Thomas, 'Imperial concerns and "women's affairs": state efforts to regulate clitoridectomy and eradicate abortion in Meru, Kenya, c.1910–1950', *Journal of African History*, 39 (1998), 121–145.
70 K. Mann, *Marrying Well: Marriage, Status and Social Change among the Educated Elite in Colonial Lagos* (Cambridge: Cambridge University Press, 1985), p. 71.
71 R. I. Pittin, *Women and Work in Northern Nigeria* (Basingstoke: Palgrave, 2002).
72 D. Jeater, *Marriage, Perversion and Power: The Construction of Moral Discourse in Southern Rhodesia 1894–1930* (Oxford: Clarendon Press, 1993).
73 E. G. Ingham, *Sierra Leone After a Hundred Years* (London: Seeley, 1894), p. 316.
74 J. Allman and V. Tashjan, *'I Will Not Eat a Stone': A Women's History of Colonial Asante* (Oxford: James Currey, 2000), p. 75.
75 African courts continued to exist in Freetown, the Gold Coast, and Lagos, mainly to hear disputes between locals: Mann and Roberts, *Law in Colonial Africa*, p. 13.
76 Mann and Roberts, *Law in Colonial Africa*, p. 14; 'The Marriage Amendment Ordinance', *Sierra Leone Weekly News* (3 September 1887), p. 2.
77 'The West Indies', *Sentinel* (April 1889), p. 41.
78 Elias, *Ghana and Sierra Leone*, p. 236.
79 A. Montagu, *Ordinances of the Colony of Sierra Leone* (London: HMSO, 1857), p. 103.
80 Montagu, *Ordinances of the Colony of Sierra Leone*, p. 109.
81 Attorney-general of Sierra Leone, *Supplement to the Laws of the Colony and Protectorate of Sierra Leone* (London: Waterlow, 1932).
82 Elias, *Ghana and Sierra Leone*, p. 305.
83 Clarke, *Description of the Manners and Customs of the Liberated Africans*, p. 88.
84 'Police intelligence', *Sierra Leone Weekly News* (6 September 1884), p. 2.
85 *Sierra Leone Weekly News* (9 May 1885), p. 2.
86 Engle Merry, *Colonizing Hawai'i*, p. 16.

87 Martens, 'Almost a public calamity'.
88 J. Sadowsky, *Imperial Bedlam: Institutions of Madness in Colonial Southwest Nigeria* (Berkeley: University of California Press, 1999).
89 A. A. Boahen (ed.), *General History of Africa*, vol. 7: *Africa Under Colonial Domination, 1880–1935* (London, James Currey, 1990), p. 14.
90 A. I. Asiwaju, *West African Transformations: Comparative Impact of French and British Colonialism* (Ikeja, Nigeria: Malthouse, 2001).
91 M. Crowder, *West Africa Under Colonial Rule* (London: Hutchinson, 1968).
92 PRO, CO 270/25, Minutes of Legislative Council (1859): in 1859, the colonial chief justice told the Legislative Council that 'the present state of health in the colony urgently demanded the services of a larger medical staff'.
93 The *Sierra Leone Ram* complained of the 'deplorable condition of Sierra Leone' and argued that 'the people . . . look in vain for new public buildings, improved roads and genuine sanitation': *Sierra Leone Ram* (20 March 1886), p. 1.
94 *Independent* (27 April 1876), p. 2.
95 Gale, 'The struggle against disease in Sierra Leone'.
96 Hewa, *Colonialism, Tropical Disease*, p. 6.
97 PRO, CO 267/331, Kortright to Carnarvon (24 February 1877).
98 Crowder, *West Africa Under Colonial Rule*, p. 396.
99 R. Phillips, 'Writing travel and mapping sexuality: Richard Burton's Sotadic Zone', in J. Duncan and D. Gregory (eds), *Writes of Passage: Reading Travel Writing* (London, Routledge, 2000), pp. 70–91.
100 Bleys, *Geography of Perversion*, p. 32; M. Vaughan, *Curing Their Ills: Colonial Power and African Illness* (Cambridge: Polity Press, 1991), p. 21; see also F. Fanon, *Black Skins, White Masks* (London: Pluto, 1986 [1952]), p. 177.
101 Martens, 'Almost a public calamity'.
102 H. Callaway, *Gender, Culture and Empire: European Women in Colonial Nigeria* (Basingstoke: Macmillan, 1987), p. 238.
103 Engle Merry, *Colonizing Hawai'i*, p. 260.
104 Burton, *Wanderings in West Africa*, vol. 1, p. 265.
105 Blunt and McEwan, *Postcolonial Geographies*, p. 5.
106 Vaughan, *Curing Their Ills*.

CHAPTER FIVE

Generative margins: introducing a stronger form of regulation in Bombay

Colonies could be proactive as well as reactive sites of sexuality politics, generating new ideas and strategies. For instance, in the British Empire, CD laws made their first appearance in colonies, initially in the form of military customs and later in civil legislation. When CD Acts were finally passed for England, they were based on schemes and statutes applied in India, the Ionian Islands, Malta, Gibraltar and Hong Kong.[1] Building on the previous chapter, which concluded somewhat tentatively that the colonial government of Sierra Leone had broken new or at least different ground in sexuality politics, this chapter investigates an important non-metropolitan cutting edge of imperial sexuality politics. It revisits one of the most thoroughly researched subjects of colonial history – regulated prostitution in India – not attempting to replicate detailed and sophisticated histories of the subject by Kenneth Ballhatchet, Philippa Levine and others, but aiming instead to explore a specific aspect of the located-ness of sexuality politics: the site-specific power and freedom that allowed colonial governors to go further than their metropolitan counterparts, in experimenting with and devising new forms of government.

The *Times of India* – a pillar of the colonial establishment, given to debating the details of British rule in India, if not to questioning that rule – alluded to the significance of regulation for Bombay, where its reintroduction was proposed in 1880:

> It is by no means certain that any organization that could be devised would make such an Act at once effective for its peculiar purpose, and tolerable by the population in a large city such as Bombay. In isolated places, in camps remote from large towns, in small islands such as Malta, in stations like Aden, the end in view can generally be attainable by a happy combination of vigour and judgement on the part of those entrusted with the powers usually conferred by such laws. But if legislation of this kind has ever proved successful in large communities, we should be glad to learn where such communities exist.[2]

This editorial argued that, if it were applied to the city as a whole, regulation in Bombay would go radically beyond its originally military origins and sphere: radical, if not unprecedented or wholly unparalleled, for the system had been tried in Bombay some years previously, and similar systems had been adopted in other Indian cities, under the same legislative provisions – the Indian CD Act (Act XIV of 1868), which provided for regulation in places specified by local government with the sanction of the governor-general in Council. As the *Times of India* accurately pointed out, Bombay's adoption of the system had been something of a departure in the history of regulation within the British Empire. The departure was one of degree rather than kind, since the policies were not in themselves new, though their extension to a wider range of people and places was significant.

The *Times of India* implied that regulation in Bombay was a function of its position within the British Empire. The editorial argued that introduction of regulation to the city in 1870 had depended on 'large powers, unsparingly exercised', and resulted in 'the most sweeping and high-handed proceedings';[3] in other words, it depended on a relationship of domination and subordination between rulers and their subjects, which it hoped was not inherent in imperialism, but identified as a danger to be guarded against. The newspaper cautioned against repeating the abuses of European countries and cities, which had adopted systems 'with a strictness and arbitrary disregard of individual rights which would never be tolerated in any country under British rule'.[4] Implicitly, it recognised that the danger of trampling on the liberties of British subjects was greater in colonies than in England. This concentration of power, which defined Bombay's place within the Empire, meant that whereas some of its other contributions to sexuality politics were more or less derivative, brought from England by figures such as Dyer (as explained in chapter 1), or tentatively productive as in Malabari's active reading and appropriation of English campaign journalism and legislative models (chapter 2), the city sometimes led rather than followed the political field.

These observations give rise to some specific and some broader questions about ways in which places cast – however problematically – as the margins of empire can be politically productive, sites of political experimentation and innovation. They suggest ways in which sexuality politics were structured by geographies of power. Dyer's derivative acts and Malabari's interventions were structured by the power relations that existed between England and the Empire, and the *Times of India* underlined the significance of power relations within each of these spheres – relationships between different members of society, and the channels open to them for political action – in structuring sexuality politics there. But these are general suggestions, calling for more specific analysis of the manner in which geographies of power structured sexuality politics, in which colonies sometimes followed but sometimes systematically led.

There are many insights in the theoretical literature as to why places on the margins may be politically productive. Some ideas about cultural change and innovation, concerned with creative (and destructive) frontiers and with generative sites of hybridity and liminality, are addressed in the next two chapters. Here, I turn to a theoretical idea that throws more direct light on regulation and governance in colonies, and both acknowledges and explains the tendency of colonial governments to innovate rather than merely replicate, negotiate or resist the actions of metropolitan Europe. I think, specifically, of Paul Rabinow's interpretation of French colonies as 'laboratories of modernity', which generated and experimented with a wide range of modern practices, from architecture to systems of social regulation. Rabinow explains that planners and architects, reduced to a state of 'melancholy' by the inertia they experienced in metropolitan France, perceived possibilities on the colonial horizons.[5] Rather than imitating the French model in North Africa, for instance, they produced something for France to imitate, 'islands of modern civilisation'.[6] Initially, these consisted of European districts, though certain spheres of urban planning reached into native towns, and these included sanitary policy, for example in regulations that required local authorities in French Morocco to collect health statistics, enforce hygiene provisions and (after the First World War) regulate prostitution.

Gwendolyn Wright argues: 'However exotic certain districts might have seemed, the European sections of colonial cities not only evoked the capitals and provincial towns of home, they sometimes suggested future directions for Western cities.'[7] She reads colonial experiments in city planning and governance as French attempts at 'working out solutions to some of the political, social, and aesthetic problems which plagued France. Urbanism, implying both policy and design, formed the core of such efforts.'[8] Ann Laura Stoler draws together these and other reassessments of *European* innovations, from modes of industrial production, surveillance and social discipline to the concept of 'culture' – all colonial formations. She argues that broad swathes of ostensibly European political, social, cultural and economic life – even *Europeanness* itself – were generated in colonial spheres 'and only then brought 'home'.[9] She makes a similar claim for European sexualities in her critique of Michel Foucault's *History of Sexuality*. As I have explained in the Introduction, she seeks to acknowledge the productivity of relationships between European and non-Europeans, and to recover the latter in the construction of European sexualities. She also argues that systems of sexual as of other forms of social regulation were produced and/or tested in colonies and/or among colonised peoples before sometimes being extended to other regions and peoples of the British Empire.

Resonant though it appears for sexuality politics, and convincingly though Stoler applies the term, the notion of the laboratory of modernity should not be imported too smoothly. It makes a series of suggestions about the function of colonial space which demand to be disentangled, their application assessed: this space accommodates experimentation and sometimes generates new ideas; it is focused on modernity; it is malleable and controllable. First, the idea that colonies were used as laboratories for all sorts of experiments in governance, including experiments in the regulation of sexualities, finds support in colonial archives. The language of laboratories and experiments was often explicit, for example in Robert Peel's comparison of Trinidad with 'a subject in an anatomy school or rather a poor patient in a country hospital and on whom all sorts of surgical experiments are tried, to be given up if they fail, and to be practised on others if they succeed'.[10] To the extent that they experimented with new forms of governance – with new and/or stronger forms of regulation, for instance – colonies could be regarded as laboratories of modernity. Second, the term 'laboratory *of modernity*' asserts that colonies produced not just the new, but the specifically modern. Each of the critics I have mentioned in relation to laboratories of modernity makes a case for the modernity of his or her particular subject. For instance, Wright argues:

> Colonial urbanism can be called modern in two senses. First, teams of professional advisers relied heavily on various social sciences to generate supposedly impartial, objective criteria and techniques. And it is here that the modern urban design developed, with its battery of legal tools and artistic guidelines, in an effort to achieve a balance of historical continuity, profitable economic development, and public amenities.[11]

Certain large colonial cities such as Bombay have been located with reference to models of urbanism and urban governance that were not only described by historians as modern, but conceived as such by contemporary planners, civic leaders and colonial governors.[12] The city was even compared with the new Paris – the quintessential model of modernity – by the *Times of India*, which argued that 'Haussman is a great deal nearer right than we are' on matters such as public expenditure, but added that Bombay should and could aspire towards modernisation in all its forms, from public works to social policy.[13]

Policies for the regulation of sexuality which the city adopted have been located within histories and geographies of modernity.[14] On the other hand, many colonial processes and places were far from modern. Megan Vaughan argues, for example, that African 'colonial states were hardly "modern states" for much of their short existence'.[15] For the purposes of this chapter, the question of whether colonial sexuality politics were more modern than their European counterparts is less important than that of whether they were innovative in some way, whether the sites of colonial sexuality politics were generative.

Finally, and crucially, the idea of the 'laboratory of modernity' underlines one of the assertions in the *Times of India* editorial, which stated that innovations in sexuality politics were possible because of the particular configurations of power that existed in colonies. The laboratory is, of course, a controlled and controllable space, in this context one in which Europeans could get away with things that they could not at home. In Europe, they might be limited by the fear of failure – with its electoral consequences – or by greater civil liberties which limited their ability to interfere in people's lives. The image of the laboratory of modernity is defined, fundamentally, by the figure of the powerful scientist, empowered to conduct experiments within his domain. But this is just an analogy, of course; the reality demands closer inspection.

Intersections of power

The special conditions that allowed certain parts of certain colonies to become laboratories were a function of specific dynamic situated intersections of colonial power. To understand laboratories of modernity, Rabinow acknowledges, it is first necessary to gain 'a more complex understanding of power in the colonies'.[16] For Fred Cooper and Ann Laura Stoler, that means understanding the role of the State, asking questions about its unity and coherence – in other words, understanding its fractures, conflicts and instability, and its textured history and geography.[17] To show how specific configurations of colonial power facilitated experiments with the regulation of sexuality, it is first necessary to disentangle the various forms of power, thus to identify the forces operating – not always in harmony – within the wider field of sexuality politics. This section traces those broad forces, setting the stage for the subsequent discussions of how they came together in Bombay in the late 1860s. Concentrating on the city of Bombay, the chapter departs somewhat from other studies of regulation in India, which have tended to concentrate on India as a whole, albeit with reservations. Levine, for instance, regards India as a geographical and political whole, but she recognises that it is not directly comparable in this respect with other constituents of the Empire, such as those in her comparative study – the much smaller and differently ordered Hong Kong, Straits Settlements and Queensland – and acknowledges that there is no easy answer to the question posed by Immanuel Wallerstein: 'does India exist?'[18] Locating sexuality politics within spaces of power – composed, as I here explain, of nested and roughly hierarchical geopolitical entities and local or regional regimes of political and social power – it can also be meaningful to concentrate on a colonial city such as Bombay.

At the most general level, this power was a function of relationships between the coloniser and the colonised, even though, refusing to conform to any simple binary, it was complicated by multiple social, ethnic and religious positions. More specifically, the relationship, for example, between the municipal authorities in Bombay and the people they governed was structured by imperialism: thus, health officers in Bombay's municipal administration deployed a series of Orientalist clichés to assert the need for strong government in the city:

> I cannot speak too strongly in condemnation of the dark, ill-lighted, and still worse ventilated buildings in which so many of the people of this city are condemned to live. The baneful effects of habitually breathing impure air are everywhere visible on the face of the population, whether one visits the lumbering and ill-adjusted pile in which the rich with their numerous relations and followers seclude themselves, or the hovel between whose mud walls the poor crouch and nestle together. That apathy, that indifference to danger on the part of the people which so startles and astonishes a stranger on first walking through our streets, is but one of its many effects. The hawking and spitting observed at every corner in our morning walks, and the violent and protracted attempts to empty the stomach of contents that it is too feeble to digest, which is so painful a spectacle on every side one turns to, are other links in the train of symptoms by which overcrowding of the population makes itself evident to the observant mind.[19]

Imperial power was also expressed in other levels of government and in the institutions that underpinned British India, particularly those associated with the medical and the military.

With a strong presence of both the Indian Army and the Royal Navy, Bombay was an important centre for the British military (figure 5.1). As the headquarters for troops in western India, it was home to many soldiers: approximately 25,000 native and 10,500 European troops were stationed in the presidency, of which 2,000 and 500, respectively, were based in the city.[20] There was also a naval dockyard, maintained by the Bombay Marine (subsequently the Indian

[141]

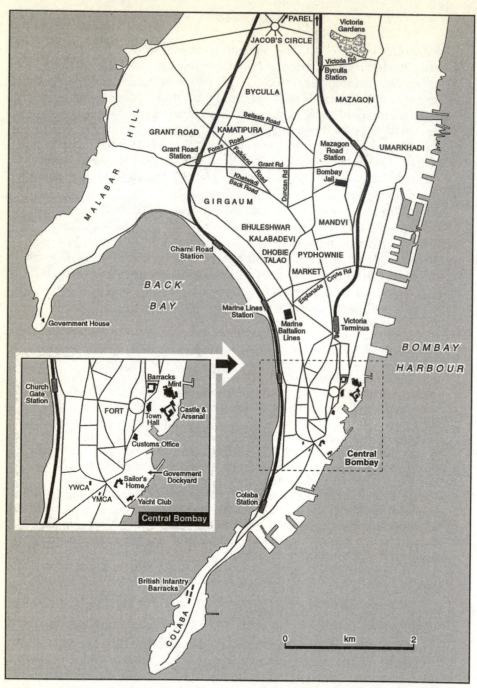

5.1 Map of Bombay (c.1880) showing merchant and military docks and army barracks. Alfred Dyer spoke of a 'red light district' between and along Falkland Road and Duncan Road

Marine), which provided for the transportation of troops and stores, and maintained station ships and government vessels and launches.[21] The Royal Navy maintained a strong presence in Bombay, and its vessels and sailors were frequently seen in the city.

In India as a whole, the military traditionally provided soldiers with prostitutes, whose appearance and health they monitored. This system was formalised in the Cantonments Act (1864) and extended in the Indian CD Act (1868), which was passed in response to an enquiry – the Royal Commission on the Sanitary State of the Army of India (appointed in 1859, reported in 1863) – which found that a significant portion of mortality and sickness among soldiers in India was due to venereal disease.[22] The sexual health of military personnel was also addressed at the regional level: the Government of Bombay commissioned an ongoing survey of sanitary conditions within its jurisdiction by establishing a Bombay Sanitary Commission, which submitted annual reports, the first of them published in 1865.[23] This generally replicated the findings of the national Commission at the presidency level, reporting a large and growing number of cases of venereal disease among military personnel and calling for regulation within its jurisdiction.[24] Military interests and voices were also represented more locally within the presidency. For example, the Admiralty, which launched an enquiry of its own into the sexual health of its personnel worldwide, compared the effects of shore leave in specific ports and intervened in local politics of regulation. Royal Naval officers frequently intervened on the subject in Bombay, claiming that the system worked when it was in force and that it was needed when it was not, lobbying for its introduction, retention and then reintroduction in the city.[25]

The military did not operate in isolation, nor was it necessarily the dominant force within colonial Bombay, with respect to regulation. As was discussed in chapter 4, Levine forcefully and convincingly argues that, whereas regulation in England may have been a principally military policy, the system had a broader function in colonies:

> Unlike their domestic British counterparts, colonial CD laws looked beyond as well as at the military, justifying often intrusive measures on the grounds not just of military necessity but the need to bring to heel sexual disorder among colonised peoples. These ordinances were not just about soldiers and prostitutes, not just about the control of VD. They also tell us much about British colonialism and the culturally specific assumptions on which it rested.[26]

The military depended on contact with civilians, and this – as the Royal Commission of 1863 recognised – made it impossible to neatly

5.2 Bombay bazaar street scene (c.1870)

separate military and civilian areas, practices and policies. It concerned itself not only with the barracks, hospitals and cantonments
(areas set apart for military personnel and their entourage) of European troops but with the sanitary state of towns and cities.[27] Sanitary
commissioners, appointed as a result of this and subsequent enquir-
ies, were asked to do the same. The remit of the Bombay Sanitary
Commission, composed of military and civilian doctors, included responsibility to advise and assist in 'all matters relating to public health',
including stations and bazaars, barracks and hospitals, and 'to exercise a constant oversight on the sanitary condition of the population,
European and Native' (figure 5.2).[28] There was therefore some recognition that military and civilian sexual health could not be separated.
The military had tried to isolate its personnel within safe, controllable spaces, designating cantonments in which special arrangements
and systems of government existed. But in the wider sphere the
military operated alongside other forces, in particular the medical
establishment and the government – the composition of which is
explained below.

The professional biography of one public health professional,
Thomas Gillham Hewlett (1832–1889), illustrates this intermingling
of spheres and sources of power. Hewlett served as surgeon to the

Bombay Army, as well as health officer and coroner to the city of Bombay in which capacity he produced numerous reports on sanitation and health in India and Bombay.[29] Despite the military initiation of and the continued involvement in wider sanitary and health policy and practice in Bombay, medical officers and administrative departments emerged from the shadow of the military, transforming this particular wing of the medical establishment into a force in its own right. The power of doctors and of the medical establishment can be located within the broader structures of imperialism. In *Curing Their Ills: Colonial Power and African Illness*, Vaughan locates colonial medicine within the political economy of imperialism, but acknowledges that relationships between medicine and imperialism were varied, complex and ambivalent. She identifies medicine as a distinct, if complex, strand of imperial power, a force in itself, with a degree of autonomy.[30] Levine shows that the introduction and operation of regulation coincided with and contributed to the 'self-conscious rise and remodelling of the medical profession', as an agent of welfare and social improvement.[31]

Doctors in the colonies presented themselves as leaders of civilisation and pillars of the new society, and regulation as one aspect of their progressive and scientific agenda.[32] In Bombay, as elsewhere in the British Empire, medical professionals and organisations variously interfered in the lives of colonial subjects, neglected them and attempted to adopt benevolent and/or humanitarian attitudes to them. One way in which medical power was manifest at this time was in municipal reforms, which were justified in India, as they had been in England, on general – not specifically military – medical grounds.[33] The remit of municipal governments, including municipal health officers and departments, was correspondingly broad.[34] Municipal authorities did not simply execute medical power, however. On the contrary, they formed one tier in the hierarchical system of government, within which regulation was conceived.

After the Government of India was transferred from the East India Company to the Crown, following the uprising of 1857, Bombay was subject to the rule of three main tiers of government: the British Government; the Government of India; and the government of Bombay (presidency). The former – including the elected government and the India Office – passed legislation, handed down decisions and oversaw imperial institutions (such as the military) that determined broadly how the million residents of Bombay and 230 million other Indians would be governed.[35] But much of the governance of India took place in India. Though the various tiers of government were originally created by the British or were ultimately answerable to them, they nevertheless retained or carved out for themselves degrees of autonomy, which led in a number of different directions. The process that led to the adoption of regulation at particular places within India was correspondingly complex, involving multiple levels and agents, particularly the presidency and the municipal governments of Bombay.

The government of Bombay, which ruled 23 million of India's 250 million people, was headed by a governor and three members of Council, one of whom was commander-in-chief of the Bombay Army.[36] This government oversaw the extension of Indian laws at the local level – sometimes mechanically, but sometimes with discretion and proactively – and by amending Indian laws on the basis of feedback and experience at the local level. In the case of the Indian CD Act, which had to be actively adopted at the local level, the government of Bombay actively mediated the application of the Act, though it could not always force it on its subordinate tiers of government, as I explain below. It also communicated with the Government of India (headed by the governor-general, after 1877 the viceroy, with the support of appointed Executive and Legislative Councils), informing it of the working of the Act within its jurisdiction, enabling the Indian Government to track and amend the system.[37] Thus, for example, Bombay kept the Government fully informed on the introduction of regulation within the city in 1870, forwarding reports and information from the municipal authorities, including letters from the municipal commissioner,[38] and reassuring central government that the 'operation of the Act has been, and will be, carefully watched'.[39]

The government of Bombay also used its power, specifically the powers granted to it under the Indian Councils Act of 1861, to establish a new authority. It responded to the rapid growth and the deteriorating health of Bombay by creating a municipal government.[40] Mariam Dossal interprets the Municipal Act (1865) as an attempt to compete with European cities, which had adopted similar provisions – those in England, for example, through the Health Act of 1855.[41] A municipal commissioner was to have sweeping powers, subject only to the financial scrutiny of an appointed bench of justices.[42] As the chairman of the bench reminded his fellow justices in 1868, 'We presented a report in which we [suggested] that the executive control of the Municipality should be placed in the hands of one individual.'[43] Neither answerable to the population of the city nor controllable by the bench – much to their chagrin, the justices were charged only to oversee the budget – the municipal commissioner was invested with considerable power.[44] This is an understatement – one of the justices described the municipal system as 'a satire on representative institutions'.[45] The *Times of India* compared his regime with that of Louis XIV.[46]

Arthur Crawford, the first municipal commissioner, used his powers fully and boldly, quickly and expensively reforming drainage, constructing new roads and markets, and introducing measures against cholera and smallpox. His ambitious administration involved great expenditure, which gained him friends and enemies alike, the latter eventually accusing him of financial irregularity.[47] Crawford had not long been in office before the bench formally asked the government of Bombay to appoint a commission of enquiry into the municipal government and to consider proposals for its reform.[48] Its interventions against Crawford resonated with wider criticism of his regime and arguments that his power and that of his administration should be curtailed. The justices proposed municipal government reform, securing Crawford's resignation in 1871 and ushering in a period of less dictatorial if less than democratic city government. Crawford's short-lived regime coincided with the enactment of India's CD Act, and it played an instrumental part in binding together supporters of the system – the military and medical establishments, and the governments of India and the presidency – and thereby ensuring its introduction in the city, as the sections below explain.

Power to regulate

Having identified the main forces behind the introduction and extension of regulation in Bombay and traced their general interests in and positions on regulation, it is now possible to ask how they used that power and with what effect, with specific reference to the city of Bombay. As Jo Sharp argues, structures and agents of domination and resistance do not operate in the abstract, but come together in rounded contexts – 'material spaces, places and networks which sustain, practically as well as imaginatively and symbolically, the knottings' of domination and resistance.[49] This section traces the individual and collective actions of the colonial establishment – and specifically the military, medical and governmental forces identified above – that effected the extension of a system of regulation throughout the city for a brief period, beginning on 7 May 1870 when the *Bombay Gazette* reported simply that 'the Indian Contagious Diseases Act has come into operation in Bombay'.[50]

Most generally, the events leading up to the introduction of regulation reflected the imperial order, which framed the specific if overlapping and intersecting powers of medical, military, governmental and other individuals, institutions and organisations. Bombay Health Officer John Lumsdaine betrayed this more general attitude to, and very real power over, those subjected to sanitary policy in the city when he referred to the 'ineradicable untrustiness of the lower order of natives' who, he claimed, were 'seldom in sight, and always exposed to temptation' that rendered them unsuitable for employment as health inspectors, and suitable instead for health inspection themselves.[51] Similarly, another health officer in Bombay argued that prostitutes did not deserve the respect accorded to others, claiming that 'a woman who is prepared to expose her charms to the lewd gaze of the stranger, is not likely to have her feelings outraged, or her modesty hurt, by a medical inspection'.[52]

Of course, this power was neither unbounded nor uncontested. These interventions presented regulation in Bombay as a product of the power not only to deploy resources and infrastructure, but also to over-rule the possible objections of those affected by the system, as well as their allies and advocates. Yet the municipal and presidential governments of Bombay did not totally ignore the real or perceived concerns of prostitutes and other women, or the possibility that these colonial subjects would resist the system. They took these into account in their decision not to charge prostitutes for their registration and, where necessary, their treatment, determining that such a policy would be 'unpopular to the women' concerned.[53] The health officer tried to legitimise the system by citing claims that elsewhere it had been 'of the greatest benefit to the women themselves'.[54] The assistant surgeon claimed that experience in England had shown that 'women will readily submit, and voluntarily present themselves at the hospital where they meet with kindness and relief', and concluded that 'native women of this country, so soon as they see that this Act will benefit their miserable condition, will put aside all prejudices of caste and race, and readily conform to the rules of those placed in Medical charge of them'.[55] When women objected to the system, in petitions and other representations, the authorities did not completely ignore them.[56] For example, it was decided that the 'dancing girls of Belgaum', who submitted one such petition, should be 'not unnecessarily interfered with'.[57] Other women defended themselves in other ways, sometimes successfully, ranging from court actions to verbal complaints and letters of protest.[58] Still others often the majority – simply failed to submit to registration or examination. But, if imperial power was not unlimited, it nevertheless remained a great force, providing those who governed and dominated Bombay with a relatively free hand. Neither the Indian women affected by regulation, nor the English social purity activists who campaigned against it, proved able to defy the fundamental inequality between dominating and dominated groups, which resulted in the heavy-handed introduction of a system of regulation in Bombay.

The military was another, more specific, force behind the extension of regulation in Bombay. Venereal disease among soldiers, which had been used to justify the Indian CD Act (1868), was also used as an argument for the adoption of the system in the presidency and city of Bombay. On the basis of its detailed local reports, the Bombay Sanitary Commission made recommendations about where regulation was most needed.[59] Through this and other channels, military doctors and other officers directed the implementation at the presidential and local level of the Cantonments Act and then the Indian CD Act. As a system that monitored and closely regulated the lives of its personnel, the military provided a model for the intrusive form of regulation that was introduced to Bombay. Leith's sanitary report addressed issues of environmental health with an attention to minute detail. The report provided included instructions and plans for barracks for single and married soldiers, respectively. No stone was left unturned by Leith's Commission, which considered such details as the preparation of soldiers' bread and the distance between barracks and gardens, the tea strainers approved for soldiers' use, the reading rooms and gymnasia designed for them.[60] The military took a close look at the places in which soldiers mixed with civilians, ate local food, breathed local air and met local women. Leith paid particular attention to 'the habitations of the native civil population in the neighbourhood of the barracks'.[61] He wanted a 'neutral interval' between soldiers and civilians, which might ensure the 'isolation of the barracks' from military bazaars and the wider 'population of the town'.[62] It was recognised, however, that this was not entirely practicable. Bombay's Sanitary Commission thought it desirable to distance barracks from bazaars, but did not expect to eliminate contact between military personnel and civilians.[63] Since soldiers could not be kept from prostitutes – on the contrary, military rules prevented most soldiers from marrying, effectively forcing them to find alternative sexual outlets – the military tried to control their contact with local women. The traditional practice had been to provide dedicated prostitutes, but the legislation passed in 1868 allowed for something more ambitious, regulating prostitution in wider areas. Nevertheless, for all the precedents it set, the demands it made and the pressure it brought to bear, the military did not force regulation on the wider sphere, nor could it have done so: for that, it relied on civilian allies, led by medical professionals and certain members of the colonial government.

When regulation was debated and implemented in Bombay, doctors played an important part by virtue of their position in the military and the municipal (and other tiers of) government, their socially sanctioned authority in matters of sexuality and sexual health, and their professional involvement in operating the system. When Crawford introduced regulation in Bombay, he decided that it should be 'worked under the immediate orders of the Health Officer'.[64] Later, exercising their special licence to speak about sexual matters, doctors played an important part in lobbying and petitioning for the introduction, and later reintroduction, of regulation in Bombay. They collated medical statistics that appeared to show steady increases in the number of cases of venereal disease and, as the city's sanitary commissioner put it, to 'prove that the disease has assumed proportions which are becoming matters of grave anxiety to those entrusted with the superintendence of the public health'.[65] Doctors actively defended their privileged position within the politics of sexual health and regulation, asserting the ignorance of others. Health Officer Weir attributed 'violent opposition' to regulation to ignorance – 'the nature and vitality of syphilis being imperfectly understood'.[66] Consequently, when opponents of regulation entered the political fray, they were forced to justify and defend themselves against explicit or implicit charges that they acted without adequate medical knowledge. Thus, for example, an editorial in the *Times of India* explained previous silence on the subject, and justified a late intervention:

> We have hitherto refrained from even alluding to a subject which has an importance of its own, but which is so unsavoury that as long as the public interests did not urgently call for its treatment we thought it best to pass over the question *sub silentio*. But as it is quite evident that the official mind is revolving the propriety of re-introducing the Contagious Diseases Act, and as the advantages of that course are set forth at length in pamphlets and letters, the time has come to point out to those who are ventilating the subject the real tendency of the measure which they recommend.[67]

The editorial went on to charge those who administered the Act – doctors – with 'corruption, extortion, and oppression'.[68] Doing so, it both challenged *and* acknowledged the privileged power of doctors over the whole question of regulation. More generally, the contestation of medical power, together with the failure of doctors – and of military and other champions of the system – to retain the system or secure its speedy reintroduction, qualify any assertions about medical and military influence, pointing to the significance of other political forces, particularly those in local government. The chequered history of regulation in Bombay was a product not simply of the military, or the medical or the government, but of intersections between each of these forces.

As explained above, the Government of India oversaw the adoption and administration of the Indian CD Act in Bombay, as in other localities, though it did not impose or administer the system directly.[69] It advised and directed the Bombay authorities, through a series of memoranda on medical, administrative and financial aspects of the subject. The inspector-general of the Indian Medical Department wrote to the government of Bombay, commenting on the means by which it had introduced the Act to Bombay.[70] The Government of India also determined how the system should be funded in Bombay, deciding – in the face of local disagreements – that half the cost should be provided at the municipal level, half by the presidential government.[71] The government of Bombay, responding to the enactment of the Indian CD Act (1868), appointed a committee – including representation from the new municipal government – to consider whether the Act should be extended to the city; the committee promptly recommending that it should.[72] The Bombay government duly agreed to match the municipal government's expenditure on the system of Rs (rupees) 40,000, later reduced to 30,000.[73] It then monitored the way in which its money was spent, and intervened in the day-to-day administration of regulation, for example in the selection of premises for a lock hospital.[74]

The municipal authority also played an important part in the adoption of the Indian CD Act in Bombay. As already explained, this tier of government had been established largely to combat sanitary problems in the city.[75] Reflecting on the first years of the municipal authority, the chair of the bench of justices reflected that the first commissioner had 'acted boldly' and 'acted effectively'.[76] Crawford continued, as he had begun, to use his considerable powers to bring about sanitary reform. Thus it was that he managed, in the face of moral and financial objections to the system, to extend the Indian CD Act to the city of Bombay. The system was not to be in force for long, however, for the bench ultimately refused to pay for it, or to bankroll Crawford's allegedly extravagant administration. The justices represented the view that, since Bombay's finances were precarious – its brief boom had not outlasted the American Civil War, which had temporarily diverted English cotton buyers from their traditional suppliers – its expenditure should be cautious.[77] They had initially agreed to pay half the costs of regulation in the city, but when they found they could not charge prostitutes for their registration and licences,[78] and that the system would therefore cost more than originally anticipated, they decided to reduce their contribution,[79] and then refused to pay anything at all, forcing the termination of the system after less than two years' operation.[80] Regulation – which in its first year consumed Rs 41,280 of the total municipal budget of Rs 34,38,294[81] – was one of the casualties of Crawford's regime, which the justices ultimately brought down, vetoing his budget and forcing his resignation in 1871.[82]

A stronger form of regulation

Crawford's desire to outdo British municipal government extended to his policy on regulation, which went beyond its metropolitan counterparts, while it realised the potential that was inherent – but latent, until adopted and adapted at the local level – in Indian legislation.[83] Bombay's CD Act, which remained in force from 1 May 1870 through 30 March 1872, included a series of provisions under the Indian CD Act (1868).[84] The Bombay Act provided for the registration and medical examination of 'all common prostitutes' living within the city, under the supervision of a health officer.[85] It would be unlawful 'for any female known to be a common prostitute to reside within any part of the city of Bombay . . . without the permission of the Commissioner of Police', or for anyone to 'keep a brothel within the limits of the city of Bombay, except by permission of the Commissioner of Police'.[86] Once registered, prostitutes were required either to attend weekly examinations at a designated inspection office or, if found to be diseased, to submit to medical treatment at the Lock Hospital.

Statistical summaries of registration, published in the quarterly and annual health reports, show that in the first year of registration, a total of 1,875 prostitutes were registered, and of these 346 (18 per cent) were found to be diseased. A close look at table 5.1 shows that registered and diseased prostitutes were spread between a number of wards, and were not only resident in the most predictable areas – the European cantonment and suburb on the southern tip of the island (Colaba) and the Native Old Town (including Bhoolwshwur, or Bhuleshwar) – but were present in similar numbers in the Native New Town (Girgaum, Kamateepoora, or Kamathipura) and the semi-rural fringes of the city (including Mazagon). In a typical month – September 1871 – 765 women were examined, 102 of whom were confined.[87] The system's detailed surveillance – it recorded each woman's name, caste, age, birth-place, previous occupation, duration of residence in Bombay and marital status – showed that the typical prostitute was an Indian woman under 30 years of age, who had been born in India and migrated to the city of Bombay, and was either a widow or unmarried. The profile of prostitutes broadly reflected that of the city, comprising approximately two-thirds Hindu, one-fifth Muslim, and one-twentieth each Christian and Parsi.[88] Table 5.1 shows that, in comparison with their numerical presence in the city, Muslims were over-represented and Parsis under-represented among registered

Table 5.1 *Statistical digest of registration of prostitutes in Bombay, 1870*

Area/caste	Colaba, Dobytulao	Bhoolwshwur	Market	Girgaum
Hindu	210	204	112	131
Mussulman	8	257	198	69
Parsi	–	–	–	–
Christian	2	27	3	17
Total	220	488	313	217
Found to be diseased	52	78	75	48

	Mazagon	Kamateepoora and Parell	Total reg.	Diseased
Hindu	133	237	1027	19
Mussulman	131	73	736	130
Parsi	–	2	2	–
Christian	10	51	110	23
Total	274	363	1875	–
Found to be diseased	52	41	–	346

Source: IOL, PP3800GF, T. G. Hewlett, Report of the Bombay Health Officer, in *Annual Report of the Municipal Commissioner of Bombay, for 1870* (Bombay: Education Society's Press, 1871), p. 12.
Note: Place names in the table are as they appear in Reports of the Health Officer, from which this data is taken. Camateepoora is spelled with a K in some reports, a C in others; it also appears as Kamathipura and Kamatipura. Most spellings vary widely between different sources.

prostitutes. Among the prostitute community there were also small minorities of over-40s, Europeans and married women.[89] The medical officer, writing in 1872, was 'glad to say that [he had] not as yet found any native of the United Kingdom among the Prostitutes'.[90] The mother country was better represented among the clients of registered prostitutes: sailors, who were known to favour brothels (which were also regulated under the Indian CD Act) and soldiers, who tended to wander the city when they wanted a prostitute.[91]

As Crawford intended, regulation in Bombay – as more widely in India – outdid its metropolitan counterparts, both substantively and geographically. The experience in Bombay bears out Levine's general conclusion that 'Indian women were subject to closer control than were British women'.[92] Whereas the domestic Acts concentrated on street-walking and stopped short of regulating brothels, their colonial counterparts went further, intruding into private spaces and actively

[153]

working to keep prostitutes off the streets.[93] Ballhatchet concurs that the Indian law was harsher, with no fixed limit to the time a woman could be detained in hospital and no mechanism with which she could appeal. In India, a woman was held 'until cured',[94] whereas in England she was held 'until discharged'[95] – but for no more than 3 months without special certification (from the 'Chief Medical Officer of the Hospital in which she is detained, or the Visiting Surgeon for the place whence she came or was brought'), and no more than 6 months under any 'One Certificate'.[96] In India a woman had no right of appeal, whereas in England she had the right to be 'conveyed before a Justice' for that purpose.[97]

The relative strength of the Indian provisions should, however, be qualified. Though the *Times of India* claimed that women lived 'in constant terror of being brought within [regulation's] hateful meshes', many escaped those entanglements.[98] In Bombay the majority of prostitutes failed to register, and many of those who did register failed to attend examinations. The authorities rarely imposed the penalties that were available to them, and non-compliance became a subject for debate and scrutiny. In one review of the system, the Bombay government reported, for example, that of 356 defaulting prostitutes only 83 were brought before the magistrates. For no apparent reason, no action was taken with the rest. Some explanation on this point is necessary. Of those prosecuted 25 were warned and discharged, one was sentenced to simple imprisonment for a day and fines of Rs 1–10 were inflicted on the others.[99] The government of Bombay acknowledged the limited extents to which the Act was enforced in its principal city and to which 'clandestine prostitution' remained beyond the reach of the system and the law.[100]

There was, however, one area in which the system adopted by Crawford went well beyond its English counterparts. In England the system applied only to 'certain Naval and Military Stations',[101] whereas in India it was extended much more widely – in Bombay to 'every common prostitute residing within the limits of the city'.[102] This is consistent with Levine's more general argument that whereas the domestic CD Acts were never extended to the civil population, their colonial counterparts 'grew quickly beyond the strictly military purview'.[103] Attempts to extend the English system – championed by organisations such as the Association for Promoting the Extension of the CD Act of 1866 to the Civilian Population – were weakened by a rising tide of opposition to the system. Arguments for extension were rewarded to a limited extent in 1869, when the new CD law extended provisions well beyond their initially defined military limits.[104]

Walkowitz argues that, applying to larger urban areas, which were not completely controlled by the military and which had substantial civilian communities, the new laws 'broke new ground as domestic social measures, creating new medical institutions and new precedents for police and medical supervision of the lives of the poor'.[105] Nevertheless, the system's application to a number of medium-sized port cities represented a tentative extension, in comparison to provisions for India, which directly affected the indigenous population in cities where the legislation was in force.[106] Regulation in India, and specifically in Bombay, did not reach tentatively into civilian quarters; it systematically encompassed them, reaching throughout the 'limits of the city'.[107] Whereas the Cantonment Act (1864) distinguished and regulated only those prostitutes who worked for European soldiers, the new law applied more widely, regulating the prostitutes who worked outside cantonments.[108]

The form of regulation adopted in Bombay, stronger and more geographically extensive than its English counterpart, was an effect not only of the Indian statute but also the city's ambitious, authoritarian, colonial government. Crawford and his colleagues wanted the city they governed to be larger, more prosperous and – as they often put it – more modern than its metropolitan counterparts. The municipal health officer had begun his work with an official fact-finding visit to England, studying the sanitary arrangements in thirty or more towns and cities.[109] Hewlett was not content to copy England, and his report recommended sanitary solutions that had been contemplated in England but would not be introduced there for some years, including what would later be known as slum clearance and reconstruction.[110] He contributed to the move, which Crawford championed, from *laissez-faire* government to comprehensive planning.[111] The city's pretensions towards the cutting edge of municipal government were taken seriously. Florence Nightingale complimented the governor of Bombay: 'If we do not take care, Bombay will outstrip us in the sanitary race.'[112] The *Times of India* concurred: in an editorial printed in 1869,[113] the paper compared Bombay with Paris, presenting the former as a contender in the race for modernity in which the French city was widely regarded as a frontrunner. It argued that the city must play a full part in 'the race of improvement side by side with the great cities of Europe'.[114] The rhetoric of modernisation was deployed to justify ever greater interventions in the lives of colonial subjects. Though many plans remained on the drawing board, in the dreams of planners and governors, those for the regulation of prostitution were executed, within a broader drive towards modernity.

Conclusions

This chapter has illustrated how and why colonies sometimes set the agenda in the field of imperial sexuality politics. Their leading role was shaped by the possibilities that lay within geographically concentrated regimes of colonial power, which generated political and governmental ideas and forms.

The consequences of this were mixed, contradicting strands of Eurocentrism, but not in any challenge to imperialism. On the contrary, colonial regimes such as Crawford's may have represented the Empire's cutting edge, generating colonial solutions to colonial problems and then potentially re-exporting them. Far from challenging the imperial order, this illustrated the commonplace practice of allowing colonial representatives latitude to generate solutions locally – through the relative autonomy of responsible governments. The imperial order was also upheld – caricatured even – in the substance of this system, as represented by Butler. Writing to Dyer, she claimed:

> A Bombay magistrate wrote to me that on the first introduction of British State harlotry in Bombay, hundreds of poor women fled affrighted from the town; many were never heard of; some perished in the forests; others were found dead at the bottom of wells, having committed suicide to escape an infamy which they could endure not even to contemplate.[115]

Unfettered by the moral dilemmas and accountability that restricted domestic legislation, the British in India were apparently free to do whatever they needed – subject only to financial constraints; and in Bombay, unlike some colonies, money flowed relatively freely, albeit for limited periods of time. When Crawford claimed that 'large towns like Bombay cannot be managed without large funds', he alluded to the kind of management of which most municipal governments only dreamed.[116] And though Crawford was not able to keep regulation in force for very long, those who opposed it proved equally unable to keep it from the city's statute books. In 1880, when reintroduction was proposed, disparate voices of opposition coalesced, including those of the journalists (in particular, of the *Times of India*, discussed above) and activists quoted throughout this chapter, religious leaders and municipal officials.[117] In the event, they proved unequal to the champions of regulation. These localised forces – led once again by a combination of military,[118] medical[119] and governmental[120] bodies – helped keep the system in place until the Act was suspended in 1888[121] (only to be replaced with further Cantonments Acts in 1889 and subsequent years[122]).

Yet regulation relied on the forces of imperialism – including the specific strands of the colonial establishment – lining up against the many obstacles to this evidently objectionable system, something that proved difficult to sustain for long periods. The brief time for which regulation remained in force in Bombay emphasises that while colonies were often the product of intense concentrations of situated power, that power was tenuous due to the contradictions and fractures within the eclectic colonial order, and also its constant contestation. Had the discussions of regulation in Bombay and Sierra Leone, in this and the last chapter, not focused so specifically on colonial power, they might have traced the voices of a range of others, which also played significant parts in sexuality politics. Other discussions of regulation have been limited in similar ways: for instance, Stoler could be criticised for marginalising the experiences and voices of colonised peoples in *Carnal Knowledge and Imperial Power* – not before page 162, in a book of 217 pages of text, does she turn from the perspectives of colonisers and colonial authorities to those of the colonised, finally considering how Javanese men and women who worked as servants in late colonial Indonesia saw their Dutch employers, and in particular how they perceived physically intimate relationships with Dutch children in their care. This empirical bias reflects both a stated emphasis on colonial governments' positions on regulation and the limitations of what are essentially imperial archives, the bases for partial research and provisional knowledge. But, as the subaltern studies movement also showed, there are other ways to do research, other sources to tap and ways to interpret them, through and beyond a critique of the imperial archive. Of course, it is not easy to trace the experiences of colonial subjects who were drawn into or actively involved themselves in sexuality politics. Sources on prostitutes, for instance, are more elusive than those on colonial governments, though researchers have been able to trace and produce a range of materials, including oral histories and less conventionally social scientific sources such as songs, sayings and street vocabularies, and textual sources including chapbooks, poems, letters and non-European newspapers.[123]

The final chapter of this book brings the discussion back from elites and centres of colonial power to colonial subjects and colonisers. Doing so, it challenges overstatements about the reach and dominance of imperial power, and about the ways in which geographies of power may have permitted progressive or extreme forms of governance. First, however, there is more to say about the generative possibilities of colonial space. Whereas this chapter has examined the productivity of the margins with reference to material colonial geographies, the next turns to their metaphorical counterparts, exploring the form and significance for sexuality politics of imaginative and discursive colonial geographies.

Notes

1 P. Levine, 'Rereading the 1890s: venereal disease as "constitutional crisis" in Britain and British India', *Journal of Asian Studies*, 55:3 (1996), 585–612, at 590.
2 Editorial, *Times of India* (6 September 1876), p. 2.
3 Editorial, *Times of India* (6 September 1876), p. 2.
4 Editorial, *Times of India* (6 September 1876), p. 2.
5 P. Rabinow, *French Modern: Norms and Forms of the Social Environment* (Cambridge, MA: MIT Press, 1989), p. 289.
6 Rabinow, *French Modern*, p. 295.
7 G. Wright, *Politics of Design in French Colonial Urbanism* (Chicago, IL: University of Chicago Press, 1991), p. 2.
8 Wright, *Politics of Design in French Colonial Urbanism*, p. 3.
9 Stoler, *Race and the Education of Desire*, p. 16.
10 Robert Peel, 1812, quoted by D. Wood, *Trinidad in Transition: The Years After Slavery* (Oxford: Oxford University Press, 1968), p. 31; see also R. Home, *Of Planting and Planning: The Making of British Colonial Cities* (London: E. & F. N. Spon, 1997), p. 7.
11 Wright, *Politics of Design in French Colonial Urbanism*, p. 6.
12 Home, *Of Planting and Planning*.
13 'The revenue of Bombay', *Times of India* (9 January 1869), p. 2.
14 Ogborn, 'Law and discipline'; Ogborn, *Spaces of Modernity*, p. 45.
15 Vaughan, *Curing Their Ills*, p. 10.
16 Rabinow, *French Modern*, p. 259.
17 F. Cooper and L. A. Stoler, *Tensions of Empire: Colonial Cultures in a Bourgeois World* (Berkeley: University of California Press, 1997), p. 20.
18 Levine, *Prostitution, Race and Politics*, p. 31.
19 India Office Library, British Library, London (hereafter IOL), PP3800GF, T. S. Weir, Health Officer's Annual Report, in *Annual Report of the Municipal Commissioner of Bombay for 1873* (Bombay: Education Society's Press, 1874), p. 5.
20 In 1872 there were 25,194 native and 10,454 European troops in the presidency, of which 1,887 and 470 respectively were garrisoned in Bombay city: IOL, V/24/3717, *Ninth Annual Report of the Sanitary Commissioner for the Government of Bombay* (Bombay: Government Central Press, 1872), pp. D24, E1.
21 D. J. Hastings (ed.), *Bombay Buccaneers: Memories and Reminiscences of the Royal Indian Navy* (London: Basca, 1986), p. 6.
22 H. J. Wilson, *Rough Record of Events and Incidents Connected with the Repeal of the 'Contagious Diseases Acts, 1864–69', in the United Kingdom, and of the Movement Against State Regulation of Vice in India and the Colonies, 1858–1906* (Sheffield: Parker, 1907), p. 7.
23 IOL, V/24/3709, A. H. Leith, *Report by President of the Sanitary Commission for Bombay, for the year 1864* (Bombay: Education Society's Press, 1865).
24 In 1867, for instance, it stated that in the space of a year there had been 2,556 admissions, representing 212 per 1,000 men, and 15 per cent of the entire sickness: Report of the Sanitary Commission for Bombay for the year 1866, House of Commons Command Paper 27 (1867), p. 11.
25 For example, a naval spokesman praised the system for reducing to 10 the instances of primary syphilis among a combined crew of 1,482, who spent 9 days' shore leave in the city in 1883: India Office Records, British Library, London (hereafter IOR), V/24/2289, Report by B. Gordon, Chief Medical Officer at the Lock Hospital Bombay, on the Contagious Diseases Acts in Bombay (12 June 1883), p. 8.
26 Levine, *Prostitution, Race and Politics*, p. 2.
27 J. B. Harrison, 'Allahabad: a sanitary history', in K. Ballhatchet and J. Harrison (eds), *City in South Asia* (London: Curzon Press, 1980), pp. 166–195.
28 IOL, V/24/3709, Leith, *Report of the Sanitary Commission for Bombay, for the year 1864*, p. 1.

29 'Thomas Gillham Hewlett', in F. Boase, *Modern English Biography* (London: Frank Cass, 1965), vol. 1, p. 1458.
30 Vaughan, *Curing Their Ills*.
31 Levine, *Prostitution, Race and Politics*, p. 61.
32 Levine, *Prostitution, Race and Politics*.
33 Home, *Of Planting and Planning*.
34 A. H. Leith, *Report on the Sanitary State of the Island of Bombay* (Bombay: Education Society's Press, 1864), pp. 24–25.
35 A. P. Kaminsky, *India Office 1880–1910* (London: Mansell, 1986).
36 E. C. Cox, *A Short History of the Bombay Presidency* (Bombay: Thacker & Co., 1887).
37 WL, JB345.02534, T. S. Weir (Health Officer), *Report on the Prevention of Venereal Diseases in Bombay* (Bombay: Times of India Steam Press, 1877), p. 18.
38 IOR, P/441/53, Report by the Municipal Commissioner for the City of Bombay (23 September 1870).
39 IOR, P/441/53, Abstract of Proceedings of the Government of Bombay, General Department (1870), p. 298.
40 M. Dossal, *Imperial Designs and Indian Realities: The Planning of Bombay City, 1845–1875* (Oxford: Oxford University Press, 1991), p. 143.
41 Dossal, *Imperial Designs and Indian Realities*, p. 84.
42 IOR, SV252, *Bombay Municipal Record for 1868* (Bombay: Bombay Gazette Press, 1869), p. 100; Home, *Of Planting and Planning*.
43 Maclean speaking at a quarterly meeting of the bench of justices in Bombay in April 1869, as reported in the *Times of India* (3 April 1869), p. 2.
44 IOR, SV252, *Bombay Municipal Record for 1868*, p. 100.
45 Maclean, at quarterly meeting of the bench of justices, April 1869, *Times of India* (3 April 1869), p. 2.
46 Dossal, *Imperial Designs and Indian Realities*, p. 213.
47 Anonymous, *Broken Pledge: A Brief Summary of Facts and Arguments. On the Immunity of Prosecution Offered by the Government of Bombay to Persons Giving Evidence on Charges of Corruption Brought Against A. T. Crawford* (London: A. Bonner, 1890), p. 2.
48 *Times of India* (3 April 1869), p. 2.
49 Sharp, Routledge, Philo and Paddison, *Entanglements of Power*, p. 1.
50 *Bombay Gazette Overland Summary* (7 May 1870), p. 1.
51 IOL, PP3800GF, J. Lumsdaine, Report of Health Officer, in *Annual Report of the Municipal Commissioner of Bombay for 1868*, p. 15.
52 WL, JB345.02534, Weir, *Report on the Prevention of Venereal Diseases in Bombay*, p. 14.
53 IOR P/441/53, Abstract of Proceedings of the Government of Bombay, General Department (6 October 1870), p. 285: Letter dated 30 September 1870 from the Inspector-General, Indian Medical Department.
54 WL, JB345.02534, Weir, *Report on the Prevention of Venereal Diseases in Bombay*, p. 14.
55 IOR P/441/53, Abstract of proceedings of the Government of Bombay, General Department (6 April 1870), pp. 15–20: Letter dated 23 March 1870 from W. F. Knapp to the Chief Secretary to Government.
56 See also Levine, *Prostitution, Race and Politics*, p. 31.
57 IOR, P/439, Abstract of Proceedings of the Government of Bombay, General Department (1 June 1872), No. 2,185: 'Petition from certain dancing girls of Belgaum, dated 22nd May 1872'; IOR, P/439, Abstract of Proceedings of the Government of Bombay, General Department (16 October 1872): No. 4009: Government resolution.
58 S. Banerjee, *Under the Raj: Prostitution in Colonial Bengal* (New York: Monthly Review Press, 1998).
59 See, for example: Bombay Sanitary Commission, Report of the Sanitary Commission for Bombay for 1866, House of Commons Command Paper 27, 1867, p. 12.

60 IOR, V/25/840/4, *Proceedings of Meetings of the Sanitary Commission for Bombay (4 July 1865)* (Bombay: Bombay Education Society's Press, 1865).

61 Bombay Sanitary Commission, *Report of the Sanitary Commission for Bombay for 1865*, House of Commons Command Paper 529, 1866, p. 13.

62 Bombay Sanitary Commission, *Report of the Sanitary Commission for Bombay for 1865*, p. 4.

63 IOR, V/25/840/4, *Proceedings of Meetings of the Sanitary Commission for Bombay (22 August 1865)*, p. 76.

64 WL, JB3940119972, T. G. Hewlett, Acting Sanitary Commissioner, *Reports on the Prevention of Venereal Diseases in Bombay* (Bombay: Times of India Steam Press, 1877), p. 4.

65 WL, JB3940119972, Hewlett, *Reports on the Prevention of Venereal Diseases in Bombay*, p. 3.

66 WL, JB345.02534, Weir, *Report on the Prevention of Venereal Diseases in Bombay*, p. 7.

67 Editorial, *Times of India* (6 September 1876), p. 2.

68 Editorial, *Times of India* (6 September 1876), p. 2.

69 Levine, 'Rereading the 1890s', p. 590.

70 IOR, P/441/53, Abstract of Proceedings of the Government of Bombay, General Department (26 March 1870), No. 852: Report by the Inspector General, Indian Medical Department.

71 Ballhatchet, *Race, Sex and Class under the Raj.*

72 'The extension of the Contagious Diseases Act to Bombay', *Bombay Gazette Overland Summary* (10 April 1869), p. 3; 'Report of the committee', *Bombay Gazette Overland Summary* (17 August 1868), p. 1.

73 IOR, P/441/53, Abstract of Proceedings of the Government of Bombay, General Department (16 December 1870), No. 3,072: Letter from Municipal Commissioner for the City of Bombay.

74 IOR, P/441/53, Abstract of Proceedings of the Government of Bombay, General Department (20 February 1869), p. 408: Letter from Acting Collector of Bombay.

75 IOR, SV252, *Bombay Municipal Record for 1868* (Bombay: Bombay Gazette Press, 1869), p. 99.

76 IOR, SV252, *Bombay Municipal Record for 1868*, p. 100.

77 Dossal, *Imperial Designs and Indian Realities*, p. 202.

78 IOR, P/441/53, Abstract of Proceedings of the Government of Bombay, General Department (1870), pp. 79–80.

79 Report on meeting of bench of justices: 'Introduction of the Contagious Diseases Prevention Act', *Times of India* (8 April 1869), p. 1; IOL, PP3800GF, *Annual Report of the Municipal Commissioner of Bombay, with Annual Reports of the Health Officer and Executive Engineer, for 1869* (Bombay: Education Society's Press, 1870), p. 1.

80 IOL, V/25/840/17, T. G. Hewlett, *Bombay Health Officer's Report for the First Quarter of 1872* (Bombay: Times of India Office, 1872), p. 5.

81 'Bombay municipal commissioner's budget for 1870', *Times of India* (21 October 1869), p. 3.

82 Home, *Of Planting and Planning.*

83 Dossal, *Imperial Designs and Indian Realities*, p. 219.

84 WL, JB345.02534, Weir, *Report on the Prevention of Venereal Diseases in Bombay*, p. 18.

85 IOR, P/441/53, Abstract of Proceedings of the Government of Bombay, General Department (April 1870), p. 21: Rules under Sections 5, 11 and 21 of Act XIV of 1868 (the Contagious Diseases Act).

86 IOR, P/441/53, Abstract of Proceedings of the Government of Bombay, General Department (April 1870), pp. 21–26: Rules under Sections 5, 11 and 21 of Act XIV of 1868 (the Contagious Diseases Act).

87 IOL, V/25/840/16, T. G. Hewlett, *Bombay Health Officer's Report for the Third Quarter of 1871* (Bombay: Times of India Office, 1871), p. 13.

88 M. Kosambi, *Bombay in Transition: The Growth and Social Ecology of a Colonial City* (Stockholm: Almqvist & Wiksell International, 1986), p. 60: figures for 1881.

89 IOR, P/441/53, Abstract of Proceedings of the Government of Bombay, General Department (April 1870), pp. 21–26: Rules under Sections 5, 11 and 21 of Act XIV of 1868 (the Contagious Diseases Act).

90 IOL, V/25/840/16, Hewlett, *Bombay Health Officer's Report for the Third Quarter of 1871*, p. 11.

91 The surgeon-general stated in 1885 that 'the soldier avails himself' to 'illicit prostitution' to a 'much larger extent than the sailor': IOR, V/24/2289, W. J. Moore, Surgeon General with the Government of Bombay, Contagious Diseases Acts, Bombay Report (9 July 1885).

92 P. Levine, 'Venereal disease, prostitution, and the politics of empire: the case of British India', *Journal of the History of Sexuality*, 4:4 (1994), 579–602, at 585.

93 Levine, *Prostitution, Race and Politics*.

94 IOR, P/441/53, Abstract of Proceedings of the Government of Bombay, General Department (April 1870), pp. 21–26: Rules under Sections 5, 11 and 21 of Act XIV of 1868 (the Contagious Diseases Act).

95 An Act for the better Prevention of Contagious Diseases at certain Naval and Military Stations (England and Ireland), 11 June 1866, 29 and 30 Vict., c.35, para.22.

96 An Act for the better Prevention of Contagious Diseases at certain Naval and Military Stations, 29 and 30 Vict., c.35, para.24.

97 An Act for the better Prevention of Contagious Diseases at certain Naval and Military Stations, 29 and 30 Vict., c.35, para.25.

98 Editorial, *Times of India* (6 September 1876), p. 2.

99 IOR, V/24/2289, J. Monteath, Acting Under Secretary to Government, Bombay Report on the Working of the Contagious Diseases Acts during the six months ending 30 November 1883.

100 This was made most explicit when the system was revived in the early 1880s, and was subject to sustained scrutiny. T. B. Beatty, surgeon general with the government of Bombay, reported in 1884 that 'the Act could never have been said to have much effect towards diminishing the civil population owing to the great prevalence of clandestine prostitution and the limited way in which the Act has been worked': IOR, V/24/2289, T. B. Beatty, Bombay Report on Contagious Diseases Acts (5 July 1884).

101 An Act for the better Prevention of Contagious Diseases at certain Naval and Military Stations, 29 and 30 Vict., c.35.

102 IOR, P/441/53, Abstract of Proceedings of the Government of Bombay, General Department (April 1870), pp. 21–26: Rules under Sections 5, 11 and 21 of Act XIV of 1868 (the Contagious Diseases Act).

103 Levine, *Prostitution, Race and Politics*, p. 5.

104 Walkowitz, *Prostitution and Victorian Society*, 88.

105 Walkowitz, *Prostitution and Victorian Society*, 88.

106 Levine, 'Venereal disease, prostitution, and the politics of empire', p. 581.

107 IOR, P/441/53, Abstract of Proceedings of the Government of Bombay, General Department (April 1870), p. 22: Rules under Sections 5, 11 and 21 of Act XIV of 1868 (the Contagious Diseases Act).

108 Banerjee, *Under the Raj*, p. 64.

109 At the request of the under secretary of state for India, Hewlett visited and reported on sanitary improvements in England and their relevance to India: T. G. Hewlett, *A Report of a Sanitary Tour by Surgeon T. G. Hewlett, Health Officer of Bombay* (London: Eyre & Spottiswoode for H.M.S.O., 1869), p. 4; IOL, PP3800GF, T. G. Hewlett, Report of the Health Officer, in *Annual Report of the Municipal Commissioner of Bombay, for 1869*, p. 5.

110 IOL, PP3800GF, T. G. Hewlett, Report of the Health Officer, in *Annual Report of the Municipal Commissioner of Bombay, for 1869*, p. 14.

111 Home, *Of Planting and Planning*, p. 73.

112 Home, *Of Planting and Planning*, p. 73.
113 Editorial, *Times of India* (1 January 1869), p. 2.
114 'The revenue of Bombay', *Times of India* (9 January 1869), p. 3.
115 Dyer, *Slavery Under the British Flag*, p. 13.
116 IOR, SV252, *Bombay Municipal Record for 1868* (Bombay: Bombay Gazette Press, 1869), p. 101.
117 Religious leaders, including the Bishop of Bombay and the senior chaplain of the Church of Scotland, and municipal officials, such as Vishvanath Narayan Mandlik, chairman of the Municipal Corporation: Ballhatchet, *Race, Sex and Class*, p. 48.
118 For example, C. L. Ridout, staff surgeon on HMS *Tourmaline*, attributed 'the small amount of disease that has prevailed among the crew of this ship' to the Contagious Diseases Act in Bombay: IOR, V/24/2289, B. Gordon, Chief Medical Officer, Lock Hospital Bombay, Contagious Diseases Acts, Bombay Report (12 June 1883), p. 17.
119 Successive surgeons-general asserted that the Acts had been effective: IOR, V/24/2289, T. B. Beatty, Surgeon General with the Government of Bombay, Contagious Diseases Acts, Bombay Report (22 June 1883), p. 2; IOR, V/24/2289, W. J. Moore, Surgeon General, Memorandum on the Contagious Diseases Act (October 1886), p. 7.
120 For example, T. D. Mackenzie credited the system with bringing about a reduction of venereal disease among sailors: IOR, V/24/2289, T. D. Mackenzie, Acting Chief Secretary to Government, Contagious Diseases Acts, Bombay Report on the Working of the Acts during the six months ending 30 September 1886.
121 IOR, V/24/2289, J. Pinkerton, Surgeon General with the Government of Bombay, Contagious Diseases Acts, Bombay Report (30 August 1888), p. 3.
122 Banerjee, *Under the Raj*, p. 167.
123 White, *Comforts of Home*; Banerjee, *Under the Raj*, p. 149; B. Joardar, *Prostitution in Nineteenth and Early Twentieth Century Calcutta* (New Delhi: Inter-India Publications, 1985).

CHAPTER SIX

Drawing distinctions: Richard Burton's interventions on sex between men

Building pictures of the spatiality of contested imperialism and the 'productivity of the margins' in imperial sexuality politics, I have focused primarily on material spaces – the concrete geographies of colonial governance and power in Sierra Leone and Bombay, for instance. I have alluded to ways of seeing these spaces, but have deferred a more detailed investigation of imaginative geographies and the parts they played in imperial sexuality politics. This chapter juxtaposes the preceding material histories and geographies with their less tangible counterparts, traced through a series of cultural and textual methods and sources. At first this might seem to break the thread of this book, but ultimately the excursion into imaginative geographies will lead back to some familiar political ground: the contested regulation of sexuality in the British Empire and sexualised imperialism in the same space.

Colonial geographical imagination, in common with colonial discourse more generally, revolves around a dualism between metropolitan and non-metropolitan spaces and spheres. This has particular resonance for sexuality politics, concerned as they often are with the representation and contestation of moral distinctions and boundaries. Stead's interventions on the age of consent, for instance, used images of pure and impure spaces, and journeys between them, to make distinctions between innocent and corrupted femininity. On one end of the moral spectrum there was London – 'Hell', in the words of one 'Christian lady' whose letter appeared in the *Pall Mall Gazette.*[1] This was set against the purity of the country and particularly the countryside: 'Young girls from the country' were 'fresh and rosy', pictures of innocence and vulnerability.[2] Stead's distinction between purity and impurity traced another, more general, between metropolitan and non-metropolitan spheres, the latter reaching beyond Britain to its colonies. Stead portrayed Britain's nearest overseas colony as an extension of

[163]

rural and provincial England, in which Irish girls were simpler and more naïve than their English counterparts: 'The Irish girl, being innocent and inexperienced, setting foot for the first time in a foreign city, without friends and not knowing where to go', was easily trapped.[3] Stead referred more obliquely to other colonies and colonial sexualities. Working-class districts of London were often identified as a domestic counterpart of 'darkest Africa', fearfully regarded by middle-class observers as unknown, unwashed and threatening. In keeping with this tradition, Stead claimed to be 'shedding a flood of light upon these dark places'.[4] Like a host of other social commentators and writers of erotic travel, he thereby portrayed racial and ethnic minorities and the under-classes in metaphorically colonial, sexualised terms. For some writers, this was a formula for pornography, in which urban travellers encountered erotic possibilities, vice and promiscuity.[5] For instance, in the anonymous *Sins of the Cities of the Plain; or, Confessions of a Mary-Anne* (1881), a symbolically racialised East End 'bootblack boy' is seduced by a wealthy West End gentleman, whose voyeurism and exploitative conduct mirrored that of colonists and sexual tourists. In other hands, sexualised metaphorically colonial discourse assumed a different potency, as a vehicle for interventions in social and cultural politics.

Stead used this conventional geographical rhetoric to literally *draw* distinctions and thereby negotiate boundaries. For all the taboos it was said to have smashed, Stead's sexual geography was deeply conventional. It worked because it was already familiar to many readers, therefore plausible as a point of departure for political intervention. It echoed stories about the erotic and moral journeys of girls and women, such as the classic work of English pornography *Fanny Hill* (1748–1749).[6] It was indebted to travel guides, which variously steered women away from sexual possibilities and men towards them.[7] It reproduced almost timeless distinctions between what Raymond Williams called the 'worldliness' of the city and the 'innocence . . . and simple virtue' of the country – the 'whole society'.[8] Stead's 'country', defined in opposition to the capital, appeared generically simple and innocent. His 'home' was the lost idealised place left behind.[9] Lamenting the fate of 'young girls who have been tenderly trained and carefully educated *at home*',[10] Stead echoed cultural conservatives such as John Ruskin, who argued that the woman in the home would be 'protected from all danger and temptation', away from the 'peril and trial' of the 'open world', a place best left to men.[11] This glossed the realities of home that many women experienced, both economically (many domestic workers were forced into part-time prostitution to supplement their inadequate incomes)[12] and sexually (the home was and is also a site of sexual danger for young people[13]). Stead's converse sexualisation of the non-metropolitan – the metaphorically colonial in 'darkest London' – was an equally false creation. These were, however, familiar and therefore accessible and plausible imagined geographies. Stead used them to great effect, drawing in readers and attracting them to a demonstration for the protection of girls and women, in the form of a higher age of consent (the Criminal Law Amendment Bill).[14]

Though he was primarily interested in the age of consent, Stead also intervened, albeit implicitly and somewhat mysteriously, in another sexual boundary dispute of his time. Male vulnerability was a subtext of the 'Maiden Tribute', based as it was on the corruption of not just seven maidens, but seven youths. Stead had chosen to introduce the youths, then to bury them with the barest of mentions, leaving them as a hidden subtext, an obvious and suggestive silence. A link might be made between this awkward silence in the 'Maiden Tribute' and new prohibitions against sex between male persons, which were included in the Criminal Law Amendment Act (1885).[15] Arguably Stead had helped place sex between men on the political agenda, if out of the reach of open debate. And there it remained. Those who spoke out against the new law tended to do so indirectly. The amendment had passed through Parliament with almost no discussion; and very little was said in public about its draconian provisions or the values behind them. Clearly, some taboos remained, the silences they engendered constraining and shaping sexuality politics.

It was in this context that Richard Francis Burton (1821–1890) charted and deployed a series of sexual geographies. Burton declared his contempt for the 'Mrs Grundyism of Victorian society'.[16] He asserted that men who have sex with men 'deserve, not prosecution but the pitiful care of the physician and the study of the psychologist';[17] but he articulated this point also in other ways, including coded sexual geographies. Burton found a number of advantages in writing geographically about sex. Like Stead, he saw that geographical writing could reach wide audiences and that its figurative imagery could be used to address metaphorical boundaries. More than Stead, Burton depended on this roundabout way of addressing sexual questions, because his subjects were particularly thorny ones. Writing geographically, he was able to assume the voice of a professional with some ostensibly scientific interest in – and authority to speak about – sex. He was also able to raise a subject while seeming to keep it at arms' length. Geographies, he found, provided a lens through which to peer at sexual subjects as if from afar; they afforded, too, a sense of imaginative control and freedom. In controllable, abstract, open, imaginative geographies it was possible to contemplate the socio-sexual order with a bird's eye view, a bigger picture in which to imagine and call for change.

Richard Burton's 'Sotadic Zone'

In the course of a long career as a soldier, adventurer and writer, Burton addressed sexual subjects on multiple levels and in a number of media. His biography demonstrates a lifelong interest in sexual cultures and attitudes. As a young soldier in India, he claimed to have been ordered to investigate the boy brothels of Karachi, writing a report for Sir Charles Napier, who commanded British forces in the recently conquered region of Sind.[18] Burton threw himself into this project, visiting 'all the porneia' in search of 'the fullest details',[19] but when his report fell into the hands of unsympathetic officials in the Bombay government, the young lieutenant was dismissed.[20] He later established a reputation as the author of and the protagonist in a series of entertaining, vividly set travel books, including *Personal Narrative of a Pilgrimage to El-Medinah and Meccah* (1855–1856), *First Footsteps in East Africa; or, An Exploration of Harar* (1856) and *The Lake Regions of Central Africa: A Picture of Exploration* (1860).[21] Burton smuggled sexual details into many of these written works, though he tended to relegate sex to the margins and allowed publishers to censor them when they insisted.[22] In his later travel writing, and more so his translations – including the *Kama Sutra of Vatsyayana* (1883) and *Ananga-Ranga, or the Hindu Art of Love* (1885) – Burton continued to write geographically, but brought sex to the forefront of his work, which he printed privately to avoid the interference of editors. His most sustained attention to sex between men appeared in his annotated translation of the *Plain and Literal Translation of* The Arabian Nights' Entertainments; or, The Book of a Thousand Nights and a Night (1885–1886).[23] The *Nights*, which included a long essay on 'pederasty', constituted Burton's most sustained contribution to a wider literature in which travel writers, anthropologists, geographers, visual artists and others mapped the non-European world in sexual terms.[24] In this essay, he drew together the sexual threads running through this text and his lifetime of reading, observation and experience.

Translating the *Nights*, Burton sexualised a collection of stories that was already a classic and a favourite in England and France.[25] As he put it, he offered readers an 'uncastrated'[26] version of stories that had suffered in the hands of censorious scholars, translators, editors and publishers. Burton claimed to translate without prejudice, resisting the temptation – that had plagued many of his predecessors

– to sanitise and censor. In addition, he took the opportunity to add sexual and other details, in extensive if often loosely tangential footnotes. And he appended extended essays on 'Pornography' and 'Pederasty' in the tenth of what grew to sixteen volumes. Burton arranged for the book to be privately printed, so he did not suffer the editorial intrusion and/or censorship of publishers, and he evaded the repercussions that might have come from formally publishing (rather than merely printing) erotica. This translation was more than competent, but, partly because it came in the wake of another, the well-crafted and literary work of John Payne, it was noted primarily for its sexual content.[27]

The sexual geography of Burton's *Nights* is spelled out most concisely in the terminal essay 'Pederasty', a practice which has been defined recently as 'sexual activity with pubertal boys',[28] though in Burton's time the term referred to relationships between older and younger males, the latter young men rather than children. Reading Burton, one must keep the nineteenth- rather than the twentieth-century definition in mind. Although fifty discursive pages are devoted to the subject, which Burton argues is 'geographical and climatic, not racial',[29] the main points are summarised neatly:

1   There exists what I shall call a 'Sotadic Zone', bounded westwards by the northern shores of the Mediterranean (N. Lat. 43°) and by the southern (N. Lat. 30°). Thus the depth would be 780 to 800 miles including meridional France, the Iberian Peninsula, Italy and Greece, with the coast-regions of Africa from Morocco to Egypt.
2   Running eastward the Sotadic Zone narrows, embracing Asia Minor, Mesopotamia and Chaldæa, Afghanistan, Sind, the Punjab and Kashmir.
3   In Indo-China, the belt begins to broaden, enfolding China, Japan and Turkistan.
4   It then embraces the South Sea Islands and the New World where, at the time of its discovery, Sotadic love was, with some exceptions, an established racial institution.
5   Within the zone the Vice is popular and endemic, held at worst to be a mere peccadillo, whilst the races to the North and South of the limits here defined practise it only sporadically amid the opprobrium of their fellows who, as a rule, are physically incapable of performing the operation and look upon it with the liveliest disgust.[30]

The Sotadic Zone is precisely bounded, with imaginary walls that seem to keep pederasty in, to contain this and other apparently deviant but just-repressible desires and sexual acts. The boundaries are precisely mapped, to particular latitudes and national borders. They hold back desires that seem to well up within the Zone and spill in from outside it. These include pederasty, which Burton referred to as *'Le Vice contre nature'*, or *'Le Vice'*, and its female counterpart (but not equivalent) 'Tribadism';[31] there is 'debauchery' and 'temptation', 'erotic perversion'[32] and 'evil'[33] – the list of 'abominations'[34] and 'corruptions'[35] is long – and pederasty is practised alongside infanticide and cannibalism, prostitution and bestiality.[36] On the surface Burton seems titillated at times, disgusted at others. Here, it seems, is evidence to support Isabel Burton's claim that (to paraphrase) her husband shared and endorsed his countrymen's homophobia and that he broke discursive taboos only to condemn and to bring deviants before the eyes of the law and/or the doctor.[37] There is, as I explain presently, much more convincing evidence to support wholly different readings.

The Sotadic Zone is distanced from England, and is both geographically and sexually disconnected. Burton employs a variety of distancing devices. Most tangibly, he reproduces geographical and imaginative distance between contemporary constructions of Occident and Orient, by pinning his Sotadic Zone roughly on the latter.[38] Within the Sotadic Zone, an area in the eastern Mediterranean from Greece to Egypt forms a centre of gravity, a historical centre, from which desire spreads out, threatening surrounding areas. Like an aggressive and dominant lover, the Zone 'embraces' Asia and the South Pacific, 'enfolding' nations in its arms, and threatening Europe with its dangerous passions. Burton traces the origins and spread of particular forms of pederasty, from Greece to Rome, and from Rome to North Africa, for example, in each case presenting the sexual practice as something forced by strong, conquering nations on their weaker counterparts.[39] Burton suggests that, despite 'sporadic' outbreaks in London and endemic pederasty among ancient Celts,[40] the English generally kept pederasty at bay.

Embellishing this sense of distance, Burton tells the reader that the sexual geography of the *Nights* is a region he imagines from afar. He says he dreamed of it while in the 'luxuriant and deadly deserts of West Africa' and the 'dull and dreary half-clearings of Brazil', where he passed years of 'official banishment' engaged in minor diplomatic duties, and where he found solace in escapist Oriental day-dreams and translations:[41]

> From my dull and commonplace and 'respectable' surroundings, the Jinn bore me at once to the land of my predilection, Arabia, a region so familiar to my mind that even at first sight, it seemed a reminiscence of some by-gone metempsychic life in the distant past.[42]

Burton further distances himself from the Sotadic Zone, and from stories set there, by assuming the seemingly passive role of the translator, who merely retells stories. He distances himself from language, details and anecdotes by emphatically quoting others, effectively disowning much of his own text. Pederasty, for example, is *'Le Vice'* – someone else's term, which Burton uses ambiguously.

Burton also distances the Sotadic Zone through a series of visual images and metaphors. His cartographic frame, which places the Sotadic Zone on an imaginary map of the world, provides the first visual abstraction, while giving it a factual appearance. In other visual metaphors, Burton claims to display 'a *landscape* of magnificent *prospects* whose *vistas* are adorned with every charm of nature and art'.[43] He sees from what seems to be a fixed, elevated position. His vision is panoramic, a grand sweep through geography and history. He 'glanc[es] over the myriad pictures of this panorama', with a gaze that is both self-effacing and voyeuristic. Even scenes of rape are regarded with casual, light-hearted detachment. In the 'Terminal essay', for example,

> A favourite Persian punishment for strangers caught in the Harem or *Gymnæceum* is to strip and throw them and expose them to the embraces of the grooms and the negro slaves. I once asked a Shirazi how penetration was possible if the patient resisted with all the force of the sphincter muscle: he smiled and said, 'Ah, we Persians know a trick to get over that; we apply a sharpened tent-peg to the crupper-bone (*os coccygis*) and knock till he opens.'[44]

Visual distance is produced, also, by Burton's graphic imagery. He echoes the 'Eastern story-teller' who, he claims, sees and tells all, ushering the listener into every situation, even 'the bridal chamber', where he describes 'everything he *sees* and *hears*'.[45] The cumulative effect is to display sex, sexuality and sexual geography that seems both realistic and remote.

The authoritative, realistic and sexually frank tone of Burton's essay and notes is licensed and augmented by the scholarly appearance he cultivates: graphic sexual images are justified on the basis of clinical and geographical interest; occupants of the Sotadic Zone are presented, like visitors to the doctor's surgery, in 'decent nudity'. Burton, who assumed the disguise of a doctor on some of his Oriental travels, also posed as a kind of doctor – a sexologist – in England.[46] As a doctor, he made sure of getting a good look at lots of 'decent nudity', and enjoyed the medical practitioner's licence to write about it. He also enjoyed the professional geographer's licence for sexual discourse. Identifying himself in print as a fellow of the Royal Geographical Society (FRGS), Burton used his geographical credentials as a form of professional licence, which granted him a relatively safe distance from the sexual subjects he craved. This licence he both exploited and extended, both in the scholarly associations and journals he co-founded to provide outlets for 'learned debauchery' and sexually explicit ethnology,[47] and also in the geographical and anthropological footnotes and essays he attached to the *Nights*. As a scholar, Burton claimed to write for 'students'.[48] He therefore asserted his licence to talk about sex professionally, with a freedom that would have been inconceivable in 'popular books',[49] and took the opportunity to chart something resembling a formal scholarly map.

Thus, with self-effacing distance and contrived scholarly licence, Burton charts a region that seems to have little to do with him, a region that is, nevertheless, a reflection of his colonial desires. In other words, he makes a typical colonial map. His role, as translator and scholar, is less passive than it appears. He selects stories, seeks out information and then decides how to retell and report, translate and annotate.[50] And, despite his stated intention of restoring the *Nights* to their original form, Burton proceeds to censor them. As Joseph Boone shows, whenever Burton 'must envision himself as a reader', and therefore become part of the picture he paints, 'he finds himself restoring the "fig-leaf" beneath which he has previously declared himself willing to glimpse'.[51] Detaching himself from the picture, in this way, Burton evaded the question of whose desire and whose sexuality is being mapped. He implies that sexual desire is universal; men are always looking for sex, however and wherever it is available to them. To Burton, as to more modern libertarians such as Ronald Hyam, the Empire just seemed to expand the range of choices, providing many new sexual outlets.[52] It will be necessary to critically address this assumption, and with it the colonial underpinnings of Burton's sexuality politics. First, however, I wish to take a closer look at Burton's *mapping* strategies, and specifically at the role of travel within them, since these had particular bearing on his interventions in sexuality politics.

Mapping strategies: realistic and travelling geographies

In the *Nights*, Burton appears to construct an orthodox colonial map of an unorthodox sexual subject. The Sotadic Zone describes sexual regions, neatly mapped with precise boundaries, which apparently marginalise and contain same-sex practices.

But this gives way, on closer inspection, to reveal a less orthodox map, one which is open and fluid, as the fundamentally slippery maps envisaged by Gilles Deleuze and Felix Guattari: 'The map is open and connectable in all of its dimensions; it is detachable, reversible, susceptible to constant modification. It can be torn, reversed, adapted to any kind of mounting, reworked by individual group or social formation'.[53] Maps are deceptively slippery. They seem to be scientific, objective, impersonal, even mechanical, images embodying what Svetlana Alpers[54] calls an 'aura of knowledge'. Maps, naturalised as facts, are received with trust. Brian Harley argued that maps construct taken-for-granted worlds in which geographies and identities are naturalised.[55] They seem to provide firm ground on which to stand, a sense of security for those who like to know where they are. But a map like these can be enabling rather than confining, a point of departure rather than an end in itself. On first inspection, despite its unorthodox subject material, Burton's map seems authoritative and objective, bounded and factual. But the Sotadic Zone, like the journeys and travel books that informed it, turns out to be more open and fluid than this.[56]

Despite the apparent separation between his careers as a travel writer and a translator, in his youth and old age respectively, Burton's travels and translations were always connected. The *Nights* gave Burton a point of entry to the Orient, and a way of seeing the land and its peoples. He tells stories from the *Nights* to travelling companions, gathered around campfires at night, and in so doing he identifies sexual and moral issues to which he returns later in life. In *First Footsteps in East Africa*,

> When Arabs are present, I usually read out a tale from 'The Thousand and One Nights', that wonderful work, so often translated, so much turned over, and so little understood at home. The most familiar of books in England, next to The Bible, it is one of the least known, the reason being that about one-fifth is utterly unfit for translation; and the most sanguine Orientalist would not dare to render literally more than three quarters of the remainder.[57]

Again, in the Preface to the *Nights*, he recalls how he assumed the role of story-teller, when travelling with Arabs:

> The Shaykhs and 'white-beards' of the tribe gravely take their places, sitting with outspread skirts like hillocks on the plain, as the Arabs say, around the camp-fire, whilst I reward their hospitality and secure its continuance by reading or reciting a few pages of their favourite tales. The women and children stand motionless as silhouettes outside the ring; and all are breathless with attention; they seem to drink in the words with eyes and mouths as well as with ears.[58]

Less tangibly, the *Nights* gave Burton with a way of seeing the Arab world when he was travelling there. The *Nights*, perhaps more than any other Oriental or Orientalist text, provided Burton and other Western travellers with a way of reading the landscapes of Arabia.

A recent travel essay on Cairo, by Jan Morris, provides an unusually explicit illustration of how European travellers, steeped in the *Nights*, have read Oriental landscapes. Morris evokes a street near the 'great bazaar quarter' of Cairo, a street she interprets as 'the true locale of the *Thousand and One Nights* – ostensibly set in Baghdad but really a reflection of this tremendous oriental capital'.[59] Similarly, if not always so explicitly, the people and places in Burton's narratives often seem to have stepped out of the *Nights*. Fatma Moussa-Mahmoud traces to the *Nights* some of the characters in European Oriental travel literature. For example, a travelling companion in Burton's *Personal Narrative of a Pilgrimmage*, the plump, unmarried, 28-year-old Omar Effendi, is compared to Kamer al-Zaman of the *Nights*, while two cookmaids in *First Footsteps* are nicknamed Sheherazade and Deenarzade. The *Nights* – 'part of the furniture of his mind' – provided Burton with ready-made *dramatis personae*, who served as travelling companions and as templates for his own disguises.[60]

While the *Nights* shaped the geography of Burton's travels, it is also true that Burton's travels shaped the geography of his *Nights*. By his own admission, in the Preface (quoted above), the narrator of Burton's *Nights* was the traveller telling stories by the campfire, and not the detached armchair dreamer – the exiled minor diplomat or the old man in his study. Burton emphasises this point by claiming to have conceived and begun the translation in Aden, where (he says) he spent the winter of 1852 with a travelling companion, Dr Steinhauser.[61] He remembers how the *Nights* was a comfort when he was on the road, and even in the midst of adventures: 'Throughout a difficult and dangerous march across the murderous Somali country', for example, the '*Nights* rendered [me] the best of service'.[62] In the footnotes and essays that accompany the *Nights*, Burton reiterates and develops lines of thought that first appear in his travel narratives, as the thoughts of a traveller. In *First Footsteps*, he introduced what was to be his thesis in the *Nights*, reflecting only '[a]fter much wandering' that 'morality is a matter of geography'.[63] In the *Nights*, Burton refers frequently to his travels and first-hand observations, including those of the boy brothels in Karachi, and he directs readers to his published travel books.[64] He attributes his command of Arabic and his fascination with the Orient, especially its deserts, to a 'succession of journeys and long visits' and 'an exploration'.[65] Referring to his travels, Burton establishes his credentials as a bona fide Orientalist scholar and translator, backs up some of his specific claims, and explains away his interest in pederasty. He also puts his travels, and himself as a traveller, into the *Nights*, and therefore links the geography of the *Nights* to the geography of his travels. Printing the work under his

own name – the name of a famous traveller – at the risk of prosecution for obscenity, Burton effectively invited readers to make a
connection between the geography of his *Nights* and the geography of
his travels.

Burton's travel narratives, unlike his translations and essays, are
adventure stories – exciting and heroic quests in *terra incognita*. They
are introduced and in some cases subtitled as adventures, typically as
records of 'personal adventure',[66] of which Burton is the hero and
narrator: unlike the self-effacing translator or scholar behind the *Nights*,
he is at the centre of this narrative. In *The Lake Regions*, for example,
Burton explains that he has 'not attempted to avoid intruding matters
of a private and personal nature upon the reader; it would have been
impossible to avoid egotism in a purely egotistical narrative'.[67] Burton
communicates the pleasure, the excitement and the danger of his
adventures. He is engaged, part of the picture he describes. Adopting
disguises, including the clothes of a Persian wanderer, the skin of an
Oriental (darkened with walnut juice), and the languages and dialects
to match, he blends into the Orient he constructs. This is not the
mapped, circumscribed space of formal geography, but the theatrical
mise en scène of a dramatic adventure. Fluid, like the landscapes
of exploration that Paul Carter explores in *The Road to Botany Bay*,
the geography of Burton's travel consists not of absolute, fixed places,
but points along a road. Burton describes the view from the road, the
vistas before and behind him, and maps path-like, linear, fluid geography. Here, boundaries are to be crossed, regions to be passed
through – as the name of one district, which Burton translates as
'put down! (*scil.* your pack)',[68] makes clear. This space of travel and
adventure seems very different from the geography of the *Nights*,
although the two are closely connected and similar.

Signalling his literary appropriation and political intervention,
Burton identifies the *Nights* as a classic not of Oriental but rather
of English adventure literature, suggesting that 'Sheherazade [was]
as familiar to the home reader as Prospero, Robinson Crusoe, Lemuel
Gulliver and Dr. Primrose'.[69] As the setting of an adventure, Burton's
Arabia is a magical place, visited for a while, or perhaps just imagined. Burton sets the scene, in the first instance, with a leap of
imagination:

> Again I stood under the diaphanous skies, in air glorious as æther,
> whose every breath raises men's spirits like sparkling wine. Once more
> I saw the evening star hanging like a solitaire from the pure front of the
> western firmament; and the after-glow transfiguring and transforming,
> as by magic, the homely and rugged features of the scene into a fairy-
> land lit with a light which never shines on other soils or seas.

Hardly a civil servant's guide to the Orient, this is the setting of an adventure, reminiscent of what Joseph Campbell calls the 'zone unknown' of adventure myths:

> This fateful region of both treasure and danger may be variously rep-
> resented: as a distant land, a forest, a kingdom underground, beneath
> the waves, or above they sky, a secret island, lofty mountaintop, or
> profound dream state; but it is always a place of strangely fluid and
> polymorphous beings, unimaginable torments, superhuman deeds, and
> impossible delight.[70]

A conventionally heroic explorer and map-maker, Burton mapped the Sotadic Zone in what, he claimed, was virtual *terra incognita*. In keeping with his image as England's most Nietzschean adventurer, who followed the philosopher's instructions to 'live dangerously!' and 'send your ships into uncharted seas',[71] Burton liked to be seen to go to new areas, where others feared to tread. Earlier in his life he had travelled to geographical *terrae incognitae*, parts of Africa and Arabia that remained as 'huge white blots' on the map.[72] In his old age, he travelled to metaphorical *terrae incognitae*, confronting silences and blanks of another sort – the deafening silences in sexuality politics which allowed the Labouchere Amendment to be introduced and passed with barely a mention, as I explain in more detail in the next section.

The *terra incognita* in which Burton mapped the Sotadic Zone was also figurative, concretely geographical – the setting of a specific-ally *utopian/dystopian* adventure.[73] When he explains that whereas '[h]istory paints or attempts to paint life as it is', '[f]iction shows or would show us life as it should be, wisely ordered and laid down on fixed lines',[74] Burton hints at the fictional and utopian dimensions of his narrative. He establishes a direct link between himself, as narrator and hero, and the famous utopian adventurer Lemuel Gulliver – he mentions in a telling footnote: 'Some years ago I was asked by my landlady if ever in the course of my travels I had come across Captain Gulliver.'[75] Like Gulliver, Burton travels to a disconnected utopian/dystopian space, off the map; in the Preface, he tells how he is trans-ported from the banal surroundings of his English home to the magical setting of the *Nights*, the malleable setting of a utopian adventure. Covering much of the Orient, the geography of the *Nights* was not, of course, a complete blank. There were, however, blank spaces on maps which Burton was able to fill. First, the gaps left by geographers, anthropologists, translators and others when they neglected to include sexual and other tabooed topics in their descrip-tions. Second, the blank, seemingly empty and timeless, geography at the heart of the Sotadic Zone, and at the heart of the *Nights*: the desert. It is in the desert that Burton feels most freedom, both the freedom to roam around in a world of men and adventure, and the freedom to imagine, to dream about the past and the future. Edward Said observed that to Orientalists such as Burton the desert 'appears historically as barren and retarded as it is geographically; the Arabian desert is thus considered to be a locale about which one can made statements regarding the past in exactly the same form (and with the same content) that one makes them regarding the present'.[76] Of course, utopian writers are concerned ultimately with the future. In his *Personal Narrative*, Burton wrote: 'Desert views . . . appeal to the Future, not to the Past: they arouse because they are by no means memorial'.[77] Timeless, empty, malleable, literally and metaphorically fluid space, the desert seemed the perfect setting for his utopian adventures.

Burton's description of the Sotadic Zone, reminiscent of the four regions in which Gulliver travelled, is not a static region, but a linear sequence of utopias and dystopias. Narrative is, of course, generally linear, compressing geography's many dimensions into one, but this does not completely explain the narrative structure in Burton's description of the Sotadic Zone. Burton chooses to represent the Zone in linear rather than areal representation. Since he is able to specify geographical coordinates and boundaries with impressive precision, it is noteworthy that Burton neglects to display the Sotadic Zone on a graphic rather than a textual map. His description is like an imaginary journey, one which begins in Arabia and ancient Greece, and then proceeds to other, variously utopian and dystopian, regions – moving through Rome and North Africa, and continuing in an easterly direction: 'Proceeding Eastward we reach Egypt, that classical region of all abominations';[78] 'Resuming our way Eastward we find the Sikhs and the Moslems of the Panjab much addicted to Le Vice';[79] 'Passing over to America we find that the Sotadic Zone contains the whole hemisphere',[80] and so on. Thus Burton, who superficially appears to lump all marginal sex together within the Sotadic Zone, actually draws distinctions between sexual practices and their morality. He distinguishes, most generally, between three types of pederasty – the funny, the grim and the wise[81] – although he goes into detail on subtle geographical variations. Arguing that the love of boys has a 'noble and ideal' side,[82] he idealises Greek and some forms of Arabic pederasty, and acknowledges the religious significance of same-sex relationships in Egypt, but criticised Roman pederasty and scoffs, for example, at the 'systematic bestiality with ducks, goats and other animals'[83] that he claims is common in China. I shall explain how these distinctions addressed specific contemporary sexuality politics.

With its graphic sexual imagery, its abstract fleshy surfaces that remind the reader not only of medical text books, but even of pornographic literature, Burton's broadly utopian geography could be read as what Steven Marcus calls 'pornotopia'.[84] Printing translated erotica, Burton borrowed many of the tricks of pornography;[85] he printed under false or concealed names, behind phoney cover organisations, with false publishers and imprints.[86] He co-founded a cover organisation for the printing of erotica – the Kama Shastra Society – with a membership of just two, himself and F. F. Arbuthnot. The Kama Shastra Society produced books including the *Kama Sutra* and the *Nights* with the false imprint of Benares. The names of translators were concealed, although not particularly well. The *Kama Sutra* was attributed to A.F.F. and B.F.R. – the initials of Burton and Arbuthnot in reverse order. The *Nights* was the first erotic translation Burton published under his own name. It is not clear whether Burton's pornographic tricks were genuine, or just playful parodies of England's burgeoning pornography industry. In either case, the tricks do establish a superficial association with pornography, an association that was cemented by Burton's public acquaintance with Monckton Milnes, Fred Hankey, Algernon Charles Swinburne and other well-known collectors of pornography and erotica, and an association that is sustained within the books.[87] The style is graphic, the stories replete with sensual sexual imagery. As Burton explained: 'The gorgeousness is in the imagery not in the language; the words are weak while the sense . . . is strong'.[88] The settings of Burton's *Nights*, like the settings of pornographic literature, are abstractions, historically and geographically vague. The mixture of sexual intimacy and sexual violence – Burton's principal obsessions[89] include bastinado (beating), castration, genital mutilation and rape – mirrors that in contemporary English pornography.[90] Yet Burton's interest was not entirely voyeuristic, and he was not just in search of titillation. Utopian/dystopian writers throughout history have generally used the medium as a form of political criticism at times when freedom of expression has been limited, and Burton was no exception. Burton's colonial pornotopia was a protest against English attitudes to sex between men, an intervention in sexuality politics, as I now explain.

Metropolitan sexuality politics: sex between men

The Labouchere Amendment was a somewhat mysterious development – proposed by and named after an otherwise socially liberal politician, and without the explicit provocation or request of purity campaigners – but was consistent with a historical drift in this area of legislation towards lighter sentences for a wider range of acts.[91] Previously, extreme penalties could be applied where men were convicted of sodomy (with either a man or woman), though in practice it had proved difficult to prosecute: the burden of proof was high, and police and judges were generally reluctant to seek and impose the severe punishments available. The Offences Against the Persons Act (1861) replaced the death penalty for sodomy with ten years' imprisonment, but added new crimes for lighter gender-specific acts such as male-to-male kissing and caressing.[92] Finally, the Criminal Law Amendment Act (1885) ruled:

> Any male person who, in public or private, commits, or is party to the commission of, or procures or attempts to procure the commission by any male person of, any act of gross indecency with another male person, shall be guilty of a misdemeanour, and being convicted thereof shall be liable at the discretion of the court to be imprisoned for any term not exceeding two years, with or without hard labour.[93]

Burton did not directly address this provision, but he did present a coded critique of its sweeping prohibition of sex between men. The vehicle for this critique, as I have explained, was a sexual geography structured around distinctions between sexual cultures and attitudes which laid the foundations for moral relativism. Though the Sotadic Zone appeared to tar with the same brush all forms of 'debauchery' and 'temptation',[94] 'erotic perversion'[95] and 'evil',[96] 'abominations'[97] and 'corruptions',[98] closer inspection reveals behavioural and ethical distinctions. Distinguishing between types of pederasty – between 'the funny, the grim and the wise',[99] between variously noble, spiritual and base forms of pederasty in ancient Greece, Egypt and Rome – Burton made the radical claim that sex between men was not necessarily bad. By traversing a series of sexual cultures, accumulating a picture of diversity, he assembled a case against the moral universalism of his time. His politics were coded but clear, as Isabel acknowledged when she argued, implicitly against her husband, that 'society must draw a line, make laws for the preservation of morality and punish those who break them'.[100] Following through, Isabel collaborated with the NVA after Richard's death to destroy 362 unsold copies of the *Nights*,[101] and she also authorised an abridged edition of the *Nights* in which the offending terminal essay was reduced to a few lines, with the explanation: 'It has been deemed necessary to omit from this volume the Article on Pederasty.'[102] Isabel rather than Richard was on the winning side in this battle. Unable to stop the new legislation, Richard had at least voiced opposition to it. His point would be recognised by contemporary critics such as Edward Carpenter[103] and modern sympathisers such as Kenneth Walker, a fellow of the Royal College of Surgeons who endorsed new editions of Burton's work, using the opportunity to argue that 'homosexuals should be the responsibility of the doctor and not of the judge'.[104]

Specific pieces of English and colonial legislation must be set in the context of a more fundamental sexuality politics. According to Foucault, as I have noted, 'the homosexual' emerged as a 'species' in Europe after around 1870.[105] Same-sex acts, previously treated as random aberrations, were increasingly understood as symptomatic of a coherent sexual orientation. A number of sexologists, using slightly different vocabularies, converged on this new way of thinking in the 1860s and 1870s.[106] Karl Heinrich Ulrichs elaborated on the distinction between normal and abnormal sexualities and sexual subjects.[107] Publishing in German in 1869,[108] with an English translation in 1892,[109] Ulrichs distinguished between what he called 'Urnings' and 'Dionings', which corresponded roughly with homosexuals and heterosexuals.[110] For some of Burton's contemporaries, the new sexology had seemed liberating. It circulated among and was welcomed by men who felt that it described, explained and legitimised their condition, and opened avenues for community formation and political action.[111] They particularly welcomed Ulrichs's argument that sexual orientations were naturally inherited, and therefore beyond condemnation or reform.[112] For others, however, the new ideas were less attractive. Rudi Bleys[113] suggests that many travellers, traders, missionaries and armchair ethnographers held on to an archaic sexual language because they were ignorant of the new sexology. But the limited extent to which sexual understandings were transformed, the limited adoption of new ideas and a new vocabulary, cannot be explained simply as a pattern of knowledge and ignorance. In particular, Burton's reference to pederasty cannot be dismissed so easily. He did not subscribe to the new ideas and he did not accept their implications, particularly for legislation which erected and policed the new boundaries between normality and abnormality, with prohibitions on sex between men and the scrutiny of those labelled 'homosexual'. Burton used an archaic sexual vocabulary because he refused the new one.

Burton's sexual theorising was not always coherent. Both Havelock Ellis and J. A. Symonds found it shallow and poorly conceived, confused by contradictions about the causes of same-sex desire – variously attributed to physiology (the 'blending of the masculine and feminine temperament' within the Zone) and to historical and cultural causes.[114] This could be seen as the result of an attempt to synthesise impossibly polarised debates about the nature and nurture of sexual life, but it could equally be understood as an intervention against the emerging categorical sexology. The sexuality that Burton both lived and described was as slippery as the geographies he charted, where boundaries existed to be crossed, places to be passed through. Although Burton has been labelled a 'dual man',[115] he rejected dualism. When biographers and historians of sexuality insist on debating whether Burton was homosexual or heterosexual – William Archer argued that he was a repressed homosexual, Robert Aldrich that he 'may have been homosexual', Frank McLynn that he was heterosexual – they miss Burton's point and impose inappropriate historical categories.[116] There are advantages in imposing terms on people who might not have recognised or accepted them – as Robert Aldrich does in *Colonialism and Homosexuality*, for instance – but this kind of strategic essentialism comes at a price: potentially misunderstanding the ways in which categories were deployed and contested.

Burton asserted sexual rights from the perspective of those empowered to enjoy them. In the great imperial civilisation of classical Greece, he noted, young men of a certain class took younger males as their lovers before they married.[117] With this reference to this accepted, even ennobled, sexual practice in an idealised civilisation, Burton sought to dignify what he asserted was its modern counterpart. In reality, there were clear differences between the forms and social meanings of ancient and modern same-sex practices.[118] But the important thing about identifying with Greek pederasty was not simply that it established a connection with a particular form of sexual life, but also that it asserted a disconnection with another. For Burton, pederasty was about civilisation, taste, pleasure and power. Pederastic acts could reinforce the status within the social hierarchies of those who performed them, since they were structured around distinct power-structured roles, organised around hierarchical differences of age and/or social status (historically, free-born men and slaves, citizens and non-citizens).[119] The Victorian pederast, like the libertine, pretended to an 'excessive but otherwise normal sexual appetite', and an elite rather than deviant, or abnormal, social position.[120] The *Nights* was addressed to 'a small section' of the public: those who could afford the high cost of subscribing (one guinea for each of the ten volumes).[121] Unlike the oral tradition from which it was derived, and without regard for its original female narrator, the *Nights* was attributed to a male author–translator and addressed to 'men and students'. Women were advised not to read the book, and even Isabel – editor of an expurgated 'household edition' – claimed (unconvincingly) never to have read the complete original.[122] Burton insisted that 'nothing could be more repugnant than the idea of [the *Nights*] being placed in any other hands than the class for whose especial use it has been prepared'.[123]

[179]

This approach to sexuality politics was embedded in colonial power relations: sex, never reciprocal, was constructed from the perspective of the powerful, dominant man. Hence Burton's interest in pederasty, in which one partner is dominant, rather than homosexuality, which may be more reciprocal.[124] Hence his tendency to speak of 'the use of boys' in place of women in some cultures, and hence his realised and desired power over those 'boys'.[125] This was a world away from the equality and reciprocity inherent in the new concept of homosexuality, in which, as Sinfield observes, with some concern, 'the ideal partner is similar to oneself – same class, background, income, age, ethnicity'.[126] Despite Burton's assumption that desire precedes power, colonial power relations were embedded in the sex he described and the sexual geography he mapped. In this sense, it was a fundamentally colonial imaginative geography that grounded and shaped Burton's intervention in English sexuality politics. But colonial geographies were more than the imaginary backdrop for Burton's sexuality politics: they were also the real subjects of those politics.

Sexualised colonial politics: colonising West Africa

Although Burton claimed to describe the 'true East',[127] and justified this work to would-be censors and critics as straightforward description of the Orient, essential background reading for would-be British conquerors and administrators, the East and the Orient were primarily vehicles for his sexual imagination. The Sotadic Zone was Burton's attempt to tell what Foucault called 'the truth about sex',[128] and perhaps about his own sexuality, but not the 'truth' about the East – despite his insistence to the contrary. However, as Edward Said, Rana Kabbani and others have shown, the material and the metaphorical are always connected. Burton's geographically coded interventions were set in and shaped by colonial realities and desires.

Most immediately, Burton spoke to sexuality politics in British colonies. English laws governing sex between men, like those on other subjects, were extended to some other parts of the Empire. Aldrich argues that, despite the perceptions among some European men that by going to the colonies they would escape the regulations and prohibitions that constrained them in their home countries, sex between men in colonies did not go unregulated or unpunished.[129] On the contrary, Bleys argues that colonising authorities regulated this area of indigenous and colonial sexuality with 'inquisitorial zeal'.[130] Like the other legal transplantations examined in this book, metropolitan laws on sex between men were variously appropriated, amended, rejected and supplemented in and for colonies. The authorities in NSW, for instance, decided to follow the British in imposing the death penalty for sodomy, and successive governors and legislators followed suit, amending their laws to reflect if not necessarily to replicate changes in the English law.[131] They did so selectively and in their own time. For example, when South Australia enacted its own version of the Criminal Law Amendment Act (1885), it excluded the Labouchere Amendment. NSW, which had only just adopted certain provisions of England's Offences Against the Persons Act (1861), within its Criminal Law Consolidation Bill (1883),[132] was also slow to react to the English development. Burton did not extend his opposition to the English law on sex between men into a coherent position on its colonial counterparts, though the Sotadic Zone did lend itself towards some vague suggestions on the subject. The logical conclusion of his assertion that pederasty was absent from most of sub-Saharan Africa – he claimed that 'the negro and negroid races to the South ignore the erotic perversion, except where imported by foreigners'[133] – is that colonial versions of the Labouchere Amendment would have been redundant there. On the other hand, where he did claim to find peder-asty – in Morocco and the Moslem world, for instance[134] – he did not conclude or imply that such laws should be introduced. But Burton did not develop a clear position, even an implicit one, on colonial sexual laws. The real subject of his colonial and global sexual geo-graphies had been closer to home.

Burton's sexual geographies did address colonial questions on an-other, more oblique, level. His imaginative geography of sex between men was part of a broader colonial landscape. Thus, for example, his location of sub-Saharan Africans outside of the Sotadic Zone – and outside the Oriental world of refined erotic arts – fed into his broader sexualisation of blackness, which advanced in a particularly strident way a contemporary racial idea. Selectively quoting an old encyclo-paedia, he asserted the immorality of Africans, stating:

> Vices the most notorious seem to be the portion of this unhappy race – idleness, treachery, revenge, cruelty, impudence, stealing, lying, profanity, debauchery, and intemperance, are said to have extinguished the principles of natural law and to have silenced the reproofs of conscience.[135]

Morality and sexuality were at the heart of Burton's assertion that there remained a 'great gulf, moral and physical, separating the black from the white races of man',[136] which spoke to debates about European relationships with Africans – it spoke, for instance, to Euro-pean debates about how to regulate the sexualities of their African subjects.

[181]

Burton was instrumental in not only reproducing but even extending ideas about the African as immorally, basely, uncontrollably sexual. His portrayal of African women as 'vicious'[137] and the men as bestial – he compared their sexual organs with those of horses[138] – informed the judgements of colonial officials such as Kortright, who decided that it would be 'impossible'[139] to regulate prostitution in Sierra Leone. As explained in chapter 4, Kortright's statement betrayed a powerful European anxiety about Africa and Africans as radically other and potentially ungovernable.[140] The European sexualisation of Africans, central to colonial discourse, spoke to a wider set of colonial questions and relationships. On the one hand, it affirmed the need for inter-racial distance. Burton joined a number of commentators in arguing for residential segregation in Freetown, ostensibly on health grounds. His proposals for a European enclave 'on the heights above the settlement'[141] appear to have gradually filtered through – along with similar views from a number of quarters – to the highest levels of colonial administration, since the colonial authorities adopted the principle of 'segregation from the native'[142] and built a European enclosure.[143] On the other hand, Burton's sexualisation of colonial and would-be colonial peoples spoke to wider relationships between Europeans and others, and contributed to the legitimation of colonisations and particular forms of colonial government. Burton's sexual geographies were located firmly within contemporary colonial discourse – Rana Kabbani argues that he 'helped only to further confirm the myth of the erotic East',[144] and I have suggested that he extended the sexual myth of sub-Saharan Africa – and as such they spoke to fundamentally colonial questions. For example, his account of Sierra Leone as a region of primal disorder, signified partly by base sexuality, portrayed a place and people languishing in savage disorder, effectively awaiting colonisation. Burton concluded his unsympathetic portrayal of the tiny colony and its yet-to-be-annexed hinterland with the suggestion that this region could (still) be developed and improved: 'With good management the colony might have become a flourishing portion of the empire, extending deep into Africa, and opening up to our commerce lands teeming with varied wealth. Now it is the mere ruin of an emporium.'[145] Burton's sexualisation of black Africans was integral to his claim that 'the Negro is still, as he has been for the last 4000 years, best when "held to labour" by better and wiser men than himself'.[146]

Conclusion

Burton has been accused of reproducing sexual and geographical stereotypes. Kabbani argues that Burton, like so many other Western travellers, 'hardly saw anything at all of the details before them',[147] and concludes: 'The East became codified and static in ways that were final; no deeper perception was permissible, nor indeed possible given the weighty heritage of prejudice.'[148] According to this view, the crudely Orientalist Burton reproduced stereotyped constructions of *here* and *there*, *us* and *them*. Said generalised that 'the details of Oriental life serve merely to reassert the Orientalness of the subject and the Westernness of the observer'.[149] I have shown, however, that Burton was rarely content to reproduce accepted ideas, nor to reproduce hegemonic constructions of geography and identity. On the subject of the Empire, he wanted to build a bigger and stronger one, with the use of force where necessary. On the subject of sex, he was equally willing to dissent from the contemporary mainstream, if this time to follow a radically permissive line. In either case, Burton charted space in which nothing stands still, boundaries are constantly transgressed, and there is little room for the conservative: generative colonial geography.

Yet sexual geographies such as these were spaces of desire as much as of reality, and largely unfulfilled desire at that. As I have explained, Burton did not manage to stem the tide of English legislation on sex between men, and even his imperial desires, much more in tune with the values of his countrymen, were only partially rewarded. Indeed, colonialism was messier and less assured than Englishmen such as he would have liked. His representations of colonial geographies were challenged by some of the people he represented: less powerful than him, they were not wholly powerless. Burton's geographical fantasies were called into question by figures such as the Sierra Leonean Creole barrister William Rainy (1819–1878). Burton had been taken to court and successfully prosecuted by Rainy during a brief visit to the colony. Later, when he took revenge in a travel book by writing against the colony and its legal system, Burton was taken to task once again. Rainy, who had successfully represented three native Africans in the case against the Englishman,[150] and who had a reputation for campaigning against racial prejudice,[151] contested Burton's portrayal of the Sierra Leone legal system as a 'caricature of justice' that was biased by predominantly African juries predisposed towards members of their own race.[152] In the pamphlet *The Censor Censured* (1865), which he dedicated to 'the African People',[153] Rainy dismissed 'the judgement pronounced by Consul Burton . . . a vile national slander',[154] the quick judgements of an 'ignorant' and 'superficial observer' who in a matter of 'moments' had arrived at unsound 'conclusions upon the morals, habits, and social qualities of nations'.[155] Evidently, Burton could not simply say what he wanted and get away with it. Colonial subjects such as Rainy, who refused to be spoken for by the likes of Burton, serve as a reminder that, though it may have been (as Said put it) 'almost an invention' and a vehicle for intervention in primarily English sexuality politics, Burton's imaginative geography was ultimately concerned with real places.[156] This leads to the more general conclusion that imaginative colonial geographies, like their material counterparts, were not as controlled or controllable as they may have appeared. Experiments were not always top–down, and power was not entirely centralised. It was not always the ruling classes and governing bodies, but also the less powerful inhabitants, that experimented socially and politically, and turned colonies into experimental spaces. Though the productive experiments of colonial rulers and subjects cannot be wholly disentangled, the complexities and distinctiveness of each call for broadly separate examinations.

While chapter 5 examined the intersections of power in Bombay in the 1870s and their implications for the regulation of sexuality, and while this one has explored the powerful geographies of colonial discourse and imagination, tracing their significance for sexuality politics and sexualised colonialism, chapter 7 explores the ways in which colonial subjects contested their regulation and representation, and intervened in sexuality politics. It considers the creativity of non-elite colonists and colonial subjects, examining dynamics between different groups and the broader implications for the regulation of sexuality – imperial sexuality politics in the broadest sense.

Notes

1 *Pall Mall Gazette* (9 July 1885), p. 4.
2 *Pall Mall Gazette* (7 July 1885), p. 5.
3 *Pall Mall Gazette* (8 July 1885), p. 4.
4 *Pall Mall Gazette* (6 July 1885), p. 1.
5 J. D. Edwards, *Exotic Journeys: Exploring the Erotics of U.S. Travel Literature, 1840–1930* (Hanover, NH: University Press of New England, 2001).
6 J. Cleland, *Memoirs of a Woman of Pleasure* (London: Fenton Griffiths, 1749).
7 E. D. Rappaport, *Shopping for Pleasure: Women in the Making of London's West End* (Princeton, NJ: Princeton University Press, 2000), pp. 109–110.
8 R. Williams, *Country and the City* (London: Hogarth Press, 1985), p. 1.
9 A. Blunt, 'Imperial geographies of home: British domesticity in India, 1886–1925', *Transactions of the Institute of British Geographers*, new series, 24 (1999), 421–440, at 421.
10 *Pall Mall Gazette* (10 July 1885), p. 4; emphasis added.
11 J. Ruskin, *Sesame and Lilies: Two Lectures, Delivered at Manchester in 1864* (London: Smith, Elder, 1865), pp. 135–137; L. McDowell and J. A. Sharp, *Feminist Glossary of Human Geography* (London: Arnold, 1999), p. 222.
12 F. Barret-Ducrocq, *Love in the Time of Victoria: Sexuality and Desire Among Working-Class Men and Women in Nineteenth-Century London*, trans. John Howe (London: Penguin, 1991), p. 52.
13 D. Finkelhor, *Child Sex Abuse* (New York: Free Press, 1984).

14 'The protection of girls: demonstration in Hyde Park', *South London Press* (29 August 1885), p. 3; Bristow, *Vice and Vigilance*, p. 112; Schults, *Crusader in Babylon*.

15 F. B. Smith, 'Labouchere's Amendment to the Criminal Law Amendment Bill', *Historical Studies*, 17 (1976), 165–175; J. Weeks, *Coming Out: Homosexual Politics in Britain from the Nineteenth Century to the Present* (London: Quartet Books, 1977).

16 F. McLynn, *Snow upon the Desert* (London: John Murray, 1990), p. 176.

17 R. F. Burton, *Plain and Literal Translation of* The Arabian Nights' Entertainments, *Now Entitled the Book of a Thousand Nights and a Night* (Benares: Kama Shastra Society, 1885–1886), vol. 10, p. 209.

18 Burton, *Arabian Nights*, vol. 10, pp. 205–206.

19 Burton, *Arabian Nights*, vol. 10, p. 206.

20 Burton, *Arabian Nights*, vol. 10, p. 205.

21 R. F. Burton, *Personal Narrative of a Pilgrimage to El-Medinah and Meccah* (London: Longman, 1855–1856); *First Footsteps in East Africa; or, An Exploration of Harar* (London: Longman, 1856); *Lake Regions of Central Africa: A Picture of Exploration* (London: Longman, 1860). Burton was the author of over forty published books, although those just listed, among his earliest works, were his most successful travel books, and have stayed in print almost continuously. *Personal Narrative of a Pilgrimage*, for example, was reprinted, and repackaged in at least five different editions between 1855 and 1893, when Isabel Burton issued a 'memorial edition': N. Penzer, *Annotated Bibliography of Sir Richard Burton* (London: Philpot, 1923).

22 Burton's Appendix to *First Footsteps in East Africa*, entitled 'Brief description of certain peculiar customs', which described acts of adultery and positions of Somali love-making, proved too much for the publisher, who ordered the Appendix to be ripped out: F. M. Brodie, *Devil Drives: A Life of Sir Richard Burton* (London: Eyre & Spottiswoode, 1967), p. 110.

23 The Title Page of Burton's *Arabian Nights* continues: 'With Introduction, Explanatory Notes on the Manners and Customs of Moslem Men and a Terminal Essay upon the History of the Nights. Printed by the Kama-shastra Society For Private Subscribers Only. 10 vols.'

24 Burton's sexual geographies can be placed alongside other works, some of which he cited, including: Dr Jacobus X (pseudonym of Louis Jacolliot), *L'Amour aux colonies* (Paris: Librairie des Bibliophiles, 1893); see also Bleys, *Geography of Perversion*.

25 F. Moussa-Mahmoud, 'English travellers and the *Arabian Nights*', in P. L. Caracciolo (ed.), *The Arabian Nights in English Literature* (Basingstoke: Macmillan, 1988), pp. 95–110.

26 Burton, *Arabian Nights*, vol. 1, p. ix.

27 Burton contributed to Payne's translation, which was published in an edition of 500 copies by subscription, and he dedicated a volume of his own translation to Payne's.

28 R. Hyam, *Empire and Sexuality: The British Experience* (Manchester: Manchester University Press, 1990), p. 226.

29 Burton, *Arabian Nights*, vol. 10, p. 207.

30 Burton, *Arabian Nights*, vol. 10, pp. 206–207.

31 Although, as Burton explains in a footnote: 'As this feminine perversion is only glanced at in the *Nights* I need hardly enlarge upon the subject': *Arabian Nights*, vol. 10, p. 209.

32 Burton, *Arabian Nights*, vol. 10, p. 222.

33 Burton, *Arabian Nights*, vol. 10, p. 233.

34 Burton, *Arabian Nights*, vol. 10, p. 224.

35 Burton, *Arabian Nights*, vol. 10, p. 233.

36 Burton, *Arabian Nights*, vol. 10, p. 240.

37   Brodie, *Devil Drives*, p. 329; R. Phillips, 'Sexual politics of authorship: rereading the travels and translations of Richard and Isabel Burton', *Gender, Place and Culture*, 6:3 (1999), 241–257.

38   J. Boone, 'Vacation cruises; or, the homoerotics of Orientalism', *Publications of the Modern Language Association*, 110 (1995), 89–107; R. Kabbani, *Imperial Fictions: Europe's Myths of Orient* (London: Pandora).

39   Burton, *Arabian Nights*, vol. 10, pp. 218–222.

40   Burton, *Arabian Nights*, vol. 10, pp. 246, 222.

41   Burton, *Arabian Nights*, vol. 1, p. vii.

42   Burton, *Arabian Nights*, vol. 1, p. vii.

43   Burton, *Arabian Nights*, vol. 10, p. 254; emphasis added.

44   Burton, *Arabian Nights*, vol. 10, p. 235.

45   Burton, *Arabian Nights*, vol. 10, p. xvi; emphasis added.

46   Brodie, *Devil Drives*; W. G. Archer (ed.), *Kama Sutra of Vatsyayana*, trans. R. F. Burton (London: Allen and Unwin, 1966).

47   Burton co-founded the Cannibal Club (1863) and the Anthropological Society of London (1873), vehicles for 'learned debauchery' and sexual ethnology, respectively: Brodie, *Devil Drives*; Archer, *Kama Sutra*.

48   Burton, *Arabian Nights*: one-page 'Memorandum' enclosure.

49   Burton, *Arabian Nights*, vol. 1, p. xviii.

50   T. J. Assad, *Three Victorian Travellers* (London: Routledge, 1964): Assad argues that Burton respected the original sources on which his translation of the *Nights* was based, making his mark mainly in the notes. To Kabbani, *Imperial Fictions*, even the 'translation' is Burton's creation.

51   Boone, 'Vacation cruises', p. 93.

52   Hyam, *Empire and Sexuality*.

53   G. Deleuze and F. Guattari, *A Thousand Plateaus: Capitalism and Schizophrenia* (London: Athlone, 1988), p. 12.

54   S. Alpers, *The Art of Describing* (Chicago, IL: University of Chicago Press, 1983), p. 133.

55   J. B. Harley, 'Deconstructing the map', in T. Barnes and J. Duncan (eds), *Writing Worlds* (London: Routledge, 1992), pp. 231–247, at 233.

56   See McLynn, *Snow upon the Desert*.

57   Burton, *First Footsteps in East Africa*, p. 26.

58   Burton, *Arabian Nights*, vol. 1, p. viii.

59   J. Morris, 'In a family embrace', *Guardian* (9 March 1996), p. 29.

60   Moussa-Mahmoud, 'English travellers and the *Arabian Nights*', p. 105.

61   Burton, *Arabian Nights*, vol. 1, p. ix.

62   R. F. Burton, *Supplemental Nights to the Book of a Thousand Nights and a Night* (Benares: Kama Shastra Society, 1886–1888), vol. 6, p. 388.

63   Burton, *Lake Regions of Central Africa*, p. 84.

64   In a typical footnote, he writes: 'For full details I must refer readers to my "Personal Narrative of a Pilgrimmage to El-Medinah and Meccah" . . . I shall have often to refer to it': Burton, *Arabian Nights*, vol. 1, p. 28.

65   Burton, *Supplemental Nights*, vol. 6, p. 416.

66   Burton, *Lake Regions Of Central Africa*, vol. 1, p. vii.

67   Burton, *Lake Regions Of Central Africa*, vol. 1, p. viii.

68   Burton, *Lake Regions Of Central Africa*, vol. 1, p. 313.

69   Burton, *Arabian Nights*, vol. 10, p. 95.

70   J. Campbell, *The Hero with a Thousand Faces* (New York: Pantheon, 1949), p. 58.

71   Cited by P. Zweig, *The Adventurer* (London: Dent, 1974), p. 204.

72   Burton, *First Footsteps in East Africa*, vol. 1, p. 1.

73   L. Marin, *Utopics: Spatial Play*, trans. R. A. Vollrath (London: Macmillan, 1984).

74   Burton, *Arabian Nights*, vol. 10, p. 123.

75   Burton, *Arabian Nights*, vol. 10, p. 125.

76   E. Said, *Orientalism: Western Representations of the Orient* (New York: Pantheon, 1978), p. 235.

77 Burton, *First Footsteps in East Africa*, vol. 1, p. 149.
78 Burton, *Arabian Nights*, vol. 10, p. 224.
79 Burton, *Arabian Nights*, vol. 10, p. 236.
80 Burton, *Arabian Nights*, vol. 10, p. 240.
81 Burton, *Arabian Nights*, vol. 10, p. 253.
82 Burton, *Arabian Nights*, vol. 10, p. 218.
83 Burton, *Arabian Nights*, vol. 10, p. 238.
84 S. Marcus, *Other Victorians: A Study of Sexuality and Pornography in Mid-Nineteenth Century England* (London: Weidenfeld & Nicolson, 1966), p. 269.
85 Burton frequently pointed out that literary works by Shakespeare, Swift, Rabelais and others were replete with sexual references which would probably have been considered scandalous if printed in other media.
86 Archer, *Kama Sutra*.
87 Burton dedicated a volume of the *Nights* to Monckton Milnes, a well-known collector of erotica. He cites Pisanus Fraxi's virtually definitive bibliographies of pornography and sexual literature: *Index Librorum Prohibitorum* (London, 1877), *Centuria Librorum Absconditorum* (London, 1879) and *Catena Librorum Tacendorum* (London, 1885): Burton, *Arabian Nights*, vol. 10, p. 252.
88 Burton, *Arabian Nights*, vol. 10, p. 170.
89 Burton's obsession with these themes was sustained throughout his writing career, some of his works, such as *A Mission to Gelele, King of Dahome* (1864), being almost entirely devoted to them.
90 Marcus, *Other Victorians*.
91 In 'Labouchere's Amendment', p. 170, Smith states: 'Male homosexuality was not reported as having been mentioned at any of the mass meetings called by the Purity Leaguers, before or after the adoption of the clause.'
92 Aldrich, *Colonialism and Homosexuality*, p. 221; Offences Against the Person Act of 1861 (24 & 25 Vic., Cap. 100); Smith, 'Labouchere's Amendment', p. 165.
93 Criminal Law Amendment Act (48 & 49 Vic., Cap. 69): Smith, 'Labouchere's Amendment', p. 165.
94 Burton, *Arabian Nights*, vol. 10, p. 222.
95 Burton, *Arabian Nights*, vol. 10, p. 222.
96 Burton, *Arabian Nights*, vol. 10, p. 233.
97 Burton, *Arabian Nights*, vol. 10, p. 224.
98 Burton, *Arabian Nights*, vol. 10, p. 233.
99 Burton, *Arabian Nights*, vol. 10, p. 253.
100 I. Burton, *Inner Life of Syria, Palestine, and the Holy Land from My Private Journal* (London: Henry S. King, 1875), p. 132.
101 In the NVA's ninth annual report (1892–1894), for instance, Isabel's financial and practical contributions are acknowledged: Women's Library, London (hereafter WL), *National Vigilance Association Annual Report* (1894), p. 38; see also W. A. Coote and A. Baker, *Romance of Philanthropy: Being a Record of Work of the NVA* (London: NVA, 1916).
102 Richard Burton, *Arabian Nights' Entertainments; or, The Book Of A Thousand Nights and a Night*, 12 vols, ed. L. C. Smithers (London: H. S. Nichols, 1894), vol. 8, p. 185.
103 E. Carpenter, *Selected Writings*, vol. 1: *Sex* (London: Gay Men's Press, 1984), pp. 257, 260.
104 K. Walker (ed.), *Love, War and Fancy: The Customs and Manners of the East from Writings of the Arabian Nights* (London: William Kimber, 1964), p. 20.
105 Foucault, *History of Sexuality*, vol. 1, p. 43.
106 Foucault, *History of Sexuality*, vol. 1, p. 43.
107 J. Bristow, *Sexuality* (London: Routledge, 1997), pp. 20–21.
108 D. M. Halperin, *How to Do the History of Homosexuality* (Chicago, IL: University of Chicago Press, 2002), p. 131.
109 Bristow, *Sexuality*, p. 4.

110 J. A. Symonds, *A Problem in Modern Ethics* (London: privately printed, 1896), p. 88. These two groups were subdivided into numerous sub-groups on the basis of their sexual preferences and gender identities.

111 Bristow, *Sexuality*, pp. 20–21.

112 Symonds, *A Problem in Modern Ethics*, p. 85.

113 Bleys, *Geography of Perversion*, p. 189.

114 Norman Penzer reproduced extracts from the works of Havelock Ellis and John Addington Symonds. These show that the latter, author of an early and favourable review of Burton's Nights, was more impressed by Burton's translations and notes than by his most general remarks and theories: N. Penzer (ed.), *Anthropological Notes on the Sotadic Zone* (New York: Falstaff, undated); Symonds, *Problem in Modern Ethics*, p. 80. For Burton's response to Symonds, see *Supplemental Nights*, vol. 6, pp. 406, 412.

115 F. McLynn, *Of No Country: Anthology of the Works of Richard Burton* (London: Scribners, 1990), p. 2; Brodie, *Devil Drives*, p. 175.

116 McLynn, *Snow upon the Desert* and *Of No Country*; Archer, *Kama Sutra*, p. 19; R. Aldrich, *Seduction of the Mediterranean: Writing, Art and Homosexual Fantasy* (London: Routledge, 1993), p. 173.

117 W. A. Percy, *Pederasty and Pedagogy in Archaic Greece* (Chicago: University of Illinois Press, 1996).

118 Halperin, *How to Do the History of Homosexuality*, p. 139.

119 Halperin, *How to Do the History of Homosexuality*, p. 121.

120 Halperin, *How to Do the History of Homosexuality*, p. 114.

121 While he described Payne's *Nights*, of which 500 copies were printed, as 'caviare to the general – practically unprocurable', Burton issued just 1,000 copies of his own version: *Arabian Nights*, vol. 1, p. xiii.

122 In a letter to *The Academy*, dated 6 March 1886, Isabel Burton wrote: 'I have not read, nor do I intend to read, my husband's *Arabian Nights*.'

123 Burton, *Arabian Nights*: one-page 'Memorandum' enclosure.

124 Burton was probably familiar with the relatively new notion of 'homosexuality', which dates to 1869. He is said to have discussed the work of Karl Heinrich Ulrichs, who coined the term, in the manuscript of his revised translation of *The Scented Garden*, which contained a lengthy discourse on same-sex love.

125 For example, Burton, *Arabian Nights*, vol. 1, p. 211.

126 A. Sinfield, 'The production of gay and the return of power', in R. Phillips, D. Watt and D. Shuttleton (eds), *De-Centring Sexualities: Politics and Representations Beyond the Metropolis* (London: Routledge, 2000), pp. 21–36, at 25.

127 Burton, *Arabian Nights*, vol. 1, p. xiii.

128 M. Foucault, *History of Sexuality*, vol. 1, p. 58.

129 Aldrich, *Colonialism and Homosexuality*, p. 5.

130 Bleys, *Geography of Perversion*, p. 50.

131 Aldrich, *Colonialism and Homosexuality*.

132 Aldrich, *Colonialism and Homosexuality*, p. 221.

133 Burton, *Arabian Nights*, vol. 10, p. 223.

134 Burton, *Arabian Nights*, vol. 10, p. 223.

135 R. F. Burton, *Mission to Gelele, King of Dahomey*, 2 vols (London: Tinsley, 1864), vol. 2, p. 177.

136 Burton, *Mission to Gelele, King of Dahomey*, vol. 2, p. 178.

137 R. F. Burton, *To the Gold Coast for Gold: A Personal Narrative*, 2 vols (London: Chatto & Windus, 1883), vol. 1, p. 267.

138 Burton, *Arabian Nights*, vol. 1, p. 6.

139 PRO, CO 267/331, Kortright to the Earl of Carnarvon, Colonial Office (24 February 1877).

140 G. Mosse, *Nationalism and Sexuality* (New York, Fertig, 1985), cited by White, *Comforts of Home*, p. 176.

141 R. F. Burton, *Wanderings in West Africa*, 2 vols (London: Tinsley, 1863), vol. 1, p. 200.

142 Dr W. Prout, quoted by S. Frenkel and J. Western, 'Pretext or prophylaxis: racial segregation and malarial mosquitoes in a British tropical colony: Sierra Leone', *Annals of the Association of American Geographers*, 78 (1988), 211–228, at 211.

143 T. Gale, 'The struggle against disease in Sierra Leone: early sanitary reforms in Freetown', *Africana Research Bulletin*, 6:2 (1976), 29–44.

144 Kabbani, *Imperial Fictions*, p. 66.

145 Burton, *Wanderings in West Africa*, vol. 1, p. 265.

146 Burton, *Mission to Gelele, King of Dahomey*, vol. 2, p. 204.

147 Kabbani, *Imperial Fictions*, p. 66.

148 Kabbani, *Imperial Fictions*, p. 139.

149 Said, *Orientalism*, p. 247.

150 Brodie, *Devil Drives*, p. 208.

151 He 'exercised considerable if not proprietary rights' over local papers, including the *Sierra Leone Observer*, the *Interpreter*, the *West African Liberator*, and others overseas, like the *African Times*: C. P. Foray, *Historical Dictionary of Sierra Leone* (London: Methuen, 1977), pp. 180–181.

152 Burton, *To the Gold Coast for Gold*, vol. 1, p. 220.

153 W. Rainy, *The Censor Censured; or, The Calumnies of Captain Burton on the Africans of Sierra Leone* (London: George Chalfont, 1865), p. 3.

154 Rainy, *The Censor Censured*, p. 5.

155 Rainy, *The Censor Censured*, p. 5.

156 Said, *Orientalism*.

CHAPTER SEVEN

Experimental and creative places:
Creole interventions in Sierra Leone

An editorial printed in the *Artisan*, a Creole newspaper published in Sierra Leone, suggests the generative power of ordinary colonial geographies – the real and imagined worlds of colonial subjects rather than government officials or metropolitan travel writers – within imperial sexuality politics.

> Here in the numerous dark approaches are imparted and received many first lessons in a course of error, hard to be removed, if even repented of. Perhaps unadvisedly, young and inexperienced persons are sent on the most frivolous errands, to jostle and form the doubtful acquaintances of some street oldsters, rarely for any good purpose. The scenes of debauchery and lewdness too that meet the eye, the offensive language and indecent utterances that cannot bear the light of day, are among the numerous reasons that may be advanced against the practice recited above.[1]

The 1885 editorial evoked a place in which encounters between different peoples presented moral and specifically sexual dangers – and opportunities for action. It signified difference through the goods on sale, associated with different places and cultures, and the words – in Krio, the local Creole language,[2] transcribed into English – in which they were named and advertised: passers-by are exposed to 'the noise and screams of the vendors announcing and describing the special qualities of their stock, "Fish yar", "Bullom Palm Oil yar", "Dis Agidi he big O" . . .'.[3] Allegedly the colour and 'sublime confusion' of the market (figure 7.1) were 'not unmixed with evil in various forms', and were to be approached cautiously or avoided.[4]

This pointed geographical description paralleled a number of interventions in English sexuality politics. Whether they were addressing concretely situated questions – as for instance in Chant's campaign to close a London theatre believed to be a venue for prostitution and a meeting-place for gay men[5] – or whether their concerns were more

7.1 Freetown (c.1890) looking down on the King Jimmy Market building and wharf, with customers and traders in the foreground and King Jimmy's Bay beyond

general, metropolitan activists tended to speak about places and particular locations within the city.[6] As Judith Walkowitz, Lynda Nead and Erika Rappaport have all explored, they spoke in particular about London, about how its great mass of people, its anonymity and its juxtaposition of rich and poor, powerful and vulnerable provided an unprecedented range of sexual opportunity, which brought pleasure to some, danger and anxiety to others.[7] Disputes over obscenity, for instance, focused on particular locations in London – shops, streets and what Nead terms 'the visual environment of the city'.[8] Purity activists were interested also in other kinds of places. Miles Ogborn and Chris Philo have shown how moral judgements about such places were used to formulate and legitimise place-specific social policies. For instance, refuges for sailors were located in places that the naval authorities considered morally and medically threatening.[9] Similar ideas were expressed about the urban society found in Freetown, which was both a city–port and, more specifically, a colonial contact zone.

The encounters represented in the editorial – indeed, the editorial itself – played a two-fold function within colonial sexuality politics: they explored and used the city as a contact zone in which the moralities and sexualities of different groups were brought into relief; at the same time, they constructed Freetown as a sexualised imaginative geography, which borrowed tropes and stereotypes about cities and sexualities, but also adapted and altered them to suit their own purposes.

Experimentation and creativity in Sierra Leone

Like the geographies of colonial Bombay and of Richard Burton's imagination, examined in previous chapters, Sierra Leone was conceived as the site of a British experiment. Whereas the colonial authorities in Bombay devised and extended systems for, among many things, the regulation of sexuality, their counterparts in the principal West African British colony experimented in other, generally more progressive, ways. Poor black people living in eighteenth-century London 'were the favoured target of social experiments by philanthropists and projectors' such as the abolitionist Granville Sharp, who played an important part in founding the colony and shipping the so-called 'blackbirds of St. Giles' there.[10] The colony was conceived as a haven for emancipated slaves, even while the institution of slavery continued to operate legally within the British Empire, and it provided the base for Britain's anti-slave trade campaign in the nineteenth century, as well as a place in which to experiment with the Westernisation of former slaves and other Africans. Wyse argues that the colony 'was meant as an experiment in social and cultural engineering: the founders hoped that by creating the right conditions, an opportunity would be given to emancipated African settlers in the Peninsula to evolve a free and self-governing black community patterned on Western civilisation'.[11] In some respects, the colony served its founders and founding society well, playing an important role in British anti-slavery campaigns, and in the production and transformation of racial ideas and relations.

British control over Sierra Leone was, however, limited. First, while it was shaped – by those with the power to purchase the land (English businessmen and philanthropists founding the colony and the British Government adopting it as a Crown Colony) – as a sort of laboratory of race relations, Sierra Leone also became a site of contact and exchange. If, for many years, this socially diverse colony was at the cutting edge of a certain kind of black liberation and advancement, then that was not the work entirely of its founders and governors, in the form of companies and foreign governments, but also of the people who lived in and passed through it. Second, as the image of Freetown market makes clear (figure 7.1), colonial contact zones also had the potential to be more anarchic, sites of multiple experiments and everyday creative acts, in which numerous voices contradicted and drowned out the would-be colonial elites. William Rainy's rebuttal of Burton, mentioned at the end of the last chapter, illustrated the limited reach and authority of colonial voices in Sierra Leone. (Burton was further compromised by the distance between himself and the colonial mainstream, between his open racism and the commitment of successive British governments to ending slavery and, ostensibly, facilitating the advancement of Africans in the colony.) Rainy's intervention was anticipated and echoed in local newspapers such as the *Sierra Leone Weekly News*, which dismissed Burton as one of a number of 'noisy and blustering Anthropologists' determined to 'prove the mental and moral inferiority of the Negro' and by other advocates of the African people.[12] The leading African nationalist Edward Wilmot Blyden (1832–1912) also spoke out against what he called 'the exaggerations of Captain Burton . . . in relation to the Natives of Sierra Leone'.[13] These expressions of dissent illustrate how the control and absolute possession evoked in so much colonial discourse – from travel and adventure writing to cartography and later to colonial cinema – could be desired rather than realised. The colonial reality, as the description of Freetown's Saturday market acknowledged, was less subdued.

Both in experience and imagination, Sierra Leone could be, if not exactly anarchic, then at least a creative and experimental space. When the Creole-identified *Artisan* spoke out against the immorality it saw in Freetown, it did so from the ambivalent position of a group sandwiched between the British rulers and Arab traders on the one hand and native Africans on the other. This intervention spoke of privilege, in its particular form of literacy and access to the media, but also of marginality, in its relationship with the colonial establishment. Arguably, it was *because of* rather than despite their qualified marginality that certain colonies and colonial subjects generated new and changing ideas about sexual and other aspects of social life.

It has been argued that marginality – rarely chosen – can foster creative freedom. People on the margins, out of the frame of things and with relatively little to lose in the event of social change, can have less to lose and more to gain from radical and disruptive acts and ideas. For bell hooks, the social and spatial margin is an ambivalent place which can be reclaimed – actively chosen – 'as a site of radical openness'.[14] Victor Turner argued that in places removed from the centres of everyday life – the spatial and temporal edges of a society: its theatrical spaces and performances; and at the edges of communities and seasons, for instance – where the social order is less pervasive and where it may be possible to break the social conventions that apply elsewhere, there lie possibilities for creative, perhaps transgressive, behaviour.[15] For Homi Bhabha, extending this thesis on liminality to the colonial order, the margins or interstices of colonialism – between here and there, coloniser and colonised – can be sites of creative action which potentially disrupts the social order.[16] Mary Louise Pratt critically reclaims the margins of the imperial world order – contact zones – as animated, generative 'social spaces where disparate cultures meet, clash, and grapple with each other'.[17] Although shaped by asymmetric relations of domination and subordination, the contact zone is open-ended, a site of possibility. Pratt uses the term 'contact' to foreground 'the interactive, improvisational dimensions of colonial encounters so easily ignored or suppressed by diffusionist accounts of conquest and domination'.[18] Creative, disruptive contact took place throughout the Empire, both in colonies and in metropolitan sites. Racial and ethnic contact and exchange was not confined to colonies, but also penetrated the 'heart of empire', as Antoinette Burton has shown in her study of London at the turn of the twentieth century.[19] Contact and exchange were uneven, though, concentrated in colonial ports and trans-shipment points such as London, Bombay and Freetown, places that were consequently important for the disruption of colonial (binary and other) social relations, including formal and informal codes (such as laws on prostitution, consent and interracial sex).

Where Europeans encountered others – particularly more numerous others – they were not always able to choreograph what followed. Trading-posts and ports were the quintessential colonial contact zones. Produced and maintained as nodes in imperial systems of trade, communication, production and interdependence, colonial trading posts and ports were necessarily outward looking, open-ended. Coastal colonial settlements from Sydney to Sierra Leone looked out to sea, rather than into the continental interiors that Europeans crossed and colonised later on. (Their trade with the interior was often conducted through intermediaries who came to their coastal stations.) Australian cultural critic Ross Gibson argues that in these 'ocean settlements', social life was profoundly fluid, taking 'dynamic, improvisational shapes'.[20] In these polyglot, transient communities, people found themselves 'letting go' and 'floating about'.[21] In colonial sites such as Bombay, Sydney and Sierra Leone, daily life brought people into contact and difference into focus, and engendered creativity and social change. In their 'hidden history of the revolutionary Atlantic', Peter Linebaugh and Marcus Rediker show that the creativity and change fostered by eighteenth- and nineteenth-century maritime communities were often disruptive.[22] Produced but not contained by European imperialism, these sites of contact were fluid and unpredictable: 'Sailors, pilots, felons, lovers, translators, musicians, mobile workers of all kinds made new and unexpected connections, which variously appeared to be accidental, contingent, transient, even miraculous'.[23]

There is an aesthetic to ideas such as these, and to the way in which they are expressed – to their evocation of a world of anarchic, unfettered creativity. In reality, colonial contact zones were not quite so utopian. In many cases, different groups did not so much bounce off as scrape against each other, and their sparks were the effects of friction. Vying for position, they articulated and contested constructions of identity and difference, deploying familiar categories or inventing new ones in the process. Their sexuality politics may have been original, but it was more important that they were effective, as will be seen.

In Sierra Leone, diverse peoples were brought into daily contact, resulting in a mixture of creativity and conflict. Though small, with a population around 20,000 in the second half of the nineteenth century, Freetown was profoundly diverse.[24] Originally composed mainly of former slaves and a few white settlers from England, both groups having begun to arrive in 1787, the colony later absorbed African Americans from Nova Scotia, Afro-Caribbeans from Jamaica (Maroons) and free migrants from the immediate hinterland (mainly Temne and Mende peoples who had come to the region from Guinea and Liberia[25]) and from the region (including Kroo migrant workers).[26] Other immigrants included the liberated Africans, or recaptives, freed from foreign slave vessels intercepted by the British. The colony was also home to a relatively small but economically powerful population of Lebanese traders (numbering several thousand); and a small population of British merchants, military personnel and officials (just a few hundred, most of them men, throughout the nineteenth century). These immigrants gradually cohered and settled into a number of distinct, if internally differentiated, strands. Sierra Leone was a dynamic, multicultural and multiracial society which defied any reduction to coloniser and colonised – though distinctions between Europeans and Africans, white and black members of the colonial society were also drawn. By understanding something of these distinctions, it is possible both to outline the sorts of encounters and experiences of difference that took place and also to position the journalists and newspapers that described and commented on those encounters.

Despite the presence of powerful and wealthy European and Arab minorities, Sierra Leone was overwhelmingly African in the nineteenth century, and its social distinctions were mainly between different Africans, most generally between Creoles on the one hand and natives, or aborigines, on the other. The *Sierra Leone Times* described the mix of peoples who came together as identifiable strands, but merged to some extent in the local Creole culture:

Each tribe in its own peculiar way still maintains its beliefs and traditions and although nominally, the representatives of the age all come under the generic and singularly infelicitous term 'Creole', each is really and truly as distinct as it was in the earlier days of the Colony. Consequently, a heterogeneous conglomeration presents itself, covering a mass of people, culled and drawn from the four points of the compass.[27]

Internally, this society was stratified around interrelated axes of ethnicity, education and length of residence. Externally, Creoles tended to distinguish themselves from other Africans in a number of ways, although the boundaries proved fuzzy, changeable and contestable. In contrast to those others, to whom they generally referred as natives or aborigines, Creoles mostly descended from settlers and liberated Africans and those who 'cultivated their habits and had come to accept their way of living'.[28] They generally lived in or near Freetown, wore European clothes and asserted a connection with England.[29] Their values, according to Wyse, were Victorian, combining 'religious fervour' with 'middle-class materialism and social graces of the well-to-do'.[30] Creoles also spoke and in some cases wrote Krio, which has been explained as a hybrid of English vocabulary and African linguistic structure.[31] Krio existed alongside English, the language of administration, the Church, commerce, and education,[32] and for the most part writing and publishing. The cultural hybridity of Creoles was a matter of degree. Not wholly given over to European ways, some wore African clothes some of the time – in 1887 they formed a Dress Reform Society to revive this – and some kept or reinstated African names, customs and faiths.[33] Conversely, some Africans who did not identify as Creole nevertheless 'sacrificed' elements of their ethnic identities and adopted European dress and names, 'cultivating certain Anglicised social manners'.[34] Indeed, boundaries between Creoles and other Africans were not always clear, and most Africans – including journalists – could be located somewhere on a Creole continuum. Even Blyden, who condemned the Westernisation of Creoles and idealised the 'superiority in morality' of 'interior natives untouched by civilization', adopted and contributed to elements of European culture in the colony and advocated a limited form of colonisation in the interior.[35] His sensitivity to the realities of cultural hybridity and exchange – to questions of how much Africans should take from Europe and how they should use this to negotiate their relationships both with Europeans and with other Africans – called for recognition both of the complexity of speaking positions and of the consequences of what was said for the (re)production of those speaking positions. It called, for example, for the recognition that journalists in Sierra

Leone spoke from and produced a variety of Creole and other African
– *native* – positions.

Creole and African voices: journalists

Relatively high levels of education, combined with access to professional employment in law, medicine, education, religion and the civil
service, as well as opportunities in trade and business, contributed to
the formation of an African, largely Creole-identified, articulate and
politically aware middle class in nineteenth-century Sierra Leone.[36]
The class of colonial professionals included schoolteacher A. B. C.
Sibthorpe,[37] whose amateur 'researches into the historic lore of the
West African Settlements' were praised by the *Sierra Leone Times*
for 'imparting valuable and interesting information respecting our
country'.[38] Fourah Bay College, the preeminent academic institution
in West Africa, also employed and nurtured a number of African
educators, most notably Blyden, who taught Arabic at the college for
several years in the early 1870s.[39] As I have mentioned, a number of
Africans worked in the legal profession, dividing their training and
careers between England and British West Africa. Joseph Renner
Maxwell, for example, completed his education at Oxford before
returning to West Africa with his English wife.[40] Opinion leaders of
their day, these professionals wrote pamphlets, books and articles for
newspapers. Rainy is said to have 'dominated' the Sierra Leone press
in the 1860s, when he started several newspapers, including the
Sierra Leone Observer and Commercial Advocate (in 1864) and the
African Interpreter and Advocate (1866).[41] Blyden was deeply involved
in the colonial media, both as a journalist and a proprietor. One of his
many contributions to the Sierra Leone media was to edit the *Negro*,
a pan-African newspaper.[42]

The newspaper industry which flourished in Sierra Leone in the
second half of the nineteenth century did so largely in the hands of
Creole-identified proprietors and journalists. Start-up costs were low,
making this a relatively democratic medium. Papers published in the
colony were sold and read up and down the West African coast, giving
their publishers and journalists a larger market and an influence greater
than might have been afforded by Sierra Leone alone. The colonial
media found their feet in the 1870s, when standards of writing and
printing improved, as did circulation figures. Levels of capitalisation
increased, but wealthier Creoles were not priced out of the market:
they could afford to buy presses and paper, and to employ the increasingly skilful and fluent printers and contributors.[43] Whereas no newspaper sold more than 200 copies in the 1860s, circulations increased

in the decades following, the *West African Reporter*, for example, selling over 350 copies.[44] Despite or because of the linguistic diversity of readers in Sierra Leone and the surrounding areas, most editors worked in the medium of English. Krio was occasionally used in papers such as the *Sierra Leone Weekly News*, the *African*, the *Sierra Leone Times* and *Early Dawn*,[45] though for the most part it was the language of speech rather than of print.

Newspapers such as these were launched and run for a variety of reasons, from political projects to personal disputes. For example, A. C. Harleston, a descendent of African Americans, started the *Sierra Leone Weekly Times* and the *West African Reporter*, largely a platform from which to argue with liberated Africans.[46] T. J. Sawyerr, a businessman and civic leader, established the *Negro* and, with editorial assistance from Blyden, used it to criticise the Government.[47] There were other politically active Creole journalists and newspapers:

- Reverend Joseph May,[48] with assistance from Blyden and later from his brother Cornelius, started what became the colony's longest-running title in 1884: the *Sierra Leone Weekly News*, aimed at 'the general public, and the mercantile community in particular',[49] has been remembered for 'high journalistic standards'.[50]
- The *Sierra Leone Times*, which ran from 1890 to 1912, aimed to protect 'the welfare of the People' (according to its masthead) under the editorship of J. A. Fitzjohn, who contributed polemical editorials beneath the heading 'One thing and another'.
- S. H. A. Case,[51] the foreman of works in the Royal Engineer Department, published the *Artisan* 'to encourage native industry' and to 'advance a class hitherto much neglected and downtrodden' – the 'Artisans of the Colony'.[52]
- William Grant, a Creole businessman and member of the Legislative Council, used the *West African Reporter* to criticise British rule and call for self-determination, while also calling for the British annexation of the colonial hinterland, arguing that 'the Negro' must 'develop his civilisation on lines of his own'.[53]

A number of missionaries and religious groups launched titles, these including the *Sierra Leone Watchman*, the first non-official newspaper, started in 1843 by the Wesleyan Missionary Society, which contained a mixture of religious and general news. Finally, in Sierra Leone as in most other colonies, the Government published its own version of events. Its organ, the *Sierra Leone Gazette*, renamed the *African Herald*, subsequently the *Royal Gazette and Sierra Leone Advertiser*, and (after 1870) the *Sierra Leone Royal Gazette*, was the colony's first and (under its varied titles) longest-running publication.[54]

In its diverse and outspoken media, Sierra Leone had a forum for political debate and argument, in which individuals and groups came together, speaking to and about each other. An editorial in the *Sierra Leone Times* acknowledged 'one thousand and one native manners and customs practised' in the colony, concluding: 'The heterogeneous and irreconcilable elements which go to form our community, render it an all but impossible task to tabulate and chronicle with any degree of system these peculiar customs which permeate and affect our religious social and domestic economy.'[55]

If this refusal or inability to speak in one voice limited some political prospects, it opened others. Arguably, the juxtaposition of multiple voices established the potential both for a lot of noise and for productive interaction, whether through formal dialogue or through the clashes and engagements of the fray. Not simply the home of a colonial and regional newspaper industry, Sierra Leone was the subject and setting for many of the stories. The sections that follow explore moral arguments that emerged from the experience and representation of contact.

Generative contact zones

The *Artisan* editorial addressed encounters between different peoples – portrayed as young and old, innocent and corrupt, members of different tribes and ethnic groups – and it attributed some part in the conflict that resulted to the setting: the chaotic marketplace, with its 'dark approaches', 'scenes of debauchery and lewdness', and behaviour 'that cannot bear the light of day'.[56] This gives rise to questions about the form and the generative power associated with sites of encounter as they were seen by journalists, commonly through the lens of borrowed, adapted, altered and supplemented stereotypes about cities and sexualities.

Freetown was constructed in generically moralised and sexualised geographical terms. A letter to the editor of the *Weekly News* compared the moral condition of Freetown with that of other cities, working on the assumption that immorality was an urban phenomenon that increased proportionately with the size of a city. Anticipating the argument that 'London and other large cities of the world are far worse in immorality than Freetown', the writer argued against complacency:

> Still we ought to remember how many Freetowns put together make up one Liverpool, or Manchester, or Paris, or London; and as Freetown increases in population and in populated area, even so would she stand in danger of becoming more and more an immoral city, were no vigorous efforts put forth to arrest the tide of licentiousness.[57]

Similarly, stereotypes about the immorality of harbours and naval ports were also mapped onto Freetown, portraying the city as a contact zone and as an immoral city in itself.

Prostitution was occasionally cited in allegations about the immorality and iniquity of colonial Sierra Leone – only occasionally, since, as an English visitor once pointed out, many aspects of the colony's 'loose' morals, including excessive drinking, selfishness, impropriety in dress, and 'brutal indecency', were 'beyond the freedom of the press to describe'.[58] An anonymous poem, printed in the *Sierra Leone Weekly News*, did address the issue head on (figure 7.2).[59] *For Dear Father Land* provoked letters to the editor and was followed by a sequel, 'Roselyn's dialogues for young girls and women':[60] the poem addressed the exploitation and degradation of Creole girls and women – (translated from the seventh stanza as) '18, 19, even 14 year olds'[61] – whom

6 (366)   **THE WEEKLY NEWS**   *JULY 13, 1907*

FOR DEAR FATHER LAND.

Whose kind contry dis, me broder,
All man do way tin he lek.
Set down mix and carry mix,
Pick and choose nor day nor way,
But nar one word are go talk
And de word nar true true word.
All man put yase down for yerry ;
All man put heart down for think,
"Creo boy for Creo girl
Sa Lone boy for Sa Lone girl
If nar wharf boy sef way tin ?
Plenty wharf boy bill tone hose.
Plenty wharf boy get character."

II.
Sa Lone girls ! dem good good one ;
Sa Lone girls ! dem clean clean one ;
Poor lek loss, nor get for eat ;
But for God sake sweh to me ;
Sweh to God and sweh to Christ ;
Blessed Sa Lone boy for me.

III.
Money ! money ! Lord have pity !
Coverslot and Silk Henkiuchief,
Body all day go for nothing,
Jarbone all day sink nar face.
Blessed, blessed Sa Leone girls
Do, for God sake, stop and think.

IV.
If the Jarbone sef nor sink down,
If the body fat lek cut hog,
Way de use when he done be say
Character nor day again.
When he be say shame done go ;
When he be say yase done cock ?

V.
Talk say—How dis ting go look,
How he look to God and Christ :
How he look to Bible Class ;
How he look to Sunday School ;
Girl lek me for turn to yooba ;
Bad word Jenny—rotten Jane,
Girl lek me for turn Rum-puncheon
Creo boy for look me down.

VI.
Ah, me God, me Fader Jesus,
Money sweet and free life sweet
But ah me God, me Fader Jesus
Please to keep me near the Cross.
Do ! nor let are turn to yooba.

VII.
O, de Yoobas,—ah, de Yoobas,
Every day the number swell,
Swell with blessed Creole girls ;
18 year, 19 year, 14 year sef day join :
Ah, me God—me Fader Jesus,
Do yah sorry for dis land.

VIII.
Days gone by ting nor tan so :
Those were days of modesty.
Yase been day for yerry word :
Shame been day for bad bad ting
Ah de wait man—ah the aliens ;
Sa Leone nar dem pone te-day
And dem mean for misa - *mash down* ;
Blessed Creole boys and girls.

IX.
Goverment nore care Fardin
Church again—me God ; you see ;
All man say—" Jis bring de money ; "
" Are nor ask whose way you day "
" Are nor ask whose side you get am."
Ah me God, me Fader Jesus,
Do yah ! sorry for dis land.

X.
WEEKLY NEWS are beg you pardin.
Guardian paper—*Sa Lone Times.*
Get up—Get up—you our Leaders.
Woke done oam nar gron for do.
Let me ask one word for God sake
When are ask, do, answer me.

XI.
English Law nor get some clause day ?
Clause for black and clause for white ?
Clause way regulate the period
When a girl kin lef him mammy ?
When a girl kin rent adjoining ?
When a girl kin turn to yooba ?

XII.
If de clause day—O ye big men
O ye men who go to Church ;
O ye men who get the money ;
O ye men who get the voice ;
Stand up—wake up—things day bad, mind
Save de little girls from death ;
Save de Creole girls from ruin.

XIII.
O my country—O my country !
O my dear, my father land :
I am sick, aye ! I am dying ;
At the sights that meet my eyes.
Aliens ! aliens ! what do ye me in ;

Thus to spoil my dearest country ;
Thus to tread upon our daughters ;
Thus to sodomize our land ?
Goverment nor care fardin ;
Church again nor care rap.
But de Lord will surely pay you :
Jesu Christ will surely judge you.

XIV.
Finally, my dearest Sisters,
Blessed, blessed Creole girls,
All dem one way still day go School ;
All dem one still under parents ;
All dem good good Sa. Leone girls ;
All dem clean clean Sa. Leone girls ;

XV.
Take de word way are day tell you :
He nor pay for trade with Body
Temple of de Holy Ghost.
Honest labour—honest labour :
Simple bread and simple clothing :
Near to Jesus, near the Cross.
Life will be like perfumed Roses ;
Death will be a glorious gain.

XVI.
Therefore pray, my dearest sisters ;
One God—me Fader Jesus,
Money sweet and free life sweet ;
But ah me God -me Fader Jesus,
Please to keep me near the Cross ;
Do, nor let are turn to yoobas.

Amen !

UNITY CRICKET CLUB v. HART S TEAM.

MATCH PLAYED SATURDAY JUNE 6.

To the Editor of the WEEKLY NEWS
Sir,—I herewith attach results of a Cricket Match played between the parties named therein.
I shall be very thankful to have it in this week's issue.—Yours faithfully

J. G. HYDE,
Secretary.
9th July, 1907.   Hart's Cricket Team.

SCORES.
Unity Club.

1 G. Mason bowled (Jones) - 3
2 Galba Bright bowled (Jones) - 17
3 Sawyer stumped (Jones) - 13
4 Erasmus King bowled (Nylander) - 0
5 George Hamelberg caught (Mudge) - 8

7.2 *For Dear Father Land*, a poem in Krio, the Creole language of Sierra Leone

it claimed were enticed and forced into the growing ranks of the
Yoobas (also spelt *Yoogas* or *Yubas*, this Krio word for buzzards has
been translated as 'whores').[62] These allegations of British sexual
immorality were fleshed out and grounded with reference to contact
zones. Prostitution was identified as a form of colonial exploitation,
in which 'de wait man' ('the white men') 'dem mean for miss – *mash
down*' ('lead our girls astray').[63] As in other allegations about colonial
prostitution, white soldiers and their barracks were singled out.
'Roselyn's dialogues' expands upon this: a girl in a poor family explains
to her younger sister Jane why she should refuse the life of a *sojer wer*
(camp follower) and find respectable work instead. 'But for god sake
run from Barrick' it implores her, explaining that

> Barrick life nar pure ruing,
> Ruin perfect, ruin clean:
> You go surely turn to yooba.
> You go surely turn rum-puncheon.[64]

The immoral influence of the barracks and military presence were
spelt out more directly in the memoirs of a Creole who had lived in
Freetown. Though written much later, Robert Wellesley-Cole's memoir
is worth quoting because it refers to the early part of the century and
directly addresses a subject that was usually left implicit or unprinted
at the time:[65]

> As to the British Army, we saw plenty of them at school. Exactly
> outside the gates of the Model School, where Circular Road crossed the
> road connecting the main barracks of Tower Hill on the one hand and
> those of Mount Aureol and Kortright on the other, British soldiers could
> be seen daily, marching to and from either barracks, sometimes in forma-
> tion, sometimes in small groups, often in pairs or singly.
>   They were called 'Jek-Jeks'. They wore khaki shorts and shirts, heavy
> black hob-nailed boots and puttees.
>   Exactly opposite our main gate was a house where some young women
> lived, a typical wooden Freetown house. This house was a regular
> port of call for the *Jek-Jeks*. Often they would be buttoning or hitching
> their trousers or fastening their belts, or combing their hair, as they
> came out.[66]

This memoir illustrates how moral claims could be fortified when
grounded, and it also addressed the morality of the contact zone in a
broader sense, which it will be necessary to revisit through more
sustained attention to these poems. First, though, there is more to say
about the construction of Freetown as an immoral geography.
    Differentiating this generic idea of sexualised urban geography,
particular attention was paid to public spaces within Freetown.

Highlighting the dangers of the marketplace, the editorial illustrated Creole anxiety about potential contact with natives in public places. The market was presented as anarchic, anonymous, disordered – in some ways a microcosm of public space in the modern city, in others a specifically colonial contact zone. Streets, the quintessential public places, feature prominently in Creoles' accounts of their exposure to natives. The latter, associated through labels such as 'countrymen' with the hinterland – the country, land, nature – were juxtaposed uncomfortably with symbols of the modernity and civilisation with which Creoles generally identified:

> It is really saddening as one passes along Water Street, near the Battery, or East Street, hard by the establishment of Messrs Marcus Brothers, on any fine day, to see the groups of countrymen squatted on the ground, Turk-like fashion, and all deeply engaged over games in which money changes owners very rapidly. As it is in these places, so it is in nearly every other part of the city.[67]

Water Street and East Street are located in conventionally 'immoral geographies' – the former near the docks and public wharf on the River Sierra Leone, the latter near the landing-place on Susan's Bay. The *Sierra Leone Times* complained of 'primitiveness' among natives in the city which went unpunished by the colonial government.[68] Given the power attributed to juxtapositions and encounters, particular significance was attached to 'everyday scenes' and 'public thoroughfares', particularly those on the fringes of Freetown, 'the Eastern and Western ends of the City',[69] where contrasts and contacts between Creoles and natives, between a colonial city and its African hinterland, were sharpest.

The *Sierra Leone Times* wished to draw to the attention of the Government the immorality – including gambling – 'pursued in the open streets of Freetown; the aborigines being the principal actors therein'. The newspaper seemed less concerned with the offence in itself as with the space in which it took place, and the implications this had for the wider community exposed to it. It complained, for instance, that there was 'hardly a nook or corner in the public thoroughfares in which there may not be found groups of labourers, hammockboys, servants, touters, or loafers, busily engaged over the Warry Bowl or the cowry stool'.[70] Generic geographical ideas were therefore mapped onto particular places, strengthening allegations by firming them up, replacing vague suggestions with specific claims. Thus, for instance, readers were invited to think of particular ethnic groups which were either named or invoked by their association with parts of the city. The newspaper complained:

The bridges around and about Fort Thornton are not exempt from being used for this vicious pursuit, and a police raid in many houses and shops in Krootown Road, the Grassfields, Kissy and Fourah Bay Roads, would afford ample testimony in support of the assertions you made on the subject.[71]

These allegations, which concluded with calls to the Government for 'some wholesome check [to be] placed upon the practice of gambling in the public streets',[72] pointed more generally to assertions about the tense and creative possibilities of contact zones. Sexual questions were addressed in similar ways. A correspondent of the *Weekly News*, discussing issues raised by the poem *For Dear Father Land*, specified places of prostitution and argued that they must be controlled: 'Pultney Street–Silver Town and Arkanny–Silver Town and Peter Lane–Silver Town, and the rest of them, must be broken up, or else the evil will continue to spread.'[73] Once again, generic geographies of sexual danger and sexuality had been mapped onto specific places, which served as vehicles for elliptical discussions of sexual practices and how to control them.

Anxieties about contact between Creoles and natives, as between other groups, were most pronounced where young women and children were perceived to be, or could be said to be, in sexual danger. Reporting 'the abduction of a girl', the *Sierra Leone Times* claimed that 'the presence of aborigines in such numbers in our midst . . . facilitates the commission of daring crimes':

It is intolerable that their presence should occasion insecurity and danger to children. Accustomed, in their homes in the interior, to regard children as so many marketable wares, they naturally look with watering mouths at the freedom with which children move about in the city and at the ease with which they could be kidnapped and converted into cash out of British influence.[74]

The article admitted that the abduction in question turned out not to be sexually motivated,[75] but in so doing it suggested that it *could* have been, and took the opportunity to recall a 'harrowing case' in which 'a mere child' had been 'outraged and then murdered'.[76] In another column, the newspaper asked: 'Are children safe, especially girls, now-a-days in the streets of Freetown?'[77] Once again, the edges of the city were associated with immorality, in this case with aggressive native sexuality, constructed through broadly sexualised images of the hinterland and its peoples. Remembering his early twentieth-century childhood in Freetown, Wellesley-Cole portrayed himself 'surrounded by the fleshpots of Native Africa'[78] both in Kossoh Town and on occasional ventures into the hinterland, where he recalled watching a young woman bathe: 'An African nymph, her twin breasts shapely beyond compare, firm, dancing up and down with the motions of her arms, as she scrubbed and poured the crystal water over her shining brown body'.[79]

This image of a body, sexualised in the mind of the observer, rising out of the water, gestured towards a fundamental association in the colonial imagination and male gaze between nature, femininity and sexuality.[80] The same author described seeing 'dancing girls, their bodies shining with ceremonial anointing', emerge from a 'bundu bush where they had undergone their initiation rites. 'Well-developed and attractive', the 'girls' were in his view ready for marriage.[81] The mutual sexualisation of African land and people, from the Creole perspective, constructed the interior as a sexualised, dangerous place, one from which sexually dangerous Africans might emerge.

This was closely associated with another Creole representation of natives and interior Africa which also reproduced powerful strands of colonial discourse. The *Sierra Leone Times* claimed it was 'well-known' that the

> Sierra Leonean, with plenty to eat and with the superior knowledge of how best to prepare his food, becomes in his looks, more an object of especial attention to the savage gourmand, than is the ill-fed aborigine whose taste for human flesh is only equalled by that of the ferocious quadruped with which his forests abound.[82]

Invoking interior cannibalism, this Creole newspaper marked a boundary between Creoles and Europeans, on one side, and native Africans, on the other. Within colonial discourse, cannibalism functioned as a quintessential signifier of native *otherness* and immorality or amorality, which Hulme has called 'the mark of unregenerate savagery',[83] signifying 'the very borders of humanity'.[84] Cannibalism has been widely examined from 'firmly within the European or Western tradition', marking 'the world beyond European knowledge'.[85] This is mistaken, since cannibal stories are not exclusively European: West Africans have a tradition of cannibal story-telling in which the roles are reversed, Europeans eating African flesh.[86] Nevertheless, the Creole references to cannibalism, cited here, can be located within the European tradition, Creoles identifying with Europeans on one side of a great moral divide. Ideas about the spaces of sexual danger and safety were also framed, within the ideology of the public and the private spheres, with reference to the latter. The dangers of the street and the marketplace were set against the safety of the home, both as it was and as it might be. The letter to the *Weekly News*, quoted above, argued that the prevention of prostitution among girls and young women should begin within the home: '*I lay the blame chiefly on the home training of our land in the present day.* Truly God-fearing and sincerely Christian homes . . . cannot turn out Silver Town pests.'[87]

Similarly, a correspondent to the *Sierra Leone Church Times* argued that, to combat impurity, 'We must regulate our homes, sever the young from evil associates and keep them at home at nights.'[88] It was also argued, in editorials on 'the youths of Freetown', published in the 1880s and 1890s, that young people would be less 'precocious' and 'aimless' if they had the chance to retreat from the demoralising city, ideally into moral recreational facilities such as reading-rooms and debating societies.[89] These arguments were largely derivative, but they were adapted to Freetown and, specifically, to the supposed dangers that the city presented for contact with natives, the 'fearfully tainted atmosphere of immorality by which we are surrounded'.[90]

Allegations and anxieties were also directed at Europeans and at the colonial contact zones in which they operated. Renner Maxwell asserted that 'there is more immorality among the white races, whether at home or abroad, than among Negroes',[91] Blyden that professedly Christian imperialism was morally hypocritical: 'The lay white men of very bad character – greedy and unscrupulous traders, ever ready to introduce and foster drunkenness and other vices, prone to fraud and mendacity, unchristian in everything.'[92] Creole newspapers reiterated and embroidered the claim that Europeans lived immoral lives and ran an immoral empire, that they drank too much and dumped alcohol on Africans,[93] that the 'selfish interests of Commerce' were placed above those of 'the Aborigines themselves'[94] and that so-called progress had left its African customer 'as naked as it found him, with only an "empty gin box" to sit on'.[95] These general claims, like the others considered in this chapter, were fleshed out and grounded with reference to the coastal contact zone. Thus, for instance, Blyden complained that Europeans has brought syphilis, a disease 'entirely unknown in the interior of Africa away from the coast and from the influence of foreigners'.[96] The contact zone could be located within specific sites of contact between Europeans and Africans, and within a broader territorial sphere. As its title suggested, *For Dear Father Land* was concerned not only with the girls and young women directly affected by prostitution but also with the condition of the Creole people, and their homeland: 'Do yah sorry for dis land' ('Please feel sorry for this land'), the poet prayed.[97] When 'Girl lek me for turn to Yooba' ('A girl like me became a whore'[98]), not only an individual but a people and a land were corrupted. When the poet claimed that 'to tread upon our daughters' was 'to sodomize our land', he or she chose unusually strong terms in which to articulate the violation not only of individual Creoles, but of the Creole society itself and the Creole home land. This, rather than the more commonly invoked cliché of raping the land, referred to the poem's gendering of the home land – its masculinisation as father – and invoked the immoral biblical geography of Sodom and Gomorrah.

This sexual anxiety could be regarded as a displacement activity which obscured broader problems and proposed misplaced moral solutions;[99] or it could be seen as a hard-hitting expression of those tensions, at a historical juncture when they were particularly acute. The complaint that 'Sa Leone nar dem yone te-day' ('Sierra Leone is not ours today'[100]) reflected the arrival of increasing numbers of Europeans and the gradual exclusion of Creoles from the more desirable employment and housing. The shift was symbolised by the retreat of Europeans, ostensibly on health grounds, from the mixed environment of Freetown to a separate residential enclave.[101] For many Africans there was nothing new about displacement and conquest by 'de wait man',[102] but for the Creoles, some of whom had been admitted to relatively privileged positions in the colonial society, this was a development of the late nineteenth century. Creoles were increasingly lumped together irrespective of class and ethnic distinctions, and treated the same as others of their race.[103] They were also displaced by the establishment of the Protectorate, which – though administratively distinct from the colony – deprived them of their numerical majority within the greater Sierra Leone. *For Dear Father Land* did not, however, just lament the condition of Creoles in Sierra Leone: it attempted something more positive. At the time Krio was mainly a language of oral communication and domestic life.[104] The language of the street and the home, it was rarely seen in print, though several writers did adopt it as a medium for critical social comment.[105] The poem mixed English and Krio much as Creoles tended to do, improvising many of the Krio words in the absence of conventions for writing them.[106] A correspondent of the *Weekly News* welcomed the integration of political and linguistic projects, praising the poem's author 'not only for his patriotic feelings and interest on *we* the successors of our country, but especially for his grand experience in not composing his poem in the English language, but in our mother tongue'.[107]

On one level, these allegations were directed specifically against colonial attitudes to prostitution and exploitative sexual relations with Africans. The author of *For Dear Father Land* had therefore joined other Africans in speaking against the form of interracial sexual contact to which the colonial authorities were, at the very least, most tolerant. This was partly, but not wholly, a matter of individual morality, individual involvement with prostitution: it also spoke of a wider moral field. *For Dear Father Land* father land' argued that Creoles should resist the immoral influences of outsiders, both individually and collectively. They must hold the authorities to account, challenging men in positions of authority, Creole and European alike:

> If de clause day – O ye big men
> O ye men who go to Church;
> O ye men who get the money;
> O ye men who get the voice;
> Stand up – wake up – things day bad, mind
> Save de little girls from death;
> Save de Creole girls from ruin.[108]

The finger of blame was pointed both at powerful and lustful individuals, and against the wider toleration of their use as prostitutes. The allegation that 'Government nor care Fardin'[109] implicitly addressed the fact that, in spite of its decision not to introduce CD laws, the colonial Government of Sierra Leone tolerated and indirectly regulated a system of prostitution. As explained in chapter 4, prostitution was regulated and institutionalised, if not by CD laws, then by other means, laws that condemned certain forms of prostitution but implicitly tolerated and regulated others: the Police Ordinance of 1851, which prohibited loitering by 'common prostitutes or night-walkers',[110] and subsequent laws for the protection of women and children, enacted in 1926 and 1927.[111] In addition to implicit interventions with respect to the colonial Government's position on prostitution, the poet proposed something more explicit and pro-active which might shore up and defend the Creole position. *For Dear Father Land* argued for the cultivation of social and sexual distance from others, and intimacy with each other, proclaiming

> Creo boy for Creo girl
> Sa Lone boy for Sa Lone girl.[112]

Clearly, it was not just colonial authorities that tended to advocate and regulate sexual endogamy in order to reproduce and manage the boundaries of racial and ethnic groups. In this way, the author of this poem joined other Africans and Europeans who had moved away from the tradition of mixed marriage, more widely accepted during the slave years but since discredited.[113] Renner Maxwell argued that British men increasingly treated African wives as 'animals',[114] but that mixed-race marriages could be reformed. Others, including the author of *For Dear Father Land*, wanted them stopped. This overstated and over-generalised the reality, which was more textured, with many different practices of and attitudes to interracial unions. Nevertheless, the attitudes to mixed-race marriage observed by Renner Maxwell and advanced by the poem's author did reflect a broader tendency among nationalists, identified by feminist cultural critic Lynn Pearce, to call for sexual endogamy, preferably or implicitly that which is heterosexual and reproductive, as a means of self-definition and self-preservation.[115] This alludes to the wider politics of *For Dear Father Land*, an intervention *against* colonial prostitution, but more generally against the violation of the Creole people and their land through prostitution and metaphorical sodomy, and *for* something very different from this: a generalised idea of purity.

So, to return to more specific and tangible claims, it was often argued that Freetown was an immoral place, but one that could be changed. Colonial laws that provided for the adoption of European – supposedly morally superior – practices were endorsed, their enforcement encouraged. Creole newspapers frequently endorsed the provisions of the Police Ordinance of 1851, discussed in chapter 4, which sought 'to improve public morals'[116] through a series of moral codes relating to such activities as gambling, nudity and traditional dancing, drumming and religious practices.[117] They reported its enforcement positively, remembering fondly for instance how children found naked in the streets were 'taken to the Police Station, and flogged a bit'.[118] They demanded that the Government renew and extend such laws, thereby controlling such practices as public gambling and 'loud, unseemly, wild and discordant singing' and 'drinking bouts'.[119] As one Creole journalist asserted: 'We have adopted the European's dress, his language, his social, moral, political and domestic codes',[120] and natives were expected to do the same. Refusing to 'permit even these aborigines to plant *their* degrading and barbarous peculiarities in the very centre of our community', the writer condemned 'those loud and unseemly exhibitions which occasionally take place in Freetown; those grotesque and ridiculous parades along the streets'.[121] Clearly, generic moral geographies were not simply being reproduced: they were actively deployed, mainly by Creoles seeking both to describe *and* to change their moral environment.

Impacts

If Creoles were vocal within sexuality politics, what effect did their views have? One interpretation would be that, when they variously criticised and distanced themselves from Europeans on the one hand and Africans on the other, Creoles spoke to sexuality politics in conventional ways, appropriating the rhetoric and strategies of wider purity movements. I have alluded to a number of interventions, broadly along the lines of purity movements, encompassing temperance, campaigns for pure recreation and the formation of a purity association. Temperance was promoted in church sermons and special meetings, sponsored by the Evangelical Reform Association (founded in 1890)[122] and the Freetown lodge of the Independent Order of Good Templars (an international organisation, originating in the USA, that established a branch in Freetown in 1876[123]). These organisations both encouraged individuals to refuse drink and campaigned against the trade and licensed distribution of alcohol, particularly trade rum and gin.[124] Earlier in the century, Creoles organised 'Dignity Balls' to celebrate the Queen's Birthday with 'civilised dancing',[125] and in the 1870s they were involved in the establishment of societies and facilities for tennis, reading and other 'moral entertainments',[126] and finally a branch of the YMCA in 1884.[127] Cautious optimism was expressed that these efforts, 'under the patronage of some of the leading and influential men in Sierra Leone', were bringing about real reform, acting as 'mighty levers for elevating the moral and social tone of the country'.[128] In its first year, the Independent Order of Good Templars was credited with modest success, both in attracting members and campaigning for change.[129] A Purity Association branch, started in Freetown, lobbied the authorities to enforce the moral provisions of the Police Ordinance and to introduce new laws. The Creole newspapers supported many of these initiatives, including moves, for instance, to strengthen marriage, and launched some of their own.[130]

Yet these efforts failed to gather much momentum or to produce many tangible effects. The *Sierra Leone Church Times* admitted meetings – such as a lecture at the YMCA entitled 'The duties of young men as Sierra Leoneans to their country', which discussed recreation of a moral kind – were sometimes 'thinly attended'.[131] A year after the establishment of the Freetown lodge, the *Independent* conceded that it would 'share the fate of similar institutions of the land ere this', even though it proceeded to give a mixed account of the organisation's fortunes.[132] A year later it was reported that 'internal discord has shattered its frame'.[133] Sibthorpe's assessment, that the organisation had 'closed up a few grog-shops, and rescued or made temperate many drunkards',[134] was openly downbeat. The movement continued for several decades, but without much energy or momentum.[135] Attempts to introduce moral entertainments were equally modest in their achievements. In 1881 the *West African Reporter* called for the introduction of 'amusements which would not only conduce to the improvement of the mind, but also serve as places of resort to the busy multitude who often squandered their leisure hours in degrading and besotting pleasures'.[136] It admitted, however, that even such 'healthy and purifying pleasures' as the colony had known – traditional Christmas and New Year horse-racing, regattas and athletics – had fallen into decline. In 1875, the *Independent* welcomed the establishment of a Literary Institute, which, it was hoped, would 'infuse into us right notions and correct views of things'.[137] Before his article had gone to print, the Literary Institute had, as an appended editor's note put it, 'come to a premature end'.[138] The Evangelical Reform Association and the Purity Association also slipped into obscurity – it was reported that they appeared to have 'come to grief'.[139] A polemical editorial, lamenting the lack of progress in purity movements in the colony, commented:

> And, not to put too fine a point upon it, the P.A. has all its work cut out for it, to judge by the every day scenes that are transpiring even in the most public thoroughfares, particularly in the Eastern and Western ends of the City.
> If there is a Purity Association in Freetown, what is it up to, anyway?[140]

Assessments of the achievements of individual reformers and purity activists were equally cautious. Rainy's impact, according to Nemata Blyden, was intangible,[141] as was that of Renner Maxwell, whose interventions on marriage and miscegenation were hardly noticed in the colony.[142] An overall assessment of reform and purity movements, printed in the *Sierra Leone Times*, was that they hit few of their stated targets and paled in comparison with their counterparts in other places, particularly England:

> Whereas we in Sierra Leone would sit with folded arms and expect that matters will mend themselves, in England and other highly favoured countries, means are often devised and plans adopted whereby the solution of many a difficult problem affecting the social, religious and political welfare of the people, may be arrived at. Besides the Pulpit, the Law and Police, there is scarcely any recognised institution in the Colony established for the prevention of public evils and the establishment of a social order amongst the masses.[143]

Yet, though they were apparently unable to achieve many of their stated objectives, purity campaigners in Sierra Leone were not inconsequential. While it was hoped that purity movements would draw the 'various classes of society' together to work in 'common cause',[144] they were hampered in practice by disputes and divisions. As the *West African Reporter* reflected in 1878, 'conflicting interests and race considerations' brought a premature end to efforts 'to promote improvement'.[145] The *Sierra Leone Times* regretted the consequences of fragmentation, arguing that each of the colony's many groups 'has its own characteristic, habits, manners, and customs', and that it was difficult to bring these together in collective projects.[146] Although these differences inhibited and fragmented projects, they were also political issues in their own right. Even where interventions failed to bring about change in the law or society, they succeeded in commenting on the moral differences between various groups within the colony. When individuals and organisations spoke on moral questions, they did so not simply to put forward 'the Creole position', but rather or also to position themselves within the colonial society and hierarchy, negotiating their positions within a complexly dynamic, stratified society.[147] Morality formed an important strand of Creole identities, defined against both European and native others. For the *Sierra Leone Times*, Creoles distinguished themselves from natives through their alienation from 'these lands' and their rejection of 'the undesirable darkness of barbarism', and by their adoption of 'the European's dress, his language, his social, *moral*, political and domestic codes'.[148] Public statements of support for temperance, for example, were not simply moral claims, but also pretensions to a certain kind of respectability, associated with the Creole middle classes.[149] Of course, it was not only in Sierra Leone that participation in purity movements was embedded within identity claims, related to class, gender, ethnicity and religious orientation, as the previous chapters on England, India and Australia have shown. (And, as Stoler has shown, the regulation of sexuality, particularly in the form of CD Acts, was directly concerned with the reproduction of difference, on primarily racial lines.) But the heightened multiculturalism of Sierra Leone, coupled with its complexly stratified and rapidly changing social order, established a particularly close link between moral politics and the construction of social difference.

So moral politics in Sierra Leone was not as fruitless as it often seemed. The empowerment of Creoles and other Africans to speak for themselves – in many voices, not always in harmony – was particularly evident in the media. As in many other parts of the Empire, the media in Sierra Leone was an important force, probably the closest thing the colony had to a political opposition. This had been the case since the middle of the century, when the British Government had refused to let the governor restrain a Creole journalist whose frequent criticisms had provoked and irritated him.[150] Apparently the British decided that restrictions on the press might have been counterproductive, increasing its power as well as its hostility.[151] As the *West African Reporter* put it: 'The only means at present employed of representing public opinion is the press.'[152] Historians have concurred that the press did indeed rival the colonial Government, constituting what one Sierra Leonean historian has termed 'the most effective constitutional weapon for ventilating grievances and influencing the trend of events'.[153] Perhaps journalists in Sierra Leone had the ability, if not necessarily to change or secure legislation, then at least to hold the British and their administration to account, drawing attention to the alleged impurity of their ways and the inaction of their Government. Of course, the critical media should be put in perspective, for the difference between this and a real opposition is that the latter has some chance of eventually coming to power. In any case, the press in general, and the interventions examined in this chapter, did not participate in formal politics in the way a conventional opposition would. Their sexuality politics spoke to intrinsically sexual and moral questions, of course, but also to cultural politics of difference, in which Creoles defined and defended their identities and positions against Europeans on one side and native Africans on the other. The complex and creative balancing act that this entailed – variously identifying with and distancing themselves from Europeans and other Africans, and reconfiguring if not wholly reinventing sexuality politics in the process – presented the contact zone as a space of everyday creativity, rooted in the tensions and frictions of coexistence.

Conclusion

A small, poor colony such as Sierra Leone might be the last place one would expect to find an active and creative engagement with sexuality politics. Surely, in what by most accounts was a backwater of the British Empire, people had better things to do and fewer means with which to do them? This chapter has shown, however, that the configuration of peoples and place in Sierra Leone generated a political dynamic of its own. Despite or because of its apparent marginality, its geographical and political distance from the self-proclaimed centres of the Empire, Sierra Leone had long been a kind of political centre – first in the slave trade, then in the campaign against it, and in the reconfiguration of racial ideas and race relations. The convergence of peoples within Sierra Leone also generated and energised sexuality politics there. As a contact zone, the colony fostered a series of productive encounters: between Europeans and Africans, Creoles and natives, and Creoles of different class and ethnicity. The political creativity in Sierra Leone, traced in this chapter, did not always live up to the utopian playfulness and originality envisaged by critics such as Gibson, Linebaugh and Rediker. This was less a place of radical creativity-in-itself than of generative friction, of people pragmatically appropriating and inventing political ideas and strategies. This points not to radical or total newness, but to incremental creativity, generated through the necessities and conflicts of the contact zone.

Encountering each other in person and imaginatively as occupants of a common territory, these different groups perceived each other and defined themselves through a moral lens. These productive encounters were shaped both by the coexistence of peoples and by the real, perceived and imagined spaces of their coexistence. These geographies were structured by sexualised ideas and realities of the public and the private, street and home, city and country, Europe and Africa. Though they reproduced elements of these conventional sexual geographies, they also adapted and amended them, actively deploying them to fit both the particular geographical realities of the colony and the moral politics in question. These interventions were concerned with a mixture of immediate goals – attempts to counter alcoholism or sexual abuse, for example – and the advancement of narrower interests, moralised and sexualised but not primarily moral or sexual. These projects, not just the effects of difference, of friction, between different elements of the colonial society, were also deployed in the production and delineation of difference. In other words, they might become involved in morality and specifically sexuality politics for broadly the same reasons as Europeans had done – not just out of interest in morality or sexuality *per se*, but as a means of addressing, contesting and producing racial and other social boundaries, and power relations. Their ability to do so, and with some measure of autonomy and originality, was in part a function of the sites of their political action: generative colonial geographies.

These pragmatic, situated engagements with sexuality politics speak to the broader themes of the book: questions of where political ideas come from, where they go, and how they are not only located, but actually produce social and spatial locations. The Conclusion returns to these themes, and asks whether geographical imagination has led where Butler hoped it might.

Notes

1 'Saturday in Freetown', *Artisan* (24 June 1885), p. 1.
2 Wyse argues that Sierra Leoneans with hybrid (European–African) cultural identities should be called 'Krios', though most other critics use the terms 'Creole' and 'Krio', and I follow their precedent in order to distinguish clearly between the cultural group (Creole) and the language (Krio); see A. J. G. Wyse, *The Krio of Sierra Leone: An Interpretive History* (London: C. Hurst, 1989); see also: L. Spitzer, 'Creole attitudes towards Krio: an historical survey', *Sierra Leone Language Review*, 5 (1966), 39–49.
3 'Saturday in Freetown', p. 1. Bullom, or Bulom, opposite Freetown on the Sierra Leone estuary, supplied Freetown with much of its food and vegetables; *agidi* is a

food made of boiled ground corn: C. N. Fyle and E. D. Jones, *A Krio–English Dictionary* (New York: Oxford University Press, 1980), p. 56.

4   'Saturday in Freetown', p. 1.

5   T. Davis, *Actresses as Working Women: Their Social Identity in Victorian Culture* (London: Routledge, 1991).

6   L. Nead, *Victorian Babylon: People, Streets and Images in Nineteenth-Century London* (New Haven, CT: Yale University Press), p. 149.

7   J. R. Walkowitz, *City of Dreadful Delight: Narratives of Sexual Danger in Late-Victorian London* (London: Virago, 1994); E. D. Rappaport, *Shopping for Pleasure: Women in the Making of London's West End* (Princeton, NJ: Princeton University Press, 2000).

8   Nead, *Victorian Babylon*, p. 149.

9   M. Ogborn and C. Philo, 'Soldiers, sailors and moral locations in nineteenth-century Portsmouth', *Area*, 26:3 (1994), 221–231; F. Driver, 'Moral geographies: social science and the urban environment in mid-nineteenth century England', *Transactions of the Institute of British Geographers*, new series, 13 (1988), 275–287.

10 S. Aravamudan, *Tropicopolitans: Colonialism and Agency, 1688–1804* (Durham, NC: Duke University Press, 1999), p. 254.

11 Wyse, *Krio of Sierra Leone*, p. 1.

12 'African life and customs', *Sierra Leone Weekly News* (21 September 1907), p. 4.

13 Blyden to the Earl of Kimberly, British Colonial Secretary (22 October 1873), in *Selected Letters of Edward Willmot Blyden*, ed. and introduced by H. R. Lynch (New York: KTO Press, 1978), p. 145.

14 b. hooks, *Yearning: Race, Gender and Cultural Politics* (London: Turnaround, 1991).

15 V. Turner, *Ritual Process* (Chicago, IL: Aldine, 1969); R. Shields, *Places on the Margin: Alternative Geographies of Modernity* (London: Routledge, 1991).

16 H. K. Bhabha, *Location of Culture* (London: Routledge, 1994).

17 M. L. Pratt, *Imperial Eyes: Studies in Travel Writing and Transculturation* (London: Routledge, 1992), p. 4.

18 Pratt, *Imperial Eyes*, p. 7.

19 Burton, *At the Heart of Empire*, p. 1.

20 Gibson, 'Ocean settlement', p. 93.

21 Gibson, 'Ocean settlement', p. 93.

22 P. Linebaugh and M. Rediker, *The Many-Headed Hydra: The Hidden History of the Revolutionary Atlantic* (London: Verso, 2000).

23 Linebaugh and Rediker, *Many-Headed Hydra*, p. 6.

24 M. Banton, *West African City: A Study of Tribal Life in Freetown* (London: Oxford University Press, 1957).

25 J. A. D. Alie, *A New History of Sierra Leone* (London: Macmillan, 1990).

26 S. J. Braidwood, *Black Poor and White Philanthropists: London's Blacks and the Foundation of the Sierra Leone Settlement, 1786–1791* (Liverpool: Liverpool University Press, 1994).

27 'The state of the colony', *Sierra Leone Times* (17 February 1900).

28 A. T. Porter, *Creoledom: A Study of the Development of Freetown Society* (Oxford: Oxford University Press, 1963).

29 A. J. G. Wyse, 'The Krio of Sierra Leone: an ethnographic study of a West African people', *International Journal of Sierra Leone Studies*, 1 (1988), 36–63.

30 Wyse, *Krio of Sierra Leone*, p. 7.

31 Fyle and Jones, *Krio–English Dictionary*, p. xvii.

32 Fyle and Jones, *Krio–English Dictionary*, p. xviii.

33 C. P. Foray, *Historical Dictionary of Sierra Leone* (London: Methuen, 1977), p. 62; Wyse, *Krio of Sierra Leone*, p. 8.

34 L. Spitzer, *The Creoles of Sierra Leone: Responses to Colonialism, 1870–1945* (Madison: University of Wisconsin Press, 1974), p. 13.

35 Blyden to Mary Kingsley (7 May 1900), in *Black Spokesman: Selected Writings of Edward Wilmot Blyden*, ed. H. R. Lynch (London: Frank Cass, 1971), p. 462.

36 N. A. Blyden, *West Indians in West Africa: The African Diaspora in Reverse* (New York: University of Rochester Press, 2000).

37 A. B. C. Sibthorpe (1829–1916), 'probably a receptive or Liberated African from Western Nigeria, possibly an Ibo', attended the CMS Grammar School before working as a teacher and writing the first history of Sierra Leone, as well as geographies and other books: Foray, *Historical Dictionary of Sierra Leone*, p. 194.

38 'Our native manners and customs', *Sierra Leone Times* (23 June 1894), p. 20.

39 *Selected Letters of Edward Willmot Blyden.*

40 J. Renner Maxwell, *Advantages and Disadvantages of European Intercourse with the West Coast of Africa* (London: Smart & Allen; Freetown: Sawyerr, 1881); and his book-length polemic *The Negro Question or Hints for the Physical Improvement of the Negro Race, with Special Reference to West Africa* (London: T. Fisher Unwin, 1892); see also C. Fyfe, *A History of Sierra Leone* (London: Gregg, [1963] 1993), p. 406.

41 C. H. Fyfe, 'Sierra Leone press in the nineteenth century', *Sierra Leone Studies*, new series, 8 (1957), 226–236, at 230.

42 *Selected Letters of Edward Willmot Blyden.*

43 Fyfe, 'Sierra Leone press in the nineteenth century', p. 232.

44 Fyfe, 'Sierra Leone press in the nineteenth century', p. 233.

45 E. Jones, 'Krio in Sierra Leone journalism', *Sierra Leone Language Review*, 1:3 (1964), 24–31.

46 Fyfe, 'Sierra Leone press in the nineteenth century', p. 229.

47 Foray, *Historical Dictionary of Sierra Leone*, p. 189.

48 Reverend Joseph Claudius May (1845–1902), born in Freetown, son of a liberated African father and educated in England, returned in 1871 to Sierra Leone, where he started and directed the Wesleyan Boys' School; from 1882–1888 he published the *Methodist Herald* and with Blyden's help he started the *Sierra Leone Weekly News* in 1884, appointing his brother Cornelius May as editor and printer: Foray, *Historical Dictionary of Sierra Leone*, p. 138.

49 *Sierra Leone Weekly News* (6 September 1884), p. 1.

50 Jones, 'Krio in Sierra Leone journalism', p. 26.

51 Samuel H. Athanasius Case (1845–1901), a builder, printer and journalist born in the colony, organised the Mechanics' Alliance, a trade union, and contributed to the *West African Reporter* before founding the *Artisan*: Foray, *Historical Dictionary of Sierra Leone*, p. 34.

52 'Prospectus', *Artisan* (28 May 1885), p. 1.

53 William Grant (1830–1882), born in Freetown of Liberated African parentage, successful businessman, member of the Legislative Council 1870–1882, and from 1874 the senior African unofficial member: Foray, *Historical Dictionary of Sierra Leone*, p. 82; Fyfe, 'Sierra Leone press in the nineteenth century', p. 233; 'Our physical and social relations', *West African Reporter* (3 December 1879), p. 2.

54 Fyfe, 'Sierra Leone press in the nineteenth century', p. 227.

55 'Our native manners and customs', p. 2.

56 'Saturday in Freetown', p. 1.

57 Letter to the editor regarding *For Dear Father Land*, *Sierra Leone Weekly News* (20 July 1907), p. 4.

58 T. E. Poole, *Life, Scenery and Customs in Sierra Leone and the Gambia*, 2 vols (London: Richard Bentley, 1850), vol. 1, p. 296.

59 *For Dear Father Land*, *Sierra Leone Weekly News* (13 July 1907), p. 6.

60 *Sierra Leone Weekly News* (24 August 1907), p. 6.

61 Transation by Spitzer, *Creoles of Sierra Leone*, p. 22.

62 Spitzer, *Creoles of Sierra Leone*, p. 22; the word does not appear in Fyle and Jones, *Krio–English Dictionary*.

63 *For Dear Father Land*, p. 6, trans. Spitzer, *Creoles of Sierra Leone*, p. 22.

64 'Roselyn's dialogues for young girls and women', *Sierra Leone Weekly News* (24 August 1907), p. 6.
65 Robert Wellesley-Cole (1907–1985), born in Freetown, educated in Sierra Leone and England, qualified in medicine in 1935, practised in England until he returned to Freetown in the late 1960s: Foray, *Historical Dictionary of Sierra Leone*, p. 230.
66 R. Wellesley-Cole, *Kossoh Town Boy* (Cambridge: Cambridge University Press, 1960), p. 114.
67 'Gambling in Freetown', *Sierra Leone Times* (28 July 1894), p. 2.
68 'One thing and another', *Sierra Leone Times* (11 March 1899), p. 2.
69 'One thing and another', *Sierra Leone Times* (11 March 1899), p. 2.
70 'Gambling in the public thoroughfares', *Sierra Leone Times* (21 July 1894), p. 3.
71 'Gambling in Freetown', *Sierra Leone Times* (28 July 1894), p. 2.
72 'Gambling in Freetown', *Sierra Leone Times* (28 July 1894), p. 2.
73 Letter to the editor regarding *For Dear Father Land*, p. 4.
74 'Abduction of a girl', *Sierra Leone Times* (12 August 1893), p. 2.
75 'Abduction of a girl', p. 2.
76 'Abduction of a girl', p. 2.
77 'Kidnapping, by our correspondent', *Sierra Leone Times* (12 August 1893), p. 3.
78 Wellesley-Cole, *Kossoh Town Boy*, p. 124.
79 Wellesley-Cole, *Kossoh Town Boy*, p. 134.
80 A. Kolodny, *Lay of the Land* (Chapel Hill: University of North Carolina Press, 1975); A. McClintock, *Imperial Leather: Race, Gender and Sexuality in the Colonial Contest* (London: Routledge, 1994).
81 Wellesley-Cole, *Kossoh Town Boy*, p. 126.
82 'Cannibalism in the rivers', *Sierra Leone Times* (26 March 1892), p. 2.
83 P. Hulme, *Colonial Encounters: Europe and the Native Caribbean, 1492–1797* (London: Methuen, 1986), p. 3.
84 Hulme, *Colonial Encounters*, p. 14.
85 F. Barker, P. Hulme and M. Iversen (eds), *Cannibalism and the Colonial World* (Cambridge University Press, 1998), p. 3.
86 R. Shaw, *Memories of the Slave Trade: Ritual and the Historical Imagination in Sierra Leone* (Chicago, IL: University of Chicago Press, 2002).
87 Letter to the editor regarding *For Dear Father Land*, p. 4; original emphasis.
88 H.E., Letter to the editor, *Sierra Leone Church Times* (17 February 1886), p. 2.
89 'The youths of Freetown', *Sierra Leone Times* (29 January 1899), p. 2; 'The youths of Freetown', *Sierra Leone Times* (5 May 1894), p. 2.
90 'Young Men's Christian Association', *Sierra Leone Church Times* (3 September 1884), p. 2.
91 J. Renner Maxwell, *The Negro Question*, p. 4.
92 Blyden to William Coppinger, secretary of the American Colonisation Society (18 December 1885), in *Black Spokesman*, p. 358.
93 Sibthorpe argued that the colonial churches were 'filled with blacks', that the 'ill-fated' whites were 'drinking whisky or smoking cigarettes at the Bungalow, if not shooting partridges on Sunday', setting a 'bad example' for Creoles: A. B. C. Sibthorpe, *The History of Sierra Leone*, 2nd edn (London: Elliot Stock, 1881), p. 220.
94 'A review of the policy of our present executive with our aborigines', *Sierra Leone Weekly News* (10 April 1886), p. 2; Blyden generalised that this picture was repeated around the world, where European imperialism was destroying aboriginal peoples, 'fatally poisoning them by its vices, its drunkenness and debauchery': 'Banquet to Dr Blyden', *Sierra Leone Weekly News* (26 January 1907), p. 4.
95 'European trade with West Africa', *West African Reporter* (11 February 1880), p. 2; also, for example, Renner Maxwell, *Advantages and Disadvantages of European Intercourse with the West Coast of Africa*, p. 22.
96 Blyden to William Coppinger, in *Black Spokesman*, p. 397.
97 *For Dear Father Land*, p. 6, trans. Spitzer, *Creoles of Sierra Leone*, p. 22.

98 *For Dear Father Land*, p. 6; trans. Spitzer, *Creoles of Sierra Leone*, p. 22.

99 For a similar argument about Stead's interventions, see D. Gorham, ' "The Maiden Tribute of modern Babylon" re-examined: child prostitution and the idea of child-hood in late-Victorian England', *Victorian Studies*, 21:3 (1978), 355.

100 *For Dear Father Land*, p. 6.

101 Crowder, *West Africa under Colonial Rule*.

102 *For Dear Father Land*, p. 6.

103 Blyden, *West Indians in West Africa*, p. 140.

104 Spitzer, 'Creole attitudes towards Krio', p. 41; E. D. Jones, 'The business of trans-lating into Krio, in E. D. Jones, K. I. Sandred and N. Shrimpton (eds), *Reading and Writing Krio* (Uppsala: Almqvist & Wiksell, 1990).

105 The *Sierra Leone Weekly News* printed 'long poems in Krio on burning social topics, the earliest of which appeared in 1888': Jones, 'Krio in Sierra Leone journalism', p. 26.

106 Jones, 'Krio in Sierra Leone journalism', p. 26.

107 N. E. Benson Garrick, letter to the editor regarding *For Dear Father Land*, *Sierra Leone Weekly News* (27 July 1907), p. 3; see also N. Thiong'o, *Decolonising the Mind: The Politics of Language in African Literature* (London: James Currey, 1986); Spitzer, 'Creole attitudes towards Krio', p. 44; Jones, 'Krio in Sierra Leone journalism', p. 24.

108 'O you important men /O you men who go to Church; /O you men who have money; /O you men who have influence; /Stand up – wake up – things are bad, listen /Save the little girls from death; /Save the Creole girls from ruin': *For Dear Father Land*, p. 6; trans. Spitzer, *Creoles of Sierra Leone*, p. 22.

109 Jones, 'Krio in Sierra Leone journalism'; *For Dear Father Land*, p. 6.

110 A. Montagu, *Ordinances of the Colony of Sierra Leone* (London: HMSO, 1857), p. 109.

111 Attorney-general of Sierra Leone, *Supplement to the Laws of the Colony and Protectorate of Sierra Leone* (London: Waterlow, 1932), pp. 253, 264: The 'Chil-dren's Ordinance': An Ordinance to Prevent Cruelty to Children, 24 December 1926, set penalties of up to 15 years' imprisonment 'for carnal knowledge of a girl under thirteen', up to 2 years for attempted carnal knowledge with a girl under fourteen, and additional penalties for 'abduction of a girl for immoral purposes', 'procuration' and 'allowing children to be in brothels'. The 'Criminal Law Amend-ment Ordinance': An Ordinance to Make Provision for the Protection of Women and Girls, 23 April 1927, extended provisions against procuration, which origin-ally referred to 'any child not being a common prostitute' (where 'child' was defined as anyone under 16 years of age), to protect 'any girl or woman under twenty-one years of age'.

112 *For Dear Father Land*, p. 6.

113 Fyfe, *History of Sierra Leone*, p. 438.

114 Renner Maxwell, *Negro Question*, p. 160.

115 L. Pearce, 'Devolutionary desires', in Phillips, Watt and Shuttleton (eds), *De-Centring Sexualities*, pp. 241–257.

116 T. O. Elias, *Ghana and Sierra Leone: The Development of Their Laws and Constitutions* (London: Stevens, 1962), p. 236.

117 Montagu, *Ordinances of the Colony of Sierra Leone*, p. 103.

118 'One thing and another', *Sierra Leone Times* (11 March 1899), p. 2.

119 'Our native manners and customs II', *Sierra Leone Times* (30 June 1894), p. 2.

120 'Our native manners and customs', p. 2.

121 'Our native manners and customs', p. 2.

122 'Evangelical Reform Association', *Sierra Leone Times* (2 June 1894), p. 2.

123 Sibthorpe, *History of Sierra Leone*, p. 81.

124 'Temperance meeting at Wilberforce Hall', *Sierra Leone Weekly News* (13 Febru-ary 1892), p. 4.

125 Sibthorpe, *History of Sierra Leone*, p. 45.

126 'Sierra Leone Tennis Association', *Sierra Leone Weekly News* (9 April 1892), p. 5.

127 *Sierra Leone Church Times* (3 September 1884).
128 'Retrospect of the year 1878', *West African Reporter* (1 January 1879), p. 3.
129 'Independent Order of Good Templars', *Independent* (28 December 1876), p. 3: the organisation promoted '[to]tal abstinence for life from all intoxicating liquors as beverages' and 'the creation of a healthy public opinion upon the Temperance question by the active dissemination of truth'.
130 'The Marriage Amendment Ordinance', *Sierra Leone Weekly News* (3 September 1887), p. 2.
131 'Trinity Church Young Men's Christian Association', *Sierra Leone Church Times* (18 June 1884), p. 1.
132 'Independent Order of Good Templars', p. 3.
133 'Retrospect of the year 1878', p. 3.
134 Sibthorpe, *History of Sierra Leone*, p. 81.
135 Fyfe, *History of Sierra Leone*, p. 409.
136 'Public amusements', *West African Reporter* (31 December 1881), p. 2.
137 J. H. Spaine, 'The youths of Sierra Leone', *Independent* (12 August 1875), p. 2.
138 Spaine, 'The youths of Sierra Leone', p. 2.
139 'One thing and another', *Sierra Leone Times* (11 March 1899), p. 2.
140 'One thing and another', p. 2.
141 Blyden, *West Indians in West Africa*, p. 156.
142 Spitzer, *Creoles of Sierra Leone*, p. 136.
143 'Public opinion on Sierra Leone', *Sierra Leone Times* (5 March 1892), p. 2.
144 'Independent Order of Good Templars', p. 3.
145 'Retrospect of the year 1878', p. 3.
146 'The state of the colony', *Sierra Leone Times* (17 February 1900); original punctuation.
147 Porter, *Creoledom*.
148 'Our native manners and customs', p. 2; emphasis added.
149 Spitzer, *Creoles of Sierra Leone*, p. 21.
150 Fyfe, 'Sierra Leone press in the nineteenth century', p. 228.
151 F. I. A. Omu, 'The "new era" and the abortive press law of 1857', *Sierra Leone Studies*, new series, 23 (1968), 2–14, at 14.
152 Editorial, *West African Reporter* (26 March 1881), p. 2.
153 F. I. A. Omu, 'Dilemma of press freedom in colonial Africa: the West African example', *Journal of African History*, 9 (1968), 279–298, at 279.

CONCLUSION

Fields of understanding and political action

I began with some questions and suggestions. Interpreting interventions by Josephine Butler and Alfred Dyer, I suggested the promise of geographical imagination to develop new fields of understanding and political action. This pointed towards the need to cultivate a form of what Frederic Jameson once called 'cognitive mapping' – finding ways to represent sites of political action, positioning them with 'a new sense of the absent global colonial system'.[1] I explained that Jameson's suggestive, somewhat metaphorical reference to 'mapping' finds parallels in critical language, which Ann Laura Stoler, Philippa Levine, Rudi Bleys and others have used to explore and understand imperial sexuality politics. Exploring the promise inherent in these spatial suggestions, I have tried to envisage elements of a postcolonial geography, which potentially challenges and contributes to both postcolonial criticism and critical geography. Taking up questions for a postcolonial geography, posed by Alison Blunt and Cheryl McEwan, I have asked how imperial power was and is both constituted and resisted geographically.[2] As promised in the Introduction, the book has examined the spatial dynamics of power with respect to the contested regulation of sexuality, aiming to critique and contest Eurocentric accounts of the same. It is now time to take stock of the ways in which these questions have been answered, the extent to which the promise of geographical imagination has been realised in activism and can be applied to contemporary problems.

Building on Manderson's claim that there was a 'moral logic of colonialism',[3] but that it was never very coherent or transparent, this book has been able to trace some of the connections between imperial power and the regulation of sexuality. This was sometimes a matter primarily of authority and loyalty, whereby colonial deference to metropolitan precedent expressed and confirmed the imperial order – and conversely in which colonial departures threw question marks over it. It was sometimes a matter of substance, systems of regulation underpinning colonial relationships, as for example when age-of-consent laws played a part in shaping the families that colonised much of North America and Australia, or when CD laws were used to maintain the health, morale, mobility, heterosexuality and homo-sociality of young male colonial soldiers and workers. Laws, once passed, affected different people in different ways and fared differently in different places. The age of consent was enforced in England, where the NVA monitored its application and helped to hold the authorities to public account, but in many other places – in India, and by some accounts in Australia – it was widely ignored.[4] Where laws were enforced, the consequences were varied and complex. Contradicting or complicating my speculation about the colonial family, for example, it might be argued that agricultural settlement needed families less than families needed farms, and that family farms were poorly adapted to places like South Australia. Certainly, the story of agricultural colonisation presented in historical geographer Don Meinig's tragedy *The Margins of the Good Earth* is one of families awkwardly inhabiting and in many cases being defeated by an area better suited to cowboys, wine-growers or aborigines.[5] And, whatever imperial logic may have been presented for them, laws for the regulation of sexuality were often presented as unnecessary and intrusive meddling, and the hostility this aroused may have undermined any concrete imperial advantages they brought. These observations point away from a linear moral logic – devised, imposed and perhaps resisted or negotiated for straightforward imperial ends – towards something more plural, driven by the generative friction between multiple positions.

This book's most sustained contribution to postcolonial criticism revolves around its elaboration of the spatiality of imperial sexuality politics and more generally imperial power. These politics were fundamentally *situated*, shaped by the material and imaginative geographies in and between which they unfolded: geographies of domination (concentrations of colonial power) and resistance (with scope for agency). These political geographies provide insights to imperial patterns and processes. The patterns in geographies of regulation and resistance, structured but profoundly uneven and broken, have given rise to questions about the form and depth of imperial power. As Anthony Padgen shows in *Lords of All the World*, the profound heterogeneity of European imperialism spoke in some cases of its flexibility, in others of something less assured.[6] Through the devolution of power to colonial legislatures and governors, the British actively fostered a kind of heterogeneity, founded on robust flexibility.[7] For this reason, the imperial order was not necessarily compromised in any way by colonial departures from central precedents, when the latter appeared to exist. However, these departures did sometimes disturb the imperial order, going against Eurocentric assumptions about where innovations come from and where they go.

Analysing the spatial constitution of contested imperial power, I have sought to critique and move beyond Eurocentric understandings of sexuality and empire by looking beyond 'the British experience'. At times, England could certainly seem like the centre of the world, English men and women generating new ideas and exporting them by telegraph, in newspapers and letters, and most tangibly by travelling and working between and in colonies. Beginning a critique of what James Blaut called 'the colonizer's model of the world',[8] earlier chapters in this book showed how the apparent diffusion of metropolitan ideas was not structured around a simple geographical division between innovation and adoption, active and passive political action, in the so-called centre and margins respectively. On the contrary, people in colonies actively imported and appropriated ideas and strategies, and sometimes they refused them. And if metropolitan innovations travelled better to some places than to others, as the evidence shows they did, this was not always due to intentional action: arguably there was also something about places themselves that was more receptive to specific systems of regulation, or more generally to systems of power. But it would be wrong to conclude that colonies simply reacted differently to English ideas. On the contrary, they could also be productive sites in themselves, generating new forms of regulation and resistance, which in some cases were exported to other colonies or to the mother country. The 'productivity of the margins' was variously a function of the power that was concentrated, the freedom imagined and the human contact that existed there. This analysis of imperial sexuality politics, which moves beyond Eurocentric understandings of sexuality and empire, and offers something broader to the development of a postcolonial geography, has used *spatial* perspectives to look beyond the British experience. This has often been rather tentative, edging away from Eurocentric history in quite subtle ways – appropriately, because colonial political life *did* involve negotiating and working through the power of the centre, but doing so in ways that reclaimed agency and generated political direction from the margins.

The substance of this book is historical, but its themes and concerns cannot be relegated to the past. The desire to reconstruct and interpret a past, and through it a way of seeing, that bears on the present, is one I share with others who have written histories of sexuality and/or imperialism, sometimes in the face of urgent questions that can make historical work appear almost indulgent. Judith Walkowitz and Frank Mort, for instance, turned the insights of their 1980s' studies of sexuality in Victorian London and other cities to questions of contemporary sexual violence and the emerging AIDS crisis, which they made explicit in prologues and epilogues. Critical historians and histories are, of course, concerned implicitly with speaking to the present and the future. Postcolonial critics are often more explicit in that respect, adopting the postcolonial not simply or necessarily as a chronological category – concerned with the period after colonialism – but rather as a political orientation, concerned with being and writing *against* colonialism. If this study of imperial sexuality politics opens fields for understanding and political action, it speaks both to the past and the present, both to historical debates and contemporary predicaments.

Some of the most immediate connections between past and present relate to the enduring legacies of imperial sexuality politics. The laws, introduced in the period examined in this book, have a strong legacy, and though some been swept aside, others remain more or less in place, preserved or modified. The most tenacious of the Victorian laws relate to the age of consent, increases in which, conceived and achieved at this time, have survived evidence that they are variously arbitrary, harmful and ignored. In India, as I have noted, the amendment increasing the age to 12 was almost immediately pronounced a dead letter.[9] Recent evidence that 90 per cent of English teenagers feel the age in their country (still 16) is too high, and 30 per cent have sex before they reach it, has not provoked government to seriously consider changing the age.[10] By contrast, Victorian legislation on sex between men has gradually given way, since the 1960s, to something more tolerant. In England, the provisions of the Labouchere Amendment remained in place for over 80 years, until 1967 when sex between men was partially decriminalised, subject to a higher age of consent (21) than applied to heterosexual sex (16); it took another 34 years and 2 major interventions through the European Court of Human Rights for the homosexual and heterosexual ages of consent to be equalised. Similar moves were made, generally later, in Scotland, Northern Ireland, remnants of the British Empire and Commonwealth countries.

As late as 1980 Australian laws on sex between men derived in many areas from English law, and it was not until 1984 that NSW finally decriminalised male homosexual acts.[11] Sex between men was decriminalised in Britain's remaining Caribbean colonies – Anguilla, the Cayman Islands, the British Virgin Islands, Montserrat and the Turks and Caicos, with a combined population of just under 90,000 –

in 2001, following a drawn-out process in which the British tried to persuade but then forced the islanders to repeal laws that had been imposed under colonial rule, but which had fallen foul of the European Convention on Human Rights, to which Britain has subscribed.[12] Other former colonies, with more self-determination than these Caribbean islands, have retained versions of colonial law on this subject. Jeremy Seabrook has argued that laws with 'roots in Victorian morality, but . . . embraced' by postcolonial ruling classes, filtered through society and were enshrined in laws such as Section 377 of the Indian Penal Code, which forbids 'sexual acts against the order of nature'.[13] Similarly, Peter Tatchell argues that it is 'a perverse twist of history that Robert Mugabe is now espousing a homophobic agenda not dissimilar to that which was once imposed on black Zimbabweans by the colonisers that he fought a war of liberation to overthrow'.[14]

Another set of laws, concerned with prostitution, has more limited legacy in England and former colonies. Successfully contested by purity campaigners, CD laws were repealed in England and most colonies in the 1880s and 1890s. Announcing a review of English law on prostitution, ministers recently acknowledged that 'nearly every model for dealing with prostitution has been tried in Britain over the last 700 years'.[15] The main legacy of the Victorian period, in this respect, was that regulation had been discredited for a time, and some version of Butler's critique retained as a model for formulating policy. British Home Secretary David Blunkett presented a new approach to prostitution as a kind of homage to Butler. Announcing plans to help women escape the sex trade, Blunkett declared: 'We in this century must do what Josephine Butler attempted over 100 years ago, in a very different era and in a very different way.'[16]

The diverse but generally powerful legacy of imperial sexuality politics gives rise to the question of whether contemporary forms of regulation need to be *decolonised* in some way. On one level, the answer to this appears straightforward: demonstrating that laws against sex between men in developing countries such as Zimbabwe, Jamaica and India originate either in colonial statutes or in broadly colonial attitudes, activists and critics such as Tatchell and Seabrook argue the need to recognise and eradicate legacies of colonial homophobia. The straightforward liberation suggested in calls to eradicate offending remnants of colonial legislation is complicated, however, by Foucault's convincing argument that sexuality forms 'an especially dense transfer point for relations of power'.[17] If this is so, it may be possible to dismantle particularly repressive laws or customs, but it is not possible to extricate sexuality from power in a broader sense. The simplistic libertarian objective of sex without power must then be exchanged for a critical project that positions sexuality within a broader transformative politics. Alan Sinfield argues that, since the hierarchies of capitalism and patriarchy inform 'our daily interactions, the language through which we come to consciousness, our psychic formations',[18] we should not attempt to sidestep those differentials by excluding them from our relationships. On the contrary: 'We should be exploring ways to assess and recombine power, sexiness, responsibility and love.'[19] Rather than trying to extricate sexuality from power, sex should become a vehicle for the transformation of power, power for the transformation of sex and sexuality. The decolonisation of sexuality must go hand in hand with something much broader.

This explains why Victorian sexuality politics could have been so radical: the transformation of sexuality was embedded in that of the domestic and international order. Victorians could remake sexuality because, for better or for worse, they were reinventing their world. Blunkett, a most conservative Labour Home Secretary, might not have presented Josephine Butler as an inspiration for planned amendments to the law on prostitution had he recognised the radicalism in elements of her project.[20] Resisting the law on prostitution, Butler contested pillars of the militarised imperial system, putting moral questions above national political and economic interests. Leading a movement that went on to successfully change the age of consent, one of the fundamental parameters of family, she proved willing to think very laterally indeed. Of course, historical figures can be used selectively, their radical edges diluted in sepia. Were she alive today, Butler might look more like, for instance, Tatchell than some of her admirers would expect. The comparison, though obviously limited, is provocatively suggestive. Like his Victorian predecessor, Tatchell locates sexuality politics within a broader map of power. Calling for President Robert Mugabe of Zimbabwe to change specific policies on sex between men, and to recognise and eradicate the legacies of colonial homophobia, Tatchell makes a connection between sexuality and broader forms of human liberation (figure 8.1). When Tatchell attempted a citizen's arrest on Mugabe, in London in 1999, he accused him not just of repressing gays and lesbians, but of something broader: human rights abuses.[21] 'President Mugabe, you are under arrest for torture', he declared. 'Torture is a crime under international law.'[22] Like Butler, Tatchell had found a political language acceptable to middle England. Sections of the media that once pilloried his uncompromising queer politics decided they liked and even admired Tatchell. And, like Butler, Tatchell has returned to the age of consent, provoking a debate about young people's sexualities, one which

8.1 Peter Tatchell marching against President Robert Mugabe of Zimbabwe at London Pride, a gay–lesbian demonstration and street parade, in 2003

the fear of paedophilia had all but closed – despite evidence that English teenagers are not only likely to have sex before they reach that age, but that many of them are likely to catch a sexually transmitted disease or conceive a child in the process.[23] Tatchell contradicted his Victorian predecessor's logic and specific demands, but he echoed the lateral and radical nature of her thinking when he observed that 16 'is a totally arbitrary age of consent. It originates from 1885, when consent was raised to 13. There is, however, no medical or psychological evidence that 16 is the age of sexual or emotional maturity.'[24] Perhaps, if the home secretary really wanted to learn from Butler, he would listen to Tatchell.

On the other hand, while there may be much to learn from activists such as Butler and Tatchell, the inspiration should not be too deferential. I have argued that English men and women who involved themselves in sexuality politics often did so within a Eurocentric frame of reference, and the same criticism might be levelled at their successors. Tatchell's argument with Mugabe began when the latter decided to exclude GALZ, the organisation called Gays and Lesbians of Zimbabwe, from the international book fair in Harare in 1995.[25] Opening the fair, which ostensibly celebrated 'human rights and justice', Mugabe condemned homosexuals as perverts without rights. When seventy American congressmen wrote to protest, he responded angrily: 'Let the Americans keep their sodomy, bestiality, stupid and foolish ways to themselves, out of Zimbabwe', he ranted. 'We don't want those practices here.'[26] The argument was never just about sexuality. Mugabe claimed that it spoke of something broader: relationships between African and Western attitudes to homosexuality, as his response to the congressmen indicates, and more generally between Zimbabwe and former colonial or neo-colonial powers. When Tatchell was released with a caution, after the attempted citizen's arrest, Mugabe claimed that the British Government had organised the attack as a way of punishing him for seizing land from white farmers. He used an interview with the Zimbabwean media to blame British Prime Minister Tony Blair for the attack, alleging that the Foreign Office minister with whom he had held talks was 'the wife of Tatchell'.[27] Mugabe has not been the only leader of a developing country to contest queer movements as Western affectations and impositions. For instance, Nicholas Sykes, chief pastor of the Church of England in the Cayman Islands, argued that the Privy Council's decision to force British colonies in the Caribbean to decriminalise sex between men was 'totally unacceptable to the minds of the Christian community here'.[28] Short of declaring independence, an impracticable solution for islands with a combined population of less than 90,000, there was no way to block this move. The argument about sexuality had become the vehicle for a broader conflict, concerned with power and resistance, both between nations and within them.

It is tempting to dismiss protests by the likes of Mugabe and Sykes as variously unhinged and bigoted. Yet, there is something troubling about the embroilments of interventions such as these with deeply rooted international inequalities and prejudices. Interventions in support of non-Western gay and lesbian movements are problematical, in the first instance, in their imposition of what Foucault showed to be a modern Western construction of sexuality in non-Western contexts. Frank Mort locates gay and lesbian identities and identity politics within a relatively narrow 'puritan diaspora'[29] that includes Britain, North America and Australia, but does not 'travel' well to continental Europe, let alone to other parts of the world, where the gender of one's sexual partner(s) is not necessarily the defining feature of one's sexuality. Conceivably, a gay and lesbian organisation would be seen as alien in Southern Africa, though some space might be found there for sexual love between members of the same gender.

Another potentially troubling aspect of the argument between Tatchell and Mugabe was that it reflected a broader racial pattern, in which the Zimbabwean was generally condemned by white countries and supported by black ones. Before and during the 2003 Commonwealth Conference in Nigeria, at which Zimbabwe averted possible expulsion from the organisation by announcing its decision to quit, attitudes towards the country corresponded almost perfectly to the division between Old Commonwealth (wealthier countries with white majorities) and New (poorer countries with black majorities, particularly those in Africa). Might it also be worried that his interventions against Mugabe have the effect of empowering Tatchell and his movement – gaining respectability, where before he had been vilified – by appearing to speak for others, in a Western voice that stands in for Africans who cannot represent themselves? In a parallel argument, Antoinette Burton has shown how nineteenth-century English feminists made political capital by campaigning on behalf of Indian prostitutes, of whom they spoke as 'sisters'.[30] Campaigning for Indians, they strengthened and galvanised the feminist movement closer to home. This is not to suggest that their interventions were simply self-interested, or that activists such as these should have refrained from using the power and influence that they found and made for themselves in England. It is not to suggest that political activism should be paralysed with doubt. This is not an option, since there are some areas of sexuality politics in which Western interventions in non-Western countries are not only possible and desirable, but are urgently needed. The concentration of the global AIDS crisis in the world's poorest regions – in South Africa alone, 4.5 million people are currently HIV-positive and 600 die from AIDS every day[31] – means that, whether they like it or not, Western countries must act in and for their poorer counterparts

Interventions such as these depend upon what Jameson called 'cognitive maps', representations of some kind of interconnected totality, which would make the world imaginatively accessible, orienting political action. Dennis Altman reflected, after a decade's work in the international HIV/AIDS world, both as an academic researcher and an active player in UNAIDS, that the 'interconnectedness of the world' is both a danger and an opportunity.[32] 'Cognitively mapping' sexuality politics, this book has traced connections between people, places and politics, exploring both their dangers and opportunities, which revolve in each case around embroilments in global power. Its critique of Eurocentrism provides grounds for optimism. Going beyond the attention to Indian women that enabled English feminists to forge a stronger movement, and helped Tatchell renew and widen the horizons of otherwise increasingly self-absorbed, consumerist and moribund queer politics in England, genuine engagements with others might constitute the first step along an uncharted and liberating political path. To engage rather than impose, we must be prepared to depart from Western political scripts and assumptions about what constitutes liberation. This book has shown that political ideas can come from unlikely places, and be generated and transformed in connections and movements between places. To forge a truly transformative – and thus liberating – sexuality politics, we must forge connections that involve taking as well as giving, being changed as well as changing.

Notes

1 Jameson, 'Cognitive mapping', p. 349.
2 Blunt and McEwan, *Postcolonial Geographies*, p. 5.
3 L. Manderson, 'Colonial desires: sexuality, race and gender in British Malaya', *Journal of the History of Sexuality*, 7:3 (1997), 373; and *Sickness and the State: Health and Illness in Colonial Malaya, 1870–1940* (Cambridge: Cambridge University Press, 1996).
4 A correspondent in NSW reported that 'little attention seems paid to' the age of consent, then 14: letter to the editor from correspondent in Sydney, *Church Times* (London) (5 May 1899), p. 527.
5 D. Meinig, *On the Margins of the Good Earth: The South Australian Wheat Frontier 1869–1884* (London: John Murray, 1963). The colonisation of South Australia outgrew, but remained largely modelled on, the family farm, as it reached into increasingly unsuitable physical environments, with inevitable consequences.
6 A. Pagden, *Lords of All the World: Ideologies of Empire in Spain, Britain and France, c.1500–1800* (New Haven, CT, and London: Yale University Press, 1995).
7 P. Odile Goerg, *Pouvoir colonial, municipalités et espaces urbains: Conakry–Freetown des années 1880 à 1914* (Paris: L'Harmattan, 1997), reviewed by John D. Hargreaves, *Journal of African History*, 39 (1997), 494–495.
8 Blaut, *The Colonizer's Model of the World*.
9 M. Kosambi, 'Girl-brides and socio-legal change: the Age of Consent Bill (1891) controversy', *Economic and Political Weekly* (3 August 1991), p. 1866; D. Engels, 'The Age of Consent Act of 1891: colonial ideology in Bengal', *South Asia Research*, 3 (1983), 107–34.
10 A survey conducted in 2001 showed that 27 per cent of men and 20 per cent of women had sex before the age of 16; for those aged 16–19, the rates were higher: 30 and 26 per cent, respectively: S. Bosely, 'More sex please', *Guardian* (30 November 2001), p. 3. Another survey, conducted in 2000 among 42,000 girls aged 12–16, found that 87 per cent think the age of consent of 16 is too high: P. Tatchell, 'Lower the age of consent', *Guardian* (1 August 2001), p. 15.
11 G. Wotherspoon, *'City of the Plain': History of a Gay Sub-Culture* (Sydney: Hale & Iremonger, 1991), p. 21.
12 Associated Press, 'Britain scraps islands' anti-gay laws', *Guardian* (6 January 2001), p. 7; gay sex became legal in all the islands on Monday 1 January, 2001, although the age of consent is 18 for homosexuals and 16 for heterosexuals. The islands have a combined population of 86,600: 'World news: Caribbean' *Pink Paper* (12 January 2001), p. 5.

13 J. Seabrook, 'It's not natural: the developing world's homophobia is a legacy of colonial rule', *Guardian* (3 July 2004), p. 21.
14 Bleys, *Geography of Perversion*, reviewed by P. Tatchell, *Gay Times* (April 1996), p. 7; see also: P. Tatchell, *Battle for Bermondsey* (London: Heretic Books, 1983).
15 A. Travis, 'Sex laws to get major overhaul: review of prostitution will be the first for 50 years', *Guardian* (30 December 2003), p. 1.
16 M. Oliver and A. Travis, 'Victorian reformer inspired Blunkett', *Guardian* (30 December 2003), p. 2.
17 Foucault, *History of Sexuality*, vol. 1, p. 103.
18 A. Sinfield, 'The production of gay and the return of power', in Phillips, Watt and Shuttleton (eds), *De-Centring Sexualities*, pp. 21–36, at 34.
19 Sinfield, 'Production of gay and the return of power', p. 35.
20 Oliver and Travis, 'Victorian reformer inspired Blunkett', p. 2.
21 S. Chan, *Robert Mugage: A Life of Power and Violence* (London: I. B. Taurus, 2003), p. 43.
22 D. Blair, *Degrees in Violence: Robert Mugabe and the Struggle for Power in Zimbabwe* (London: Continuum, 2003), p. 134.
23 P. Tatchell, 'Lower the age of consent', *Guardian* (1 August 2001), p. 15.
24 Tatchell, 'Lower the age of consent', p. 15.
25 The following year Mugabe added to the constitution of Zimbabwe a clause against gay marriage and a provision allowing individual rights to be overruled on the grounds of 'public morality': Chan, *Robert Mugage*.
26 M. Meredith, *Mugabe: Power and Plunder in Zimbabwe* (Oxford: Public Affairs, 2002), p. 130.
27 Blair, *Degrees in Violence*, p. 135.
28 The Privy Council used the power invested in it as the highest court for the territories to decriminalise homosexual acts between consenting adults in private, effective January 2001: Associated Press, 'Britain scraps islands' anti-gay laws', *Guardian*, 6 January 2001, p. 7.
29 Mort, *Dangerous Sexualities*, Preface; Foucault, *History of Sexuality*, vol. 1; J. N. Katz, *Invention of Heterosexuality* (London: Penguin, 1995).
30 A. Burton, *Burdens of History: British Feminists, Indian Women and Imperial Culture, 1865–1915* (Chapel Hill: University of North Carolina Press, 1994).
31 Médecins sans Frontières' website: www.msf.org (20 November 2003).
32 D. Altman, *Global Sex* (Chicago, IL: University of Chicago Press, 2001), p. 164.

BIBLIOGRAPHY

PRIMARY SOURCES (ABBREVIATIONS AS USED IN NOTES)

BRITISH LIBRARY, LONDON
India Office Records (IOR)
  Colonial government records, India and Bombay (municipality, Presidency)
  Photographic collection
India Office Library (IOL)
  Colonial government publications, India, Bombay (municipality, Presidency)
CHURCH OF ENGLAND RECORD CENTRE, LONDON (CERC)
  Church of England Purity Society: reports, minutes, pamphlets.
  Miscellaneous purity pamphlets and publications.
CHURCHILL COLLEGE CAMBRIDGE ARCHIVE (CCC)
  Correspondence of W. T. Stead
FRIENDS' HOUSE LIBRARY AND ARCHIVE, LONDON (FHL)
  Bombay Guardian: minutes, papers, records
  Alfred and Helen Dyer: publications, papers
JOHN RYLANDS LIBRARY, UNIVERSITY OF MANCHESTER
  Methodist Missionary archives
NEWSPAPER LIBRARY (BRITISH LIBRARY), COLINDALE, LONDON
  Newspapers and periodicals (listed below)
PUBLIC RECORD OFFICE, LONDON (PRO)
  Colonial government records, Sierra Leone
ROYAL COMMONWEALTH SOCIETY, CAMBRIDGE
  Photographic collection
ROYAL GEOGRAPHICAL SOCIETY, LONDON
  Photographic collection
SCHOOL OF ORIENTAL AND AFRICAN STUDIES (SOAS), UNIVERSITY OF LONDON
  Methodist Missionary Archives
STATE LIBRARY OF NEW SOUTH WALES, SYDNEY
Reference Collection (SLNSW)
  New South Wales Parliamentary Debates (NSWPD)
  Newspapers and periodicals: Australia and New South Wales
Mitchell Collection of Australiana (SLNSWM)
State Library of New South Wales, Dixson Collection (SLNSWD)
  Correspondence of Dr Richard Arthur
  Australasian White Cross League: annual reports
STATE LIBRARY OF SOUTH AUSTRALIA
Reference Collection (SLSA)
  South Australia Parliamentary Debates (SAPD)
  Newspapers and periodicals: Australia and South Australia
  Correspondence and records of J. C. Kirby

BIBLIOGRAPHY

WOMEN'S LIBRARY, LONDON (WL)
  Banner of Asia, *Sentinel*, purity pamphlet collection
  Correspondence of Josephine Butler
  Ladies National Association (LNA): records, papers
  National Vigilance Association (NVA): reports, minutes, publicity
  Travellers' Aid Society (TAS): reports, minutes, publicity

NEWSPAPERS AND PERIODICALS

Artisan (Freetown)
Australian Christian World (Sydney and Melbourne)
Banner of Asia (Bombay)
Bombay Gazette; Overland Summary
Bombay Guardian
Chicago Daily Tribune
The Christian (London)
Church Times (London)
Daily Telegraph (Sydney)
The Friend (London)
Independent (Freetown)
Indian Spectator (Bombay)
Journal of the Friends' Historical Society (London)
Nation (Melbourne)
New York Herald
New York Times
On Guard: The Monthly Magazine of the Young Men's Friendly Society
Pall Mall Gazette (London)
Sentinel (London)
Sierra Leone Church Times
Sierra Leone Ram
Sierra Leone Times
Sierra Leone Weekly News
South Australian Register
South London Press
Sydney Mail
Times of India (Bombay)
Toronto Daily Mail
Vanguard (Church of England Purity Society, London)
West African Reporter

WORKS PUBLISHED BEFORE 1945

Anonymous, *Behramji M. Malabari: A Sketch of His Life and Appreciation of His Works* (Madras: Natesan, 1914).

Anonymous, *Broken Pledge: A Brief Summary of Facts and Arguments. On the Immunity of Prosecution Offered by the Government of Bombay to Persons Giving Evidence on Charges of Corruption Brought Against A. T. Crawford* (London: A. Bonner, 1890).

Arthur, R., *The Needed Change in the Age of Consent: An Appeal for the Better Protection of Our Girls* (Sydney: privately printed, 1901 [1896]).

Attorney-general of Sierra Leone, *Supplement to the Laws of the Colony and Protectorate of Sierra Leone* (London: Waterlow, 1932).

Barrett, R., *Ellice Hopkins: A Memoir* (London: Wells Gardner, 1907).

Barry, Alfred (late Bishop of Sydney and Primate), *An Address: The White Cross League* (Sydney: W. Brooks, undated).

Blyden, E. W., 'African life and customs', *Sierra Leone Weekly News* (21 September 1907).

Brabazon, Lord (vice-president of the Young Men's Friendly Society), 'Address to young men intending to form a branch of the Y.M.F.S.', *On Guard: The Monthly Magazine of the Young Men's Friendly Society*, 2:8 (1884), 113–117.

Burton, I., *The Inner Life of Syria, Palestine, and the Holy Land from My Private Journal* (London: Henry S. King, 1875).

Burton, I., *Lady Burton's Edition of Her Husband's* Arabian Nights: *Translated Literally from the Arabic and Prepared for Household Reading by Justin Huntly McCarthy* (London: Wall, Waterlow, 1886).

Burton, I., 'Sir Richard Burton: an explanation and a defence', *New Review*, 7 (1892), 572–578.

Burton, R. F., *Personal Narrative of a Pilgrimage to El-Medinah and Meccah* (London: Longman, 1855–1856).

Burton, R. F., *Plain and Literal Translation of* The Arabian Nights Entertainments, *Now Entitled The Book of a Thousand Nights and a Night* (Benares: Kama Shastra Society, 1885–1856).

Burton, R. F., *First Footsteps in East Africa; or, An Exploration of Harar* (London: Longman, 1856).

Burton, R. F., *Lake Regions of Central Africa: A Picture of Exploration* (London: Longman, 1860).

Burton, R. F., *Wanderings in West Africa*, 2 vols (London: Tinsley, 1863).

Burton, R. F., *Mission to Gelele, King of Dahomey*, 2 vols (London: Tinsley, 1864).

Burton, R. F., *To the Gold Coast for Gold: A Personal Narrative* (London: Chatto & Windus, 1883).

Burton, R. F., *Supplemental Nights to* The Book of a Thousand Nights and a Night (Benares, Kama Shastra Society, 1886–1888).

Burton, R. F., *Plain And Literal Translation of* The Arabian Nights' Entertainments; or, The Book Of A Thousand Nights and a Night, ed. L. C. Smithers, 12 vols (London: H. S. Nichols, 1894).

Butler, J. E., *Social Purity: An Address Given to Students at Cambridge* (London: Morgan & Scott, 1879).

Butler, J. E., 'A grave question that needs answering by the churches of Great Britain', reprinted from *Sentinel* (London: Sentinel, 1886).

Butler, J. E., *Our Christianity Tested by the Irish Question* (London: T. Fisher Unwin, 1887).

Butler, J. E., *Revival and Extension of the Abolitionist Cause* (Winchester: John T. Doswell, 1887).

Butler, J. E., *The Present Aspect of the Abolitionist Cause in Relation to British India* (London: World's Women's Christian Temperance Union, 1893).

Chamier, C., *Life of a Sailor, by a Captain in the Navy* (London: Richard Bentley, 1832).

Chant, L. O., *Why We Attacked the Empire* (London: Marshall, 1895).

Church Missionary Society, *Church Missionary Society's African Missions: Sierra Leone*, 2nd edn (London: CMS, 1899 [1863]).

Clarke, R., *Description of the Manners and Customs of the Liberated Africans* (London: James Ridgway, 1843).

Cleland, J., *Memoirs of a Woman of Pleasure* (London: Fenton Griffiths, 1749).

Coote, W. A. and A. Baker, *Romance of Philanthropy: Being a Record of Work of the NVA* (London: National Vigilance Association, 1916).

Cox, E. C., *Short History of the Bombay Presidency* (Bombay: Thacker, 1887).

Cox, F. (ed.), *South Australian Congregational Year Book* (Adelaide: Congregational Union, 1882).

Cugoano, O., *Thoughts and Sentiments on the Evil and Wicked Traffic of Slavery and Commerce of the Human Species* (London: T. Becket, 1787).

Digby, W., 'Native newspapers of India and Ceylon', *Calcutta Review*, 65 (1877), 356–394.

Dyer, A. S., *Facts for Men; on Moral Purity and Health* (London: Dyer, 1884).

Dyer, A. S., *Slavery Under the British Flag: Iniquities of British Rule in India and in Our Crown Colonies and Dependencies* (London: Dyer, 1886).

Dyer, A. S., 'The Government versus the Gospel at Bareilly (sketch taken on the spot by Mr. Alfred S. Dyer, 30th December, 1887)', *Sentinel*, 10:3 (1888), 26.

Dyer, A. S., *Slave trade in European girls to British India*, Reprinted from *Banner of Asia* (Bombay: Bombay Guardian Printing Works, 1893).

Dyer, H. S., *Pandita Ramabai: The Story of Her Life* (London: Morgan & Scott, 1900).

Dyer, H. S., *Revival in India* (London: Morgan & Scott, 1907).

Ellis, H., *Studies in the Psychology of Sex* (Philadelphia: F. A. Davis, 1910).

Fawcett, M. G. and E. M. Turner, *Josephine Butler: Her Work and Principles, and Their Meaning for the Twentieth Century* (London: Association for Moral and Social Hygiene, 1927).

Gidumal, D., *Behramji M Malabari: A Biographical Sketch* (Bombay: Education Society's Press, 1888), reprinted with an Introduction by Florence Nightingale (London: T. Fisher Unwin, 1892).

Gregory, M., 'Alfred Dyer', *The Friend*, new series, 66 (1926), 1026.

Handy-Volume Atlas of the British Empire (London: George Philip & Son, 1886).

Hewlett, T. G., *A Report of a Sanitary Tour by Surgeon T. G. Hewlett, Health Officer of Bombay* (London: Eyre & Spottiswoode for HMSO, 1869).

Holman, J., *Travels in Madeira, Sierra Leone, Tenerife . . .* (London: Routledge, 1840).

Hopkins, J. E., *True Manliness*, White Cross series (London: Hatchards, 1883).

Hopkins, J. E., *Conquering and to Conquer* (London: Hatchards, 1886), vol. 1.

Hopkins, J. E., *The Power of Womanhood; or, Mothers and Sons*, Australian edn (Sydney: George Robertson, 1902).

Ingham, E. G., *Sierra Leone After a Hundred Years* (London: Seeley, 1894).

Jacobus, X., Dr (pseudonym of Louis Jacolliot), *L'Amour aux colonies* (Paris: Librairie des Bibliophiles, 1893).

Karaka, D. F., *History of the Parsis* (London: Macmillan, 1884).

Kiek, E. S., *An Apostle in Australia: The Life and Reminiscences of Joseph Coles Kirby* (London: Independent Press, 1927).

Kirby, J. C., *Three Lectures Concerning the Social Evil: Its Causes, Effects and Remedies* (Port Adelaide: privately printed, 1882).

Leith, A. H., *Report on the Sanitary State of the Island of Bombay* (Bombay: Education Society's Press, 1864).

Malabari, B. M., *Infant Marriage and Enforced Widowhood in India, Being a Collection of Opinions, For and Against, Received by Mr. Behramji M. Malabari, from Representative Hindu Gentlemen and Official Other Authorities* (Bombay: Voice of India Press, 1887).

Mitchell, J. M., *In Western India: Recollections of My Early Missionary Life* (Edinburgh: David Douglas, 1899).

Montagu, A., *Ordinances of the Colony of Sierra Leone* (London: HMSO, 1857).

Moorehouse, J. (Bishop of Melbourne), *Personal Purity, Home Life and National Greatness*, Knight of Purity Series No. 1 (London: Knight of Purity, 1885).

Morris, J., *Our Sin and Our Shame* (London: J. S. Amoore, 1885).

Newman, H. S., *Days of Grace in India: A Record of Visits to Indian Missions* (London: Partridge, 1882).

NVA, *A Brief Record of 50 Years' Work of the National Vigilance Association* (London: NVA, 1935).

NVA, *Work Accomplished* (London: NVA, 1906).

Penzer, N., *Annotated Bibliography of Sir Richard Burton* (London: Philpot, 1923).

Penzer, N. (ed.), *Anthropological Notes on the Sotadic Zone* (New York: Falstaff, undated).

Poole, T. E., *Life, Scenery and Customs in Sierra Leone and the Gambia* (London, Richard Bentley, 1850).

'Pupil of the late John Woolley', *Vice and its Victims in Sydney* (Sydney, 1873).

Rainy, W., *The Censor Censured; or, The Calumnies of Captain Burton on the Africans of Sierra Leone* (London: George Chalfont, 1865).

Renner Maxwell, J., *Advantages and Disadvantages of European Intercourse with the West Coast of Africa* (London: Smart & Allen; Freetown: Sawyerr, 1881).

Renner Maxwell, J., *The Negro Question or Hints for the Physical Improvement of the Negro Race, with Special Reference to West Africa* (London: T. Fisher Unwin, 1892).

Roe, C. G., *The Horrors of the White Slave Trade: The Mighty Crusade to Protect the Purity of Our Homes* (London: Roe & Steadwell, 1911).

Ruskin, J., *Sesame and Lilies: Two Lectures, Delivered at Manchester in 1864* (London: Smith, Elder, 1865).

Sibthorpe, A. B. C., *The History of Sierra Leone*, 2nd edn (London: Elliot Stock, 1881), reprinted in 1970 by Frank Cass, London.

Singh, S. J., *B. M. Malabari: Rambles with the Pilgrim Reformer* (London: G. Bell, 1914).

Symonds, J. A., *A Problem in Modern Ethics* (London: privately printed, 1896).

Taylor, C. B., *Speech on the Second Reading of a Bill for the Repeal of the Contagious Diseases Acts, 1866–69* (London: Effingham Wilson, 1883).

Turner, F. J., *Frontier in American History* (New York: Holt, 1920).

Whyte, F., *Life of W. T. Stead* (London: Jonathan Cape, 1925).

Wilson, J., 'Short memorial of the Honourable Mountstuart Elphinstone, and of his contributions to Oriental geography and history', *Journal of the Bombay Branch of the Royal Asiatic Society*, 6 (1861), 97–111.

Wilson, H. J., *Rough Record of Events and Incidents Connected with the Repeal of the 'Contagious Diseases Acts, 1864–69', in the United Kingdom, and of the Movement Against State Regulation of Vice in India and the Colonies, 1858–1906* (Sheffield: Parker, 1907).

Wright, T., *Life of Sir Richard Burton*, 2 vols (London: Everett, 1906).

WORKS PUBLISHED AFTER 1945

Ahmed, C. C., 'God, anti-colonialism and dance: Sheekh Uways and the Uwaysiaayya', in G. Maddox (ed.), *Conquest and Resistance to Colonialism in Africa* (New York: Garland, 1993), pp. 145–167.

Aldrich, R., *The Seduction of the Mediterranean: Writing, Art and Homosexual Fantasy* (London: Routledge, 1993).

Aldrich, R., *Colonialism and Homosexuality* (London: Routledge, 2003).

Alie, J. A. D., *A New History of Sierra Leone* (London: Macmillan, 1990).

Allen, J., 'The making of a prostitute in early twentieth-century New South Wales', in K. Daniels (ed.), *So Much Hard Work: Women and Prostitution in Australian History* (Sydney: Fontana, 1984), pp. 192–232.

Allman, J. and V. Tashjan, *'I Will Not Eat a Stone': A Women's History of Colonial Asante* (Oxford: James Currey, 2000).

Alpers, S., *The Art of Describing* (Chicago, IL: University of Chicago Press, 1983), p. 133.

Altman, D., *Global Sex* (Chicago, IL: University of Chicago Press, 2001).

Aravamudan, S., *Tropicopolitans: Colonialism and Agency, 1688–1804* (Durham, NC: Duke University Press, 1999).

Asiwaju, A. I., *West African Transformations: Comparative Impact of French and British Colonialism* (Ikeja, Nigeria: Malthouse, 2001).

Assad, T. J., *Three Victorian Travellers* (London: Routledge, 1964).

Backhouse, C., 'Nineteenth century Canadian prostitution law: reflection of a discriminatory society', *Histoire Sociale/Social History*, 18 (1986), 387–423.

Ballhatchet, K., *Race, Sex and Class Under the Raj: Imperial Attitudes and Policies and Their Critics* (London: Weidenfeld & Nicolson, 1980).

Balsara, P., *Highlights of Parsi History* (Bombay: Young Collegians' Zoroastrian Association, 1981 [1963]).

Banerjee, S., *Under the Raj: Prostitution in Colonial Bengal* (New York: Monthly Review Press, 1998).

Banton, M., *West African City: A Study of the Development of Tribal Life in Freetown* (London: Oxford University Press, 1957).

Barker, F., P. Hulme and M. Iversen (eds), *Cannibalism and the Colonial World* (Cambridge: Cambridge University Press, 1998).

Barret-Ducrocq, F., *Love in the Time of Victoria: Sexuality and Desire Among Working-Class Men and Women in Nineteenth-Century London*, trans. John Howe (London: Penguin, 1991).

Basu, J. N., *The Romance of Indian Journalism* (Calcutta: Calcutta University, 1979).

Bauman, Z., *Legislators and Interpreters: Modernity, Postmodernity, and Intellectuals* (Ithaca, NY: Cornell University Press, 1987).

Bernard, J. A., *From Raj to the Republic: A Political History of India* (New Delhi: Har-Anand, 2001).

Bhabha, H. K., 'Signs taken for wonders: questions of ambivalence and authority under a tree outside Delhi, May 1817', *Critical Inquiry*, 12 (1985), 144–165.

Bhabha, H. K., *Location of Culture* (London: Routledge, 1994).

Blair, D., *Degrees in Violence: Robert Mugabe and the Struggle for Power in Zimbabwe* (London: Continuum, 2003).

Bland, L., *Banishing the Beast: English Feminism and Sexual Morality 1885–1914* (London: Penguin, 1995).

Blaut, J. M., *The Colonizer's Model of the World: Geographical Diffusionism and Eurocentric History* (New York: Guilford Press, 1993).

Bleys, R. C., *The Geography of Perversion: Male-to-Male Sexual Behaviour Outside the West and the Ethnographic Imagination 1750–1918* (London: Cassell, 1996).

Blomley, N. K., *Law, Space and the Geographies of Power* (New York: Guilford Press, 1994).

Blomley, N., D. Delaney and R. T. Ford (eds), *The Legal Geographies Reader: Law, Power and Space* (Oxford: Blackwell, 2001).

Blunt, A., 'Imperial geographies of home: British domesticity in India, 1886–1925', *Transactions of the Institute of British Geographers*, new series, 24 (1999), 421–440.

Blunt, A. and C. McEwan (eds), *Postcolonial Geographies* (London: Continuum, 2002).

Blyden, E. W., *Black Spokesman: Selected Published Writings of Edward Wilmot Blyden*, ed. H. R. Lynch (London: Frank Cass, 1971).

Blyden, E. W., *Selected Letters of Edward Wilmot Blyden*, ed. H. R. Lynch (New York: KTO Press, 1978).

Blyden, N. A., *West Indians in West Africa: The African Diaspora in Reverse* (New York: University of Rochester Press, 2000).

Boahen, A. A. (ed.), *General History of Africa*, vol. 7: *Africa Under Colonial Domination, 1880–1935* (London: James Currey, 1990).

Boase, F., *Modern English Biography* (London: Frank Cass, 1965).

Boehmer, E., *Empire, the National and the Postcolonial, 1890–1920* (Oxford: Oxford University Press, 2002).

Boone, J., 'Vacation cruises; or, the homoerotics of orientalism', *Publications of the Modern Language Association*, 110 (1995), 89–107.

Boyle, T., *Black Swine in the Sewers of Hampstead* (New York: Viking Press, 1989).

Braidwood, S. J., *Black Poor and White Philanthropists: London's Blacks and the Foundation of the Sierra Leone Settlement, 1786–1791* (Liverpool: Liverpool University Press, 1994).

Bristow, E. J., *Vice and Vigilance: Purity Movements in Britain Since 1700* (Dublin: Gill & Macmillan, 1977).

Bristow, J., *Sexuality* (London: Routledge, 1997).

Brodie, F. M., *The Devil Drives: A Life of Sir Richard Burton* (London: Eyre & Spottiswoode, 1967).

Brown, M., 'Closet geography', *Environment & Planning D, Society and Space*, 14 (1996), 762–769.

Brown, M., *Closet Space: Geographies of Metaphor from the Body to the Globe* (London: Routledge, 2000).

Burton, A., *Burdens of History: British Feminists, Indian Women, and Imperial Culture, 1865–1915* (Chapel Hill: University of North Carolina Press, 1994).

Burton, A., *At the Heart of Empire: Indians and the Colonial Encounter in Late-Victorian Britain* (Berkeley: University of California Press, 1998).

Burton, A., 'Institutionalising imperial reform: the *Indian Magazine* and late-Victorian colonial politics', in D. Finkelstein and D. M. Peers (eds), *Negotiating India in the Nineteenth-Century Media* (Basingstoke: Macmillan, 2000), pp. 23–50.

Burton, R. F., *Love, War and Fancy: The Customs and Manners of the East from Writings of* The Arabian Nights, ed. K. Walker (London: William Kimber, 1964).

Burton, R. F., *Of No Country: An Anthology of the Works of Richard Burton*, ed. F. McLynn (London: Scribners, 1990).

Bush, B., *Imperialism, Race and Resistance: Africa and Britain, 1919–1945* (London: Routledge, 1999).

Callaway, H., *Gender, Culture and Empire: European Women in Colonial Nigeria* (Basingstoke: Macmillan, 1987).

BIBLIOGRAPHY

Campbell, J., *The Hero with a Thousand Faces* (New York: Pantheon, 1949).

Carpenter, E., *Selected Writings*, vol. 1: *Sex* (London: Gay Men's Press, 1984).

Chakrabarty, D., *Provincialising Europe: Postcolonial Thought and Historical Difference* (Princeton, NJ: Princeton University Press, 2000).

Chan, S., *Robert Mugabe: A Life of Power and Violence* (London: I. B. Taurus, 2003).

Chandra, S., *Enslaved Daughters: Colonialism, Law and Women's Rights* (Delhi: Oxford University Press, 1998).

Chaudhuri, K. N., *Trade and Civilisation in the Indian Ocean: An Economic History from the Rise of Islam to 1750* (Cambridge: Cambridge University Press, 1985).

Chrisman, L., *Rereading the Imperial Romance: British Imperialism and South African Resistance in Haggard, Schreiner and Plaatje* (Oxford: Clarendon Press, 2000).

Clark, K., *Innovation Diffusion: Contemporary Geographical Approaches, Concepts and Techniques in Modern Geography* (Norwich: Geo Books, 1984).

Clayton, A. and D. Killingray, *Khaki and Blue: Military and Police in British Colonial Africa* (Athens: Ohio University Press, 1989).

Cliff, A. D., P. Haggett, J. K. Ord and G. R. Versey, *Spatial Diffusion: An Historical Geography of Epidemics in an Island Community* (Cambridge: Cambridge University Press, 1981).

Clyne, R., *Colonial Blue: A History of the South Australian Police Force, 1836–1916* (Adelaide: Wakefield Press 1987).

Cohen, A. P., *The Symbolic Construction of Community* (London: Tavistock, 1985).

Coleman, D., *Maiden Voyages and Infant Colonies: Two Women's Travel Narratives of the 1790s* (London: Leicester University Press, 1999).

Comaroff, J., and J. L. Comaroff, *Of Revelation and Revolution: Christianity, Colonialism, and Consciousness in South Africa* (Chicago, IL: University of Chicago Press, 1991), vol. 1.

Cooper, D., *Governing Out of Order: Space, Law and the Politics of Belonging* (London: Rivers Oram Press, 1998).

Cooper, F. and L. A. Stoler, *Tensions of Empire: Colonial Cultures in a Bourgeois World* (Berkeley: University of California Press, 1997).

Crowder, M., *West Africa Under Colonial Rule* (London: Hutchinson, 1968).

Daniels, S., *Fields of Vision: Landscape Imagery and National Identity in England and the United States* (Cambridge: Polity, 1993).

David, M. D., *Bombay, the City of Dreams: A History of the First City in India* (Bombay: Himalaya Publishing House, 1995).

Davis, T., *Actresses as Working Women: Their Social Identity in Victorian Culture* (London: Routledge, 1991).

Davison, G., J. W. McCarty and A. McLeary (eds), *Australians: A Historical Library*, vol. 3: *Australians, 1888* (Cambridge: Cambridge University Press, 1987).

De Certeau, M., *The Practice of Everyday Life*, trans. S. Rendall (Berkeley: University of California Press, 1984).

Deleuze, G. and F. Guattari, *A Thousand Plateaus: Capitalism and Schizophrenia* (London: Athlone, 1988).

Dossal, M., *Imperial Designs and Indian Realities: The Planning of Bombay City, 1845–1875* (Oxford: Oxford University Press, 1991).

Driver, F., 'Moral geographies: social science and the urban environment in mid-nineteenth century England, *Transactions of the Institute of British Geographers*, new series, 13 (1988), 275–287.

Eder, F. X., L. A. Hall and G. Hekma (eds), *Sexual Cultures in Europe: Themes in Sexuality* (Manchester: Manchester University Press, 1999).

Edwards, J. D., *Exotic Journeys: Exploring the Erotics of US Travel Literature, 1840–1930* (Hanover, NH: University Press of New England, 2001).

Elias, T. O., *Ghana and Sierra Leone: The Development of Their Laws and Constitutions* (London: Stevens, 1962).

Engels, D., 'The Age of Consent Act of 1891: colonial ideology in Bengal', *South Asia Research*, 3 (1983), 107–131.

Engels, D. and S. Marks (eds), *Contesting Colonial Hegemony: State and Society in Africa and India* (London: British Academic Press, 1994).

Engle Merry, S., *Colonizing Hawai'i: The Cultural Power of Law* (Princeton, NJ: Princeton University Press, 2000).

Enloe, C., *Bananas, Beaches and Bases: Making Feminist Sense of International Politics* (London: Pandora, 1989).

Fanon, F., *Black Skins, White Masks* (London: Pluto, 1986 [1952]).

Finkelhor, D., *Child Sex Abuse* (New York: Free Press, 1984).

Finkelstein, D. and D. M. Peers (eds), *Negotiating India in the Nineteenth-Century Media* (Basingstoke: Macmillan, 2000).

Fish, S., *Is There a Text in This Class?* (Cambridge, MA: Harvard University Press, 1980).

Fletcher, I. C., L. E. N. Mayhall and P. Levine, *Women's Suffrage in the British Empire: Citizenship, Nation and Race* (London: Routledge, 2000).

Fogarty, W. J., '"Certain habits": the development of a concept of the male homosexual in New South Wales law, 1788–1900', in R. Aldrich and G. Wotherspoon (eds), *Gay Perspectives: Essays in Australian Gay Culture* (Sydney: University of Sydney, 1992), pp. 59–76.

Foray, C. P., *Historical Dictionary of Sierra Leone* (London: Methuen, 1977).

Foucault, M., *History of Sexuality* (London: Penguin, 1978), vol. 1.

Foucault, M., 'Questions on geography', in C. Gordon (ed.), *Power/Knowledge: Selected Interviews and Other Writings 1972–1977* (Brighton: Harvester Press, 1980), pp. 63–77.

Foucault, M., 'The order of discourse', in R. Young (ed.), *Untying the Text: A Post-Structuralist Reader* (London: Routledge, 1981).

French, R., *Camping by a Billabong: Gay and Lesbian Stories from Australian History* (Sydney: Black Wattle Press, 1993).

Frenkel, S. and J. Western, 'Pretext or prophylaxis: racial segregation and malarial mosquitoes in a British tropical colony: Sierra Leone', *Annals of the Association of American Geographers*, 78 (1988), 211–228.

Fyfe, C. H., 'The Sierra Leone press in the nineteenth century', *Sierra Leone Studies*, new series, 8 (1957), 226–236.

Fyfe, C., *A History of Sierra Leone* (London: Gregg, 1993 [1963]).

Fyle, C. N. and E. D. Jones, *A Krio–English Dictionary* (New York: Oxford University Press, 1980).

Gale, T., 'The struggle against disease in Sierra Leone: early sanitary reforms in Freetown', *Africana Research Bulletin*, 6:2 (1976), 29–44.

Goerg, Odile, *Pouvoir colonial, municipalités et espaces urbains: Conakry–Freetown des années 1880 à 1914*, 2 vols (Paris: Harmattan, 1997).

Gibson, R., 'Ocean settlement', in R. Gibson (ed.), *Exchanges: Cross-Cultural Encounters in Australia and the Pacific* (Sydney: Museum of Sydney, 1996), pp. 91–111.

Gill, A., *Ruling Passions: Sex, Race and Empire* (London: BBC Books, 1995).

Gorham, D., ' "The Maiden Tribute of modern Babylon" ' re-examined: child prostitution and the idea of childhood in late-Victorian England', *Victorian Studies*, 21:3 (1978), 353–379.

Gregory, D., 'Geographical imagination', in R. J. Johnston, D. Gregory, G. Pratt and M. Watts, *Dictionary of Human Geography* (Oxford: Blackwell, 2000), pp. 298–301.

Gregory, D., 'Post-colonialism', in R. J. Johnston, D. Gregory, G. Pratt and M. Watts, *Dictionary of Human Geography* (Oxford: Blackwell, 2000), pp. 611–615.

Gregory, D., *Geographical Imaginations* (Oxford: Blackwell, 1994).

Gunther, J., *The Facets of Asia*, 2 vols (Delhi: Shubhi, 1999).

Hall, C., *Civilising Subjects: Metropole and Colony in the English Imagination 1830–1867* (Cambridge: Polity Press, 2002).

Halperin, D. M., *How to Do the History of Homosexuality* (Chicago, IL: University of Chicago Press, 2002).

Harley, J. B., 'Deconstructing the map', in T. Barnes and J. Duncan (eds), *Writing Worlds* (London: Routledge, 1992), pp. 231–247.

Harris, R. C., 'The simplification of Europe overseas', *Annals of the Association of American Geographers*, 67 (1977), 469–483.

Harrison, J. B., 'Allahabad: a sanitary history', in K. Ballhatchet and J. B. Harrison (eds), *The City in South Asia* (London: Curzon Press, 1980), pp. 166–195.

Hartz, L., *The Founding of New Societies* (New York: Harcourt, Brace & World, 1946).

Hastings, D. J. (ed.), *Bombay Buccaneers: Memories and Reminiscences of the Royal Indian Navy* (London: Basca, 1986).

Heimsath, C. H., 'The origin and enactment of the Indian Age of Consent Bill, 1891', *Journal of Asian Studies*, 21 (1962), 491–504.

Henriques, F., *Prostitution and Society*, vol. 1: *Primitive, Classical and Oriental* (London: Macgibbon & Kee, 1962).

Hewa, S., *Colonialism, Tropical Disease, and Imperial Medicine* (Lanham, MD: University Press of America, 1995).

Hilliard, D., 'Sydney Anglicans and homosexuality', *Journal of Homosexuality*, 33:2 (1997), 101–123.

Hilliard, D. and A. R. Hunt, 'Religion', in E. Richards (ed.), *Flinders History of South Australia: Social History* (Adelaide: Wakefield Press, 1986), pp. 194–234.

Home, R., *Of Planting and Planning: The Making of British Colonial Cities* (London: E. & F. N. Spon, 1997).

hooks, b., *Yearning: Race, Gender and Cultural Politics* (London: Turnaround, 1991).

Horan, S., '"More sinned against than sinning"? Prostitution in South Australia, 1836–1914', in K. Daniels (ed.), *So Much Hard Work: Women and Prostitution in Australian History* (Sydney: Fontana, 1984), pp. 87–126.

Howell, P., 'Prostitution and racialised sexuality: the regulation of prostitution in Britain and the British Empire before the Contagious Diseases Acts', *Environment & Planning D, Society and Space*, 18 (2000), 321–340.

Howell, P., 'Victorian sexuality and the moralisation of Cremorne Gardens, in J. P. Sharp, P. Routledge, C. Philo and R. Paddison (eds), *Entanglements of Power: Geographies of Domination/Resistance* (London: Routledge, 2000), pp. 43–66.

Huggan, G., *Territorial Disputes: Maps and Mapping Strategies in Contemporary Canadian and Australian Fiction* (Toronto: University of Toronto Press, 1994).

Hughes, R., *Fatal Shore: The Epic of Australia's Founding* (New York: Vintage, 1986).

Hulme, P., *Colonial Encounters: Europe and the Native Caribbean, 1492–1797* (London: Methuen, 1986).

Hunt, A., *This Side of Heaven: A History of Methodism in Australia* (Adelaide: Lutheran Publishing, 1985).

Hunt, A., *Governing Morals: A Social History of Moral Regulation* (Cambridge: Cambridge University Press, 1999).

Hyam, R., *Empire and Sexuality: The British Experience* (Manchester: Manchester University Press, 1990).

Jacobs, J., *Edge of Empire: Postcolonialism and the City* (London: Routledge, 1996).

Jackson, P. A., 'Mapping poststructuralism's borders: the case for poststructuralist area studies', *Sojourn*, 18:1 (2003), 42–88.

Jameson, F., 'Cognitive mapping', in C. Nelson and L. Grossberg (eds), *Marxism and the Interpretation of Culture* (Chicago: University of Illinois Press, 1988).

Janin, H., *The India–China Opium Trade in the Nineteenth Century* (London: McFarland, 1999).

Jeater, D., *Marriage, Perversion and Power: The Construction of Moral Discourse in Southern Rhodesia 1894–1930* (Oxford: Clarendon Press, 1993).

Joardar, B., *Prostitution in Nineteenth and Early Twentieth Century Calcutta* (New Delhi: Inter-India Publications, 1985).

Jones, E., 'Krio in Sierra Leone journalism', *Sierra Leone Language Review*, 1:3 (1964), 24–31.

Jones, E., 'The business of translating into Krio', in E. D. Jones, K. I. Sandred, N. Shrimpton (eds), *Reading and Writing Krio: Proceedings of a Workshop*

Held at the University of Sierra Leone, Freetown, 29–31 January 1990 (Uppsala : Almqvist & Wiksell, 1990).

Jordan, J. and I. Sharp (eds), *Josephine Butler and the Prostitution Campaigns: Diseases of the Body Politic*, 5 vols (London: Routledge, 2003).

Jose, J., 'The White Cross League and sex education in SA state schools 1916–1929', *Journal of the Historical Society of South Australia*, 25 (1996), 45–57.

Jose, J., 'Legislating for social purity, 1883–1885: the Reverend Joseph Coles Kirby and the Social Purity Society', *Journal of Historical Society of South Australia*, 18 (2000), 119–134.

Kabbani, R., *Imperial Fictions: Europe's Myths of Orient* (London: Pandora, 1986).

Kama Sutra of Vatsyayana, trans. R. F. Burton, ed. W. G. Archer (London: Allen & Unwin, 1966).

Kaminsky, A. P., *India Office 1880–1910* (London: Mansell, 1986).

Klausen, S., '"For the sake of the race": eugenic discourses of feeblemindedness and motherhood in the *South African Medical Record*, 1903–1926', *Journal of Southern African Studies*, 23:1 (1997), 27–50.

Knopp, L. and M. Brown, 'Queer diffusions', *Environment & Planning D: Society and Space*, 21 (2003), 409–424.

Kolodny, A., *The Lay of the Land: Metaphor as Experience and History in American Life and Letters* (Chapel Hill: University of North Carolina Press, 1975).

Kosambi, M., *Bombay in Transition: The Growth and Social Ecology of a Colonial City* (Uppsala: Almqvist & Wiksell International, 1986).

Kosambi, M., 'Girl-brides and socio-legal change: the Age of Consent Bill (1891) controversy', *Economic and Political Weekly* (3 August 1991), pp. 1857–1868.

Kosambi, M., *Pandita Ramabai's Feminist and Christian Conversions* (Bombay: Research Centre for Women's Studies, 1995).

Kosambi, M., *Pandita Ramabai Through Her Own Words: Selected Works* (New Delhi: Oxford University Press, 2000).

Lawton, W. J., *The Better Time to Be: Utopian Attitudes to Society Among Sydney Anglicans, 1885–1914* (Sydney: New South Wales University Press, 1990).

Lazarus, N., *Resistance in Postcolonial African Fiction* (New Haven, CT: Yale University Press, 1990).

Lester, A., *Imperial Networks: Creating Identities in Nineteenth-Century South Africa and Britain* (London: Routledge, 2001).

Levine, P., 'Venereal disease, prostitution and the politics of empire: the case of British India', *Journal of the History of Sexuality*, 4:4 (1994), 579–602.

Levine, P., 'Rereading the 1890s: venereal disease as "constitutional crisis" in Britain and British India', *Journal of Asian Studies*, 55:3 (1996), 585–612.

Levine, P., 'Orientalist sociology and the creation of colonial sexualities', *Feminist Review*, 65 (2000), 5–21.

Levine, P., *Prostitution, Race and Politics: Policing Venereal Disease in the British Empire* (London: Routledge, 2003).

Lind, C., 'Law, childhood innocence and sexuality' in L. Moran, S. Beresford and D. Monk (eds), *Legal Queeries* (London: Cassell, 1999).

Linebaugh, P. and M. Rediker, *The Many-Headed Hydra: The Hidden History of the Revolutionary Atlantic* (London: Verso, 2000).

Little, K., *African Women in Towns* (Cambridge: Cambridge University Press, 1973).

Luhrmann, T. M., *Good Parsi: The Fate of a Colonial Elite in a Postcolonial Society* (Cambridge: Harvard University Press, 1996).

Macleod, R. and M. Lewis (eds), *Disease, Medicine and Empire: Perspectives on Western Medicine and the Experience of European Expansion* (London: Routledge, 1988).

McClintock, A., *Imperial Leather: Race, Gender and Sexuality in the Colonial Contest* (London: Routledge, 1994).

McDowell, L. and J. A. Sharp, *A Feminist Glossary of Human Geography* (London: Arnold, 1999).

McLaren, J. P. S., 'Chasing the social evil: moral fervour and the evolution of Canada's prostitution laws, 1867–1917', *Canadian Journal of Law and Society*, 1 (1986), 125–165.

McLynn, F., *Snow upon the Desert* (London: John Murray, 1990).

McPherson, K., *The Indian Ocean: A History of People and the Sea* (Delhi: Oxford University Press, 1993).

Majeed, J., 'Narratives of progress and idioms of community: two Urdu periodicals of the 1870s', in D. Finkelstein and D. M. Peers (eds), *Negotiating India in the Nineteenth-Century Media* (Basingstoke: Macmillan, 2000), pp. 135–163.

Manderson, L., *Sickness and the State: Health and Illness in Colonial Malaya, 1870–1940* (Cambridge: Cambridge University Press, 1996).

Manderson, L., 'Colonial desires: sexuality, race and gender in British Malaya', *Journal of the History of Sexuality*, 7:3 (1997), 372–388.

Mann, K., *Marrying Well: Marriage, Status and Social Change among the Educated Elite in Colonial Lagos* (Cambridge: Cambridge University Press, 1985).

Mann, K. and R. Roberts, *Law in Colonial Africa* (London: Currey, 1991).

Marcus, S., *Other Victorians: A Study of Sexuality and Pornography in Mid-Nineteenth Century England* (London: Weidenfeld & Nicolson, 1966).

Marcus, S., 'Reading the illegible', in H. J. Dyos and M. Wolff (eds), *Victorian City: Images and Realities* (London: Routledge & Kegan Paul, 1973), vol. 1, pp. 257–276.

Marin, L., *Utopics: Spatial Play*, trans. R. A. Vollrath (London: Macmillan, 1984).

Marks, S., 'History, nation and empire: sniping from the periphery', *History Workshop Journal*, 29 (1990), 111–119.

Martens, J. C., '"Almost a public calamity": prostitutes, "nurseboys" and attempts to control venereal diseases in colonial Natal, 1886–1890', *South African Historical Journal*, 45 (2001), 27–52.

Mason, M., *The Making of Victorian Sexual Attitudes* (Oxford: Oxford University Press, 1994).

Mason, M., *The Making of Victorian Sexuality* (Oxford: Oxford University Press, 1995).

Massey, D., *Space, Place and Gender* (Cambridge: Polity, 1994).

Massey, D., 'Entanglements of power: reflections?' in J. P. Sharp, P. Routledge, C. Philo and R. Paddison (eds), *Entanglements of Power: Geographies of Domination/Resistance* (London: Routledge, 2000), pp. 279–286.

Mayne, A. J. C., *Fever, Squalor and Vice: Sensation and Social Policy in Victorian Sydney* (Brisbane: Queensland University Press, 1982).

Mbaeyi, P. M., *British Military and Naval Forces in West African History, 1807–1874* (London: NOK Publishers, 1978).

Meinig, D., *On the Margins of the Good Earth: The South Australian Wheat Frontier 1869–1884* (London: John Murray, 1963).

Meredith, M., *Mugabe: Power and Plunder in Zimbabwe* (Oxford: Public Affairs, 2002).

Mintz, S. W., *Caribbean Transformations* (New York: Columbia University Press, 1989).

Moore, D. S., 'Remapping resistance: ground for struggle and the politics of place', in S. Pile and M. Keith (eds), *Geographies of Resistance* (London: Routledge, 1997), pp. 87–106.

Morris, J., *Pax Britannica: Climax of an Empire* (London: Faber, 1968).

Morris, J., 'In a family embrace', *Guardian* (9 March 1996), p. 29.

Mort, F., *Dangerous Sexualities: Medico-Moral Politics in England since 1830*, 2nd edn (London: Routledge, 2000).

Mosse, G., *Nationalism and Sexuality* (New York: Fertig, 1985).

Moussa-Mahmoud, F., 'English travellers and *The Arabian Nights*', in P. L. Caracciolo (ed.), *'The Arabian Nights' in English Literature: Studies in the Reception of 'The One Thousand and One Nights' into British Culture* (Basingstoke: Macmillan, 1988), pp. 95–110.

Muga, E., *Studies in Prostitution* (Nairobi: Kenya Literature Bureau, 1980).

Nairn, B. and G. Serle, *Australian Dictionary of Biography*, vol. 7: *1891–1939* (Melbourne: Melbourne University Press, 1979).

Nance, C., 'Women, morality and prostitution in early South Australia', *The Push from the Bush*, 3 (1979), 33–43.

Nead, L., *Victorian Babylon: People, Streets, and Images in Nineteenth Century London* (New Haven, CT: Yale University Press, 2000).

Ogborn, M., 'Law and discipline in 19th century state formation: the Contagious Diseases Acts of 1864, 1866 and 1869', *Journal of Historical Sociology*, 6 (1993), 25–57.

Ogborn, M., *Spaces of Modernity: London's Geographies, 1680–1780* (New York: Guilford Press, 1998).

Ogborn, M. and C. Philo, 'Soldiers, sailors and moral locations in nineteenth-century Portsmouth', *Area*, 26:3 (1994), 221–231.

Omu, F. I. A., 'Dilemma of press freedom in colonial Africa: the West African example', *Journal of African History*, 9 (1968), 279–298.

Omu, F. I. A., 'The "new era" and the abortive press law of 1857', *Sierra Leone Studies*, new series, 23 (1968), 2–14.

Pagden, A., *Lords of All the World: Ideologies of Empire in Spain, Britain and France c.1500–1800* (New Haven, CT, and London: Yale University Press, 1995).

Pape, J., 'Black and white: the "perils of sex" in colonial Zimbabwe', *Journal of Southern African Studies*, 16 (1990), 699–720.

Parthasarathy, R., *Journalism in India from the Earliest Times to the Present Day* (New Delhi: Sterling, 1989).

Pearce, L., 'Devolutionary desires', in R. Phillips, D. Watt, and D. Shuttleton (eds), *De-Centring Sexualities: Politics and Representations Beyond the Metropolis* (London: Routledge, 2000), pp. 241–257.

Percy, W. A., *Pederasty and Pedagogy in Archaic Greece* (Chicago: University of Illinois Press, 1996).

Philip, N. and V. Neuburg, *Charles Dickens, a December Vision: Social Journalism* (London: Collins, 1986).

Phillips, R., *Mapping Men and Empire: A Geography of Adventure* (London: Routledge, 1997).

Phillips, R., 'Sexual politics of authorship: rereading the travels and translations of Richard and Isabel Burton', *Gender, Place and Culture*, 6:3 (1999), 241–257.

Phillips, R., 'Writing travel and mapping sexuality: Richard Burton's Sotadic Zone', in J. Duncan and D. Gregory (eds), *Writes of Passage: Reading Travel Writing* (London, Routledge, 2000), pp. 70–91.

Phillips, R., 'Politics of reading; decolonising children's geographies', *Ecumene: A Journal of Cultural Geographies*, 8:2 (2001), 125–150.

Phillips, R., 'Imperialism and the regulation of sexuality: colonial legislation on contagious diseases and ages of consent', *Journal of Historical Geography*, 28:3 (2002), 339–362.

Phillips, R. and D. Watt, 'Introduction', in R. Phillips, D. Watt, and D. Shuttleton (eds), *De-Centring Sexualities: Politics and Representations Beyond the Metropolis* (London: Routledge, 2000), pp. 1–18.

Phillips, W., Influence of Congregationalism in South Australia, 1837–1915, BA dissertation, University of Adelaide, 1957.

Phillips, W., *Defending a Christian Country: Churchmen and Society in New South Wales in the 1880s and After* (Brisbane: University of Queensland Press, 1981).

Pierce, R. N., *Lord Northcliffe: Trans-Atlantic Influences*, Journalism Monographs no. 40 (Lexington, KY: Association for Education in Journalism, 1975).

Pile, S. and M. Keith (eds), *Geographies of Resistance* (London: Routledge, 1997).

Pike, D., *Paradise of Dissent: South Australia 1829–1857* (Melbourne: Cambridge University Press, 1967 [1957]).

Pittin, R. I., *Women and Work in Northern Nigeria* (Basingstoke: Palgrave, 2002).

Pivar, D., *Purity Crusade: Sexual Morality and Social Control, 1868–1900* (Westport, CT: Greenwood Press, 1973).

Pivar, D., *Purity and Hygiene: Women, Prostitution and the American Plan, 1900–1930* (Westport, CT: Greenwood Press, 2002).

Porter, A. T., *Creoledom: A Study of the Development of Freetown Society* (Oxford: Oxford University Press, 1963).

Potter, S. J., 'Communication and integration: the British and Dominions press and the British world, 1876–1914', *Journal of Imperial and Commonwealth History*, 31 (2003), 190–206.

Pratt, G., 'Resistance', in R. J. Johnston, D. Gregory, G. Pratt and M. Watts, *Dictionary of Human Geography* (Oxford: Blackwell, 2000), pp. 705–706.

Pratt, M. L., *Imperial Eyes: Studies in Travel Writing and Transculturation* (London: Routledge, 1992).

Rabinow, P., *French Modern: Norms and Forms of the Social Environment* (Cambridge, MA: MIT Press, 1989).

Ramasubban, R., 'Imperial health in British India, 1857–1900', in R. Macleod and M. Lewis (eds), *Disease, Medicine and Empire: Perspectives on Western Medicine and the Experience of European Expansion* (London: Routledge, 1988), pp. 38–60.

Rappaport, E. D., *Shopping for Pleasure: Women in the Making of London's West End* (Princeton, NJ: Princeton University Press, 2000).

Rathbone, R., 'Law, lawyers and politics in Ghana in the 1940s', in D. Engels and S. Marks (eds), *Contesting Colonial Hegemony: State and Society in Africa and India* (London: British Academic Press, 1994), pp. 227–247.

Roe, M., 'Richard Arthur', in B. Nairn and G. Serle (eds), *Australian Dictionary of Biography*, vol. 7: *1891–1939* (Melbourne: Melbourne University Press, 1979), p. 3.

Royle, E., *Radicals, Secularists and Republicans: Popular Freethought in Britain, 1866–1815* (Manchester: Manchester University Press, 1980).

Sadowsky, J., *Imperial Bedlam: Institutions of Madness in Colonial Southwest Nigeria* (Berkeley: University of California Press, 1999).

Said, E., *Orientalism: Western Representations of the Orient* (New York: Pantheon, 1978).

Said, E., 'Travelling theory', in *The World, the Text and the Critic* (London: Faber & Faber, 1984), pp. 226–247.

Said, E., *Culture and Imperialism* (New York: Vintage, 1993).

Sauer, C. O., *Agricultural Origins and Dispersals: The Domestication of Animals and Foodstuffs* (Cambridge, MA: MIT Press, 1952).

Schults, R. L., *Crusader in Babylon: W. T. Stead and the Pall Mall Gazette* (Lincoln: University of Nebraska Press, 1972).

Scott, J. C., *Weapons of the Weak: Everyday Forms of Peasant Resistance* (New Haven, CT, and London: Yale University Press, 1985).

Scully, P., 'Rape, race and colonial culture: the sexual politics of identity in the nineteenth-century Cape Colony, South Africa', *American Historical Review*, 100 (1995), 335–359.

Sharp, J. P., P. Routledge, C. Philo and R. Paddison (eds), *Entanglements of Power: Geographies of Domination/Resistance* (London: Routledge, 2000).

Shaw, R., *Memories of the Slave Trade: Ritual and the Historical Imagination in Sierra Leone* (Chicago, IL: University of Chicago Press, 2002).

BIBLIOGRAPHY

Shields, R., *Places on the Margin: Alternative Geographies of Modernity* (London: Routledge, 1991).

Sinfield, A., *Cultural Politics: Queer Reading* (London: Routledge, 1994).

Sinfield, A., 'The production of gay and the return of power', in R. Phillips, D. Watt, and D. Shuttleton (eds), *De-Centring Sexualities: Politics and Representations Beyond the Metropolis* (London: Routledge, 2000), pp. 21–36.

Singh, V., *Social Realism in the Fiction of Dickens and Mulk Raj Anand* (New Delhi: Commonwealth, 1997).

Sinha, M., *Colonial Masculinity: The 'Manly Englishman' and the 'Effeminate Bengali' in the late Nineteenth Century* (Manchester: Manchester University Press, 1995).

Smith, A., *The Newspaper: An International History* (London: Thames & Hudson, 1979).

Smith, F. B., 'Labouchere's Amendment to the Criminal Law Amendment Bill', *Historical Studies*, 17 (1976), 165–175.

Smith, F. B., 'CD Acts reconsidered', *Social History of Medicine*, 3 (1990), 197–215.

Spitzer, L., 'Creole attitudes towards Krio: an historical survey', *Sierra Leone Language Review*, 5 (1966), 39–49.

Spitzer, L., *The Creoles of Sierra Leone: Responses to Colonialism, 1870–1945* (Madison: University of Wisconsin Press, 1974).

Spivak, G. C., 'Can the subaltern speak?' in C. Nelson and L. Grossberg (eds), *Marxism and the Interpretation of Culture* (Urbana: University of Illinois Press, 1988), pp. 271–313.

Spurr, D., *The Rhetoric of Empire: Colonial Discourse in Journalism, Travel Writing, and Imperial Administration* (Durham, NC: Duke University Press, 1992).

Stock, B., *The Implications of Literacy: Written Language and Models of Interpretation in the 11th and 12th Centuries* (Princeton, NJ: Princeton University Press, 1983).

Stoler, A. L., *Race and the Education of Desire: Foucault's* History of Sexuality *and the Colonial Order of Things* (Durham, NC: Duke University Press, 1996).

Stoler, A. L., *Carnal Knowledge and Imperial Power: Race and the Intimate in Colonial Rule* (Berkeley: University of California Press, 2002).

Tatchell, P., *The Battle for Bermondsey* (London: Heretic Books, 1983).

Teale, R. (ed.), *Colonial Eve: Sources of Women in Australia, 1788–1914* (Melbourne: Oxford University Press, 1978).

Thiong'o, N., *Decolonising the Mind: The Politics of Language in African Literature* (London: James Currey, 1986).

Thomas, L. M., 'Imperial concerns and "women's affairs": state efforts to regulate clitoridectomy and eradicate abortion in Meru, Kenya, c.1910–1950', *Journal of African History*, 39 (1998), 121–145.

Tilly, C., *Big Structures, Large Processes, Huge Comparisons* (New York: Russell Sage Foundation, 1984).

Trocki, C. A., *Opium, Empire and the Global Political Economy: A Study of the Asian Opium Trade, 1750–1950* (London: Routledge, 1999).

Turner, V., *Ritual Process* (Chicago, IL: Aldine, 1969).

Ussher, J. M. (ed.), *Body Talk: The Material and Discursive Regulation of Sexuality, Madness and Reproduction* (London: Routledge, 1997).

Valverde, M., *The Age of Light, Soap, and Water: Moral Reform in English Canada, 1885–1925* (Toronto: McClelland & Stuart, 1991).

Van Heyningen, E. B., 'The social evil in the Cape Colony 1868–1902: prostitution and the Contagious Diseases Acts', *Journal of Southern African Studies*, 10:2 (1984), 170–197.

Vaughan, M., *Curing Their Ills: Colonial Power and African Illness* (Cambridge: Polity, 1991).

Walker, R., 'Congregationalism in South Australia, 1837–1900', *Royal Geographical Society of Australasia, South Australia Branch*, 69 (1967), 13–28.

Walkowitz, J. R., *Prostitution and Victorian Society: Women, Class and the State* (Cambridge: Cambridge University Press, 1980).

Walkowitz, J. R., *City of Dreadful Delight: Narratives of Sexual Danger in Late-Victorian London* (London: Virago, 1994).

Ward, J. M., *Colonial Self-Government: The British Experience, 1759–1856* (London: Macmillan, 1976).

Weeks, J., *Coming Out: Homosexual Politics in Britain from the Nineteenth Century to the Present* (London: Quartet Books, 1977).

Wellesley-Cole, R., *Kossoh Town Boy* (Cambridge: Cambridge University Press, 1960).

White, D. L., *Competition and Collaboration: Parsi Merchants and the English East India Company in 18th Century India* (New Delhi: Munshiram Manoharlal, 1995).

White, L., *Comforts of Home: Prostitution and Colonial Nairobi* (Chicago, IL: University of Chicago Press 1990).

Whyte, F., *The Life of W. T. Stead* (London: Jonathan Cape, 1925).

Williams, R., *The Country and the City* (London: Hogarth Press, 1985).

Wood, D., *Trinidad in Transition: The Years After Slavery* (Oxford: Oxford University Press, 1968).

Wotherspoon, G., *'City of the Plain': History of a Gay Sub-Culture* (Sydney, Hale & Iremonger, 1991).

Wright, G., *The Politics of Design in French Colonial Urbanism* (Chicago, IL: University of Chicago Press, 1991).

Wyse, A. J. G., 'The Krio of Sierra Leone: an ethnographic study of a West African people', *International Journal of Sierra Leone Studies*, 1 (1988), 36–63.

Wyse, Akintola J. G., *The Krio of Sierra Leone: An Interpretive History* (London: C. Hurst, 1989).

Zweig, P., *The Adventurer* (London: Dent, 1974).

INDEX

Page references for figures and tables are in *italics*; those for notes are followed by n